# RELIGIOUS BUT NOT RELIGIOUS

## Living a Symbolic Life

by
Jason E. Smith

CHIRON PUBLICATIONS • ASHEVILLE, NORTH CAROLINA

© 2020 by Chiron Publications. All rights reserved. No part of this publication may be reproduced, stored in a retrieval system, or transmitted, in any form by any means, electronic, mechanical, photocopying, recording, or otherwise, without the prior written permission of the publisher, Chiron Publications, P.O. Box 19690, Asheville, N.C. 28815-1690.

www.ChironPublications.com

Interior and cover design by Danijela Mijailovic
Printed primarily in the United States of America.

ISBN  978-1-63051-899-8 paperback
ISBN  978-1-63051-900-1 hardcover
ISBN  978-1-63051-901-8 electronic
ISBN  978-1-63051-902-5 limited edition paperback


Library of Congress Cataloging-in-Publication Data

Names: Smith, Jason E. (Training Analyst), author.
Title: Religious but not religious : living a symbolic life / by Jason E. Smith.
Description: Asheville, North Carolina : Chiron Publications, [2021] | Includes
    bibliographical references. | Summary: "In Religious but Not Religious,
    Jungian analyst Jason E. Smith explores the idea, expressed by C. G. Jung, that
    the religious sense is a natural and vital function of the human psyche. We
    suffer from its lack"— Provided by publisher.
Identifiers: LCCN 2020049329 (print) | LCCN 2020049330 (ebook) | ISBN
    9781630518998 (paperback) | ISBN 9781630519001 (hardcover) | ISBN
    9781630519025 (limited edition paperback) | ISBN 9781630519018 (electronic)
Subjects: LCSH: Religion—Philosophy. | Jung, C. G. (Carl Gustav), 1875-1961. |
    Psychoanalysis and religion.
Classification: LCC BL51 .S5729 2021  (print) | LCC BL51  (ebook) | DDC
    200.1/9—dc23
LC record available at https://lccn.loc.gov/2020049329
LC ebook record available at https://lccn.loc.gov/2020049330

For Carla

# Table of Contents

# Introduction

## The Decisive Question

In 1939, Carl Jung gave a wide-ranging talk on the psychological importance of religion to the Guild for Pastoral Psychology. Founded just two years earlier with Jung as its patron, the Guild had been formed "to encourage the study of psychology among clergy and other spiritual leaders," and to be a forum devoted to the exploration of the common ground between religion and psychology.[1] In that talk, called "The Symbolic Life," Jung made the following declaration:

> Now, we have no symbolic life, and we are all badly in need of the symbolic life. Only the symbolic life can express the need of the soul—the daily need of the soul, mind you! And because people have no such thing, they can never step out of this mill—this awful, grinding, banal life in which they are "nothing but."... Everything is banal, everything is "nothing but"; and that is the reason why people are neurotic.[2]

This often-quoted passage is a powerful statement about the dangers associated with a human life that has become emptied of the kinds of experiences that enable a person to access a dimension of living beyond the daily grind. Whatever Jung meant to indicate with the idea of "the symbolic life," it is clear from this quote that it refers to something that stands in contrast to the mundane and concrete struggles of everyday living. But more than this, it is to be understood as something crucial to emotional and psychological health and well-being. When people are unable to escape from the banal, the ordinary, or the merely rational, Jung is suggesting, they become more susceptible to suffering and neurosis.[3]

The phrase *the symbolic life* encapsulates an important core of Jung's psychology; indeed, the editors of his *Collected Works* chose it for the title of one of the volumes of that 21-book set. It is a phrase that continues to have resonance in the Jungian world and has been put into use by several theorists and authors since Jung's time.[4] It is not, however, a phrase that appears in Jung's writings with any frequency; a quick glance in the General Index of Jung's *Collected Works* reveals that there is no other reference to it apart from its use in the 1939 talk quoted above.

Given Jung's insistence that it is only the symbolic life that can satisfy "the daily need of the soul," we are left wanting a deeper understanding of what he clearly believes to be a crucial expression of human life. What are the components of the symbolic life and why is it that we are "badly in need" of it? And if we are, in fact, cut off from this essential aspect of life, how can we find our way back to it? It is these questions with which this book is concerned.

## Psychology and Religion

The examples of the symbolic life to which Jung refers at different points in this particular talk—Catholic ritual, personal devotions in India, the religious beliefs of the Pueblo peoples, and the rabbinical lineage of a Jewish family—all make it apparent that he is talking about a lived and living engagement with the religious dimension. Jung does not explain why he chooses to speak of "the symbolic life" instead of, say, "the religious life" in this instance. As I noted, it is a formulation that is unique to this talk. Elsewhere in his writings, Jung speaks of "the religious function," "the religious attitude," "a religious outlook," and other similar variations including, simply, "religion," to refer to the same dimension of experience. It is possible that because, for this talk, he was speaking to an audience primarily composed of clergy, Jung felt he needed a more neutral term to differentiate his perspective from whatever fixed associations a clerical audience might have to the words *religion* and *religious*. It is also conceivable that this was a phrase that came to Jung in the spur of the moment in what was apparently a mostly extemporaneous talk—a phrase he later set aside in favor of those variations of religion just mentioned.

It is only possible to speculate as to Jung's reasons for both coining and, ostensibly, abandoning this term. Regardless, it is clear that the phrase *the symbolic life* refers to religious experience. Furthermore, it is a helpful phrase to examine, as it provides insight into Jung's understanding of the psychological dimensions of religion. The Jungian understanding of the symbol[5] and its relationship to the individual psyche, as well as to the religious dimension of experience, lies at the heart of Jung's opus and serves to differentiate his understanding of the human psyche[6] from other schools of psychology.

One key instance of this difference can be seen in the contrast between the development of Jung's psychology and that of his one-time mentor and colleague, Sigmund Freud. The fundamental insight of depth psychology—that at the root of psychological disturbances there lies a dynamism that is outside the field and the control of conscious awareness—is usually attributed to Freud. He pointed out, however, that the idea of an unconscious had been known to the poets and philosophers before he ever began his own study of it.[7] The vehicle through which Freud made his study was the dream, which he saw as "the royal road to a knowledge of the unconscious."[8] In taking this road, Freud drew our attention to that which is produced outside of the directed willing and wanting of the conscious ego personality.[9] There is more in us than we know, and that "more" is often in conflict with what we believe we want. In Freud's pithy phrase, "the ego is not master in its own house."[10]

Jung made his own journey along this same royal road but ended up in a very different place. Put simply, where Freud's attention was on the activity of one's personal dynamics as reflected in the images of dreams, Jung's attention went to the transpersonal depths conveyed by the very same material. As the word *transpersonal* suggests, Jung cast his vision to that which was beyond the merely personal history of the individual. For Jung, the meaning of a human life could not be exhausted exclusively by reference to one's biography, such as the details of family history or the accumulation of life events. Underlying the busy hum of personal life were the steady reverberations of the archetypal[11] experience of human life. The vital question was not just "Who am I in relation to my family and my past experience?" but also "Who am I in relation to life in the world and to the experience of the infinite?" Accordingly, when Jung studied dreams, he discovered a remarkable similarity between the dream images of individuals and the images contained in the collective symbol systems of the world's religions.

This is an essential point to grasp. There is a mutual relation and resonance between the collective symbols of humankind, such as those found in the religious traditions, and the individual symbols of the person, such as those encountered in one's dreams. Collective symbols are not only expressions of general human truths but they can also reveal something of the nature of individual existence. Similarly, individual symbols not only reflect personal concerns but they also reveal something about our participation in the universal experience of being human. In an essay contrasting his own views with Freud's, Jung noted that human beings have always produced religious forms. He saw this fact as evidence of an essential relation between the psyche and religious symbolism. "The human psyche," he wrote, "from time immemorial has been shot through with religious feelings and ideas."[12]

Jung rejected any approach that sought to reduce the religious expressions of the psyche to something more rational or presumably enlightened. To do so, he felt, was to devalue the natural mode of the psyche's expression. In other words, the religious is not an accidental quality of psychic life, nor is it a distortion of some other underlying, and more rational, dynamic. Religious feelings and ideas, rather, are one of the primary forms through which the psyche expresses itself. Viewed in this light, the symbols and images of the world's religions reveal the nature of the human psyche even as they function to mediate the experience of transcendence to it. They are, so to speak, the language of the psyche.

Because of this, Jung asserted that psychology was better able to address certain questions of human life than other disciplines that were either exclusively rational or exclusively metaphysical. The activity of the psyche includes not only rational functions, such as thought, evaluation, and conceptualization, but also nonrational functions, such as intuition, symbolic imagination, and the capacity to experience awe. Approached with this awareness, then, the psyche can be recognized as being the ideal medium through which the apparent conflict between science and religion might be reconciled.[13] Such a reconciliation, however, involves the holding of a tension between two divergent attitudes and, because of this, it is extremely difficult to maintain over time. As a result, psychology since Jung has tended to collapse this tension in the exclusive direction of the rationalistic pole.

Nonrational experiences are generally those that happen *to* the individual, and, as such, they lie outside the sphere of one's conscious control. The specific quality of an intuition, to take one example, is that a sudden idea spontaneously occurs to a person without the need for any prior deliberation. An intuition, in other words, is not noticed until it emerges into the field of consciousness. A person cannot "decide" to have an intuitive idea, because then it would no longer be an intuition but rather a thought. Unlike directed thought, the person is not the initiator of intuition, but rather the receiver. The center of initiative of intuition is not the will, but something unconscious, which means something unknown—that is, something not accessible to rational formulation. A person may strengthen his capacity to perceive and to give attention to the working of intuition but will never be able to produce it as an act of will. Such is the case with any nonrational experience—from the symbolic productions of the dreaming mind, to the demanding grip of creative inspiration, to the sublime encounter with the ineffable—the individual is not actor but acted upon, not initiator but receiver, not agent but patient.

I would argue that psychology, for the most part, has succumbed to a way of thinking that expects the rational to succeed and supplant what is nonrational in human psychological experience. Psychology tends to see the nonrational as *pre-rational*—something that is not yet, but eventually will be, subject to cognition. It does not know how to deal with the nonrational in and of itself, and so excludes it as a possibility. What this means in connection to the subject of this book is that symbolic experience tends to be interpreted as a preliminary and temporary stage that *should* and—if it is to be revealed as "real"— ultimately *will* give way to a more conceptual formulation. In other words, the nonrational symbol is expected to be translated into rational terms. This is the habit of mind of our age. We think in concepts rather than in images, and we need to have our images translated into conceptual language in order to understand them. Put another way, we privilege the meaning that speaks to our minds over that which touches the heart, resonates in our bodies, or awakens the soul.

*

One especially consequential example of the way in which this habit of thinking manifests can be seen in contemporary psychotherapy with its emphasis on so-called evidence-based treatments. Although admittedly it is important to have some way of measuring the effectiveness of psychotherapeutic treatment, the practical effect of the focus on evidence-based treatments is that the value of the individual is diminished. This is because evidence-based treatments reflect a statistical norm that necessarily omits or obscures the personal and the unique. The statistical is unquestionably helpful in providing some orientation, but there is a real danger in making a Procrustean bed[14] of such a norm to the effect that essential aspects of the individual's experience are distorted, potentially causing psychic injury to the person. A rigidly applied evidence-based mindset fails to recognize that an individual is not a statistical unit but an unfolding of subjective, existential experiences—the deepest core of each individual being unrepeatable and, ultimately, unknowable.

It is just this unknowable, subjective core that is the stumbling block for evidence-based treatments because it is essentially impervious to statistical measurement. The evidence-based approach must limit the range of outcomes that it measures to what is objective and observable, which means primarily behavioral activity. When it does attend to the inner experience of the individual, its focus is again limited, this time to thought or cognition. But as I have already suggested, the inner life of a human being is vaster than cognitions and behaviors. Still, today we have taken to speaking of "mental health" or "behavioral health" while rarely speaking of emotional, spiritual, or, even for that matter, *psychological* health. After all, how do you measure the soul?

What constitutes a successful outcome in so much of modern psychotherapy is not the subjective happiness, the psychological wholeness, or the spiritual well-being of the individual. Rather, it is merely the ability of the person to be functional, which is measured by how well one is able to perform what are called the daily activities of living.[15]

But what if simply being functional is the cause of a person's suffering? In my own practice as a Jungian analyst, I see many people who are able to function very well but who do not know *why* they should. For these individuals, it is not daily functioning that is at issue; it is the experience of meaning. Focusing on the ability to function as a therapeutic goal is, in many cases, to prescribe the problem as the solution. What Jung named in the quote with which this book began as the danger of the "awful, grinding, banal life in which [one is] 'nothing but,'" contemporary psychology has set up as a goal. Our age is desperately in need of an understanding of the symbolic life, which, as Jung reminds us, is the best means of meeting and expressing the needs of the human soul.

## The Religious Approach to Psyche

To be sure, it is a challenge in our rationalistic age to even notice, let alone to attend effectively to, the nonrational expression of the symbolic life. We fail to recognize what Jung saw very clearly—that our conceptual and psychological interpretations of religious symbols do not represent a more enlightened understanding over previous eras of human knowledge, but instead are "only more or less successful translations into *another metaphorical language.*"[16] Such translations may very well be a necessary stage in our understanding of religious symbols today. To give a religious symbol a psychological name can help to orient a consciousness that is thoroughly permeated by rationalistic premises. However, this situation represents as much a loss of an older wisdom as it does a gain of new knowledge.

It is my contention that the psychological task of our present age in relation to the understanding and experience of religion is not met in identifying the rational premises that are believed to be "masked" by religious symbolism. At best, this might be a preliminary stage of a far more essential process. What is merely conceptual can be known, but it cannot be *lived,* for life is something experienced, not just something thought. There is no doubt, for instance, that we can understand human love in terms of the evolutionary benefits of pair-bonding or as the result of the brain being flooded by dopamine. These are fascinating, even helpful, ways to look at this fundamental life experience. Still, such understandings are totally extraneous when it comes to helping a human being face the trials and the joys of an actual encounter with love. In such a case, one would be better served by, say, Shakespeare's 116th sonnet or the 13th verse of St. Paul's first letter to the Corinthians, both of which resonate not only with the power and depth of love but also with the ultimate mystery that resides at the heart of it.

The crucial task today is, in fact, the reverse—to learn to dissolve our conceptual knowledge in a direct experience of the symbolic. This, I believe, is a vital necessity. We must rediscover how to make direct contact with living symbols if we are to gain a full experience of their reality and benefit from the infusion of meaning that they can bring to our lives. In other words, we need a means of becoming conversant with the nonrational domain. It is to this end that a familiarity with religion can be an invaluable aid. For where attention to the rational leads us in the direction of the scientific mindset, so recovery of the nonrational brings us into the sphere of the religious.

*

This book, then, is an attempt at something more than just a psychological interpretation of religion. Psychology has often had a great deal to say about religion, but it has not always been so good at listening first to what religion has to say about itself. In these pages, I intend to make what the anthropologist Victor Turner called an "empathetic exploration"[17] of religion and the religious life. It is not my goal to rationalize, psychologize, or pathologize religion. I will not seek to reduce religious experience to a biological impulse, an evolutionary development, a defense against trauma, or a response to the parental environment. All of these types of approaches, Turner reminds us, take an "implicitly theological position of trying to explain, or explain away, religious phenomena."[18] My attempt will be, to the best of my ability, to approach religious experience on its own terms.

That said, it is also important to recognize that depth psychology has a great deal to offer to the understanding of religious symbols and religious experience, and that religion necessarily involves the psychological life of the individual. The dividing line between religion and psychology is blurry at best, and, to a certain degree, arbitrary. As I noted above, Jung called them different "metaphorical languages." This is a helpful image to use. If we imagine each discipline as its own language, we can easily understand that each one would make use of its own—often very different—terms to refer to the same ideas or experiences. It would be absurd to think that just because I do not understand the meaning and reference of a term from a certain language it therefore must be wrong. Yet this is often what happens when one discipline, such as psychology, views another discipline, such as religion, through its own perspective, even if only implicitly.

The language metaphor is helpful in another way, as well. When one first learns a new language, it is often necessary to translate the new terms to be learned into one's native language. This helps the beginner make sense of what is being talked about. Eventually, however, one comes to learn that one language never translates exactly into another. Each one has its own rules and its own structures. It includes particular idioms and ways of thinking that are specific to the culture in which the language developed. At a certain point, it becomes clear that the best way to learn a new language is to immerse oneself in it. No one, for instance, learns his language of origin through rational means—studying the rules of grammar in a systematic way. It is learned by a full immersion in the conversational milieu in which one lives, through what the philosopher Michael Polyani calls the transfer of tacit knowing.[19] Colloquially, we speak of this kind of transfer as gaining understanding through "osmosis." In other words, we "pick it up" through nonrational means. We do not cognitively categorize which words refer to which categories or ideas. The meaning of words is absorbed by living in the context in which the language is used. To fully understand the language of religion, then, one must approach it *as* religion and not impose the categories of another discipline on it.

Yet another useful metaphor for thinking about the relationship of psychology and religion is as two of the many different stories we tell about the human condition. It is a primary characteristic of human beings to tell stories. We are, as one author puts it, "The Storytelling

Animal."[20] In a very real sense, all the ways that we try to understand the world and our place in it are, in fact, just so many stories. Which story we choose to follow, whether it is called psychology, theology, mythology, biology, philosophy, science, or religion, depends on our particular temperament and preference. Each domain is one way of telling the story of human existence, and they overlap each other repeatedly like a complicated Venn diagram.

My approach in this book, then, is not only to seek a psychological understanding of religion but also to make what might be called a religious approach to the human psyche. To put it another way, it is to bring a religious sensibility to the encounter with the psyche. For Jung, psychology represented a middle ground between matter and spirit— that is, between the domain of life primarily addressed by science and that addressed by religion. However, as I have stated, psychology has increasingly emphasized the scientific materialist position since Jung's time. The polyvalent resonance that Jung heard in the word *psychology* has been all but lost to our modern sensibilities. To speak of a religious approach to the psyche, then, is to try to recover something of that middle ground. It is not meant to be understood as a position that is opposed to the scientific approach, but rather complementary to it. I do not in any way deny the value of the scientific study of the psyche, but I do think it is important to recognize that, in the realm of the human soul, it has crucial limitations.

Psychology cannot do justice to the human experience of religion if it attempts to view it only through a scientific lens. This is because the goal of the scientific method is qualitatively different from that of the religious life. Science necessarily proceeds through a process of discrimination and differentiation. Through the scientific approach, we see how one thing is different from another, we sort and categorize and analyze. This is helpful and necessary, and the benefits of the scientific method toward the advancement of knowledge are undeniable. Still, such an approach often proves to be thin food for a spirit hungering for an encounter with the transcendent.

A religious approach to the psyche, on the other hand, is less concerned with the categorization and definition of psychological events as it is attentive to the value and meaning of psychological *experiences.* Because of this, it follows a very different path of knowing. It is not exclusively rational, in the sense of discriminating how one thing is *different* from another. It tends, rather, to the mythical, meaning that it comprehends through correspondences, how one thing is *like* another. Another way of saying this would be that it speaks in stories and not through the transmission of information.

A religious approach to the psyche does not mean making a religion of psychology, though it may, at times, mean challenging psychological dogma. Such an approach does not in any way disdain facts but seeks to remain open to truth however it may disclose itself. It looks to hold open a space for the encounter with what is unknowable, even mysterious, as it manifests in the only way in which it is possible for us to have this encounter—on the field of the human psyche. The goal of this approach is to experience the understanding of the heart and not only the knowledge of the mind. It proceeds by love and reverence, not objectivity and dispassion. Above all, it does not merely stand apart and observe, but rather enters in and participates.

## A Relationship to the Religious Dimension

I am aware that the use of the word *religious* in this context might be the cause of difficulty for many readers. It is a word that can elicit strong reactions and powerful associations for people. These reactions range from outright hostility to a kind of fierce defensiveness to just plain indifference. Still, my use of the words *religion* and *religious* in this book is deliberate. It is meant to be *more* challenging, not less. To stick solely with the phrase *the symbolic life* might be less controversial, but I believe it would only serve to keep the discussion at too much of a theoretical and abstract level. As a result, it would keep us—both reader and writer—at too safe a distance from the subject matter. It is for this same reason that I speak of a "religious approach to psyche" instead of calling it, for instance, a "phenomenological approach," an "empirical approach," or something else of a like nature. These conceptual frameworks provide important intellectual orientation and I make use of them throughout this book for just that purpose. But if, as I said, a religious approach means to "enter in and participate," then we must also find a way to allow this material to engage us and involve us personally, even viscerally.

Far too much of the discussion about religion that we hear these days centers on the not very interesting and not very edifying question of whether it is true or false, right or wrong. That is, popular culture tends to look at it through something like a consumerist lens, as a concrete product that one must decide whether or not to "buy." This is a question meant to arrive at a simple, clear, and unambiguous answer, and to do so quickly. It is a question that has little tolerance for complexity and prefers a clever sound bite to a nuanced discussion.

There is another kind of questioning, however—one that seeks to open and explore, and that is propelled by curiosity—a word whose etymology suggests care, diligence, inquisitiveness, and attention to detail. These, in fact, are the very qualities, as I will discuss in Chapter 11, that Jung appeals to in setting forth his own understanding and definition of religion.

A much more interesting and generative question, then, might be "What is my relationship to religion and to the dimensions of experience with which it is concerned?" For such a relationship, in fact, already exists. As the religious scholar Diana Eck suggests, each of us already has our own theology. She notes that each of us has come to some conclusion for ourselves about what the word *God* means: "Even those who are uncomfortable with the term *God*, who quarrel with God or who reject God, have an idea and an image of God."[21] The problem of God, in other words, is already inside us. And it does not reside there as a merely intellectual problem, but rather as one that concerns our very being and our relation to the world. It is for this reason that I choose to use the word *religion* and to emphasize a religious approach in this book, because I believe that it challenges us to confront our thoughts and feelings—good and bad, for and against—about this essential dimension of human life. Whether it is conscious or unconscious, positive or negative, our relationship to religion is not simply an academic matter but is profoundly implicated in how we see and experience the world, not to mention shaping our foremost concerns and commitments. This relationship sets the stakes for our particular life venture, determining those domains of personal investment to which we attribute both primary value and fundamental meaning.[22] Whether we ultimately accept or reject the object of religious belief and practice, it is a domain of life that must be engaged at the most personal level.

*

I remember when this question of one's relationship to religion became acute in my own life. I did not grow up in an explicitly religious household. As a family, we rarely entered a church, with the exception of the yearly Christmas Eve service. This, in my memory, was little more than a community Christmas caroling event during which we often had to stand somewhere in the back, uncomfortably crammed together because there was no room for us to sit. Undoubtedly, there was more to these services, but the truth is I stopped listening when the music stopped.

I cannot exactly say that I was intentionally given a nonreligious upbringing. My siblings and I knew, for instance, that we couldn't say the words *God* or *Jesus* casually around the house without receiving a sharp rebuke, but we never really knew *why* that should be the case. Still, my upbringing was *effectively* nonreligious, the result more of neglect or indifference as opposed to any professed atheistic or agnostic beliefs from either of my parents.

When I look back now, I can see the many ways in which my own religious sensibilities were stirring even at a very young age. What I lacked was some form, some set of images and stories, through which those feelings could become fully realized experiences with which I could engage and toward which I could develop a conscious relationship. My family's religious heritage was Christian, and although the image of Jesus was always very compelling and mysterious to me, I only really gleaned the elements of his story by eavesdropping on my older sister as she played her soundtracks from the shows *Godspell* and *Jesus Christ Superstar* over and over in her room on a tinny, plastic turntable.

I came of age in the 1980s during the rise of the Moral Majority and public religious figures such as Jerry Falwell and Pat Robertson. Those figures and the news stories about them were my main source of religious education in my teens and early twenties. My response to them was a powerful and visceral repulsion. I could not countenance the intolerance, the casual condemnation of large segments of the human family, or the anti-intellectualism and absurd literalism they promoted. It all seemed so un-Christian to me and yet, at the same time, it became in my mind synonymous with the word *Christianity*. I can't say that I rejected religion at that time, because I possessed no conscious religion to reject. It was more that it appeared obvious to me that that world of strained beliefs about an apparently petty and tyrannical God held no value that I could perceive. It required no reflection and no thought, and I gave it none. I possessed no personal experience to counter the image of religion that regularly played across my television screen, and the result was an agnosticism borne of a vacuum. My interests leaned toward theater and the arts, and the world in which I lived was liberal, artistic, intellectual, and secular.

It was not until I came across the works of Joseph Campbell, and through him those of Carl Jung, that my innate religious temperament was reawakened. From their writings I was introduced to the symbolic nature of religious symbols and began to understand that the truth of such symbols did not rely on a concrete and literal understanding of them. My resistance to Christianity remained fairly strong, but I began to immerse myself in books on Buddhism and Taoism. The *Tao Te Ching* became for me the first scripture in which the sacred truly disclosed itself in a powerful and transformative way. But even though I felt enlivened by my studies, I sensed something important remained untouched and unrecognized.

This "something" announced itself to me in a series of dreams that I found fascinating and inviting and, simultaneously, disturbing. To put it plainly, my dreams began to be filled with religious imagery. They were not, however, generically religious. I was not dreaming of universal, nonspecific Jungian archetypes, such as the Great Mother, the Wise Old Man, the World Tree, or even abstract mandala images, as I had imagined and even hoped I might. No. My images were specifically Christian images—Jesus, Mary, priests, baptism, and the church. This provoked a great deal of ambivalence in me.

In one particularly vivid dream, *I found myself going down a river on a boat. The boat came to a spot where the river forked in two directions. Somehow I knew that to the left was the path of Christianity. I could see that it was a dark, difficult path that led deep into a jungle. It was a hard path with lots of struggles, and I felt afraid at the thought of entering it. To the right stretched the path of Buddhism—a sunny, open, and easy passage. I chose to go to the right. At first, I felt I'd made the wrong choice, but soon set that feeling aside as I entered into a land filled with giant smiling Buddha statues, hot-air balloons, and, oddly, several police officers.*

Initially, in reflecting on this dream, I felt pleased about my choice. Certainly, it resonated with my conscious feelings about the two traditions. At the time, any choice between following either a Christian or a Buddhist path was a no-brainer. Buddhism held none of the cultural baggage for me that Christianity did and, in the social circles in which I moved, it was, quite simply, a cool thing to try. In a very superficial way, then, I understood the qualities of the two paths, as portrayed in my dream, to represent their respective values. The path of Christianity on the left was dark and difficult because it was "bad," and the path of Buddhism on the right was light and easy because it was "good." Still, I could not entirely shake that doubt about my choice that I had initially felt in the dream, and it hovered around me uncomfortably.

Working with this dream and others from that period of time, I came to understand that the "happy Buddhist land" with its smiling Buddhas and hot-air balloons was, for me, something of a dead end. It was a land of easy spirituality where I could go to feel good, but not necessarily to grow. Buddhism—in the way that I engaged it—kept me floating above the earth, when what I needed was to dig more deeply into it. This had nothing to do with the relative value of Buddhism and everything to do with me. I have no doubt that others could and, indeed, have found in the Buddhist tradition a rigorous path of growth and transformation. For me, it reinforced a kind of sterile disengagement from the world, rather than fostering an authentic engagement with it. I soon came to understand the presence of the policemen in this land of my dream as images of a kind of "arrested" development. Without question, I had chosen the wrong path.

This eventually led me to the insight that I could not justify rejecting the tradition of my heritage—as faint as it may be—without first having a more complete understanding of it. To do so would be to decide a critical question of my life based solely on unexamined assumptions. It would be following the path of least resistance without adequate knowledge, not only of *what* I would be rejecting but, more importantly, *why*. In other words, I had to enter the dark and difficult jungle of Christianity and discover the ways that it lived and moved in my psyche. Jung once spoke of the need to recognize that there is an unconscious religious attitude that lives deep in a person which may, in fact, be completely different from whatever attitude that person might consciously profess to hold.[23] This is what I knew I had to understand for myself.

For me, this meant I had to follow a path that would challenge me, that would test me, where I might encounter things that I wouldn't necessarily like but might have to struggle with and even fight against. Furthermore, I sensed that any understanding that I gained in taking this path needed to come "from within." Mere academic knowledge would not be enough. I had to make my experiment with full participation. From the outside, it may seem like a simple enough thing to do, but internally it caused me a great deal of difficulty. It was a challenge to my most basic sense of who I was, and it felt like it could cut me off from the world in which I lived. Frankly, the idea of reading the Bible, saying prayers, or going to church felt embarrassing. What would my friends think? What would my family say? What if, God forbid, someone found out? With more than a little ambivalence and a large dose of secrecy, I began a study of and engagement with Christianity that, to my perpetual surprise, has lasted to this very day.

I tell this story not to extol the virtues of Christianity nor to deride those of Buddhism. I remain deeply interested in the Buddhist tradition and continue to find enormous value within it. I make no claim about the merits of one tradition over any other for anyone but myself. I also recognize that my engagement with the Christian path is possible in large part because I had no history of being wounded by my religion that I needed to confront, as is the case with far too many people. I cannot claim to have overcome all my struggles with certain elements of the Christian tradition, and certainly not with a good deal of the way in which Christianity is professed and practiced. But it is through my experience that I have learned the value of engaging in the struggle, of seeking out and staying in an encounter with religion that not only soothes and comforts but also challenges, provokes, disturbs, and even sometimes disappoints.

My personal experience has confirmed for me the truth of that idea that both Eck and Jung refer to—that each of us already has a relationship to the religious dimension. We each have some image and idea of God, and if we do not establish a conscious relationship to our god-images, they will remain an unconscious and, therefore, potentially disruptive presence in the psyche. If we are not to be unconsciously driven by our god-images, we must find forms through which we can be consciously related to them. Such a conscious relationship—which is what religion ultimately is—is a work. It is safe to assume that there is much that the religious traditions of the world can teach us about the nature of this work, if we are willing to wrestle with these storehouses of our collective human wisdom and their role in our lives.

## Religious but Not Religious

The title of this book, *Religious but Not Religious,* is meant as a variation on the well-known phrase "spiritual but not religious." This latter phrase has become a common way for many people to describe their relationship to the spiritual life. The implication of the idea of being spiritual but not religious is clear. Religion—by which is usually meant "organized religion"—is problematic in some way and stands in opposition to the sense of individual freedom that is implied by the popular idea of spirituality. Because religion is seen as mostly being too rigid, too dogmatic, and too restrictive, the spirit, so it is imagined from this point of view, is more accessible outside of religion than inside it.

There is a great deal of justification for this point of view. Many people have been terribly wounded by their experiences of religion, whereas others are repulsed by the cruelty that has been expressed and performed in the name of one religion or another throughout human history. Diana Eck reminds us that all religions have a shadow of the ugly and the perverse. Religion is subject to distortions such as these because "religious traditions, especially religious institutions, are not dropped from heaven, but are our human creations as we struggle to respond to our sense of the Transcendent."[24] Furthermore, as I discuss in Chapter 4, the increasing diversity of our communities has made more exclusive, fundamentalist expressions of religion untenable for greater and greater numbers of people. To be "not religious," then, is an affirmation of the dignity of the individual and his or her personal experience as against the preservation of the collective institution or the demand to adopt a fixed belief system. Simultaneously, it expresses an openness to the reality and the richness of our cultural diversity over any narrow and exclusive claims to truth.

At the same time, there is a problem with the "spiritual but not religious" attitude. All too easily it becomes an approach by which someone can shape a kind of do-it-yourself spirituality that reflects who and what the person *already is,* but that does not challenge that person to become what he or she could be but *is not yet.* To reject the structures of religion out of hand because of what one does not like about religion is to run the risk of constructing a merely congenial spirituality that may feel good and may even sometimes be a comfort, but that may lack the capacity to accomplish the kind of growth and transformation that all religious traditions seek to effect. To be "religious," then, is to affirm the value of looking beyond one's individuality and to expose oneself to a profound encounter with life and with the human condition through which one may be tested, tried, and transformed.

Calling this book *Religious but Not Religious* is not meant simply to be a play on words. It suggests an attitude toward religion that involves both a rigorous engagement with the institutions of religion and a spirit of psychological independence and maturity. It is an attempt to articulate a way beyond a merely binary choice of "either/ or"—either religion or not religion—to a position of "both/and," religious but not religious. Among other things, the word *religion* denotes discipline, structure, and tradition, and is therefore more concrete and specific than the often vague notion of *spirituality.* In truth, however, this book could just as easily have been called "Spiritual but Not Spiritual," as there are many degrees of disciplined engagement that can be denoted by the word *spirituality*.

*

Late in his life, Jung wrote of the importance of our human connection to the transcendent dimension of life. "The decisive question for man," he declared, "is: Is he related to something infinite or not?"[25] Only when people are in relation to the infinite can they center their lives on crucial matters and not on futile activities and the trivialities that surround everyday life. This book is for those people for whom Jung's question is particularly resonant, for those who feel the call of the infinite and seek to develop an adequate means of listening and responding to it. It is for those people for whom the religious dimension is not appealed to as an answer to their questions about life, but is, in fact, a question that they cannot help but pose *to* life.

In this book, I take the position that religion is necessary for human life. This book is not an attempt to persuade, convince, or cajole. I do not expect that what follows will change anyone's deeply held convictions either for or against the value of the religious. Although religion may be necessary, it is also true that it may not be sufficient in and of itself for expressing the full meaning of a human life. From this point of view, religion is more important as a point of departure, than it is as a place of arrival. It is a path and not a destination, a psychological attitude and not a body of beliefs. Approached in this way, religion becomes, as the Buddha taught, the vessel that we leave behind once it has helped us to reach the distant shore, something we aim to move beyond as we step into a place of freedom and meaning. Paradoxically, the freedom to leave religion behind is simultaneously and surprisingly the freedom through which one can freely engage it. In this way religion *does* become a place of arrival, but not in the sense of being a fixed and final destination. Rather, it becomes the possibility of a field of aliveness that one can enter or depart readily and, as such, may choose freely again and again. This, I believe, is what it means to be religious but not religious.

# Part 1
# What Is the Symbolic Life?

# Chapter 1
## Symbols and the Symbolic

The primary unit of the symbolic life is the symbol. Jungian psychology has a very specific understanding of the nature of the symbol, which it is essential to grasp at the outset of this exploration. To fully understand this particular conception of the symbol, however, it will be helpful to ground it first in the Jungian understanding of the psyche itself.

### The Nature of the Psyche

One of the more challenging ideas of Jung's psychology is also the most fundamental—that of the autonomy of the psyche. From a Jungian perspective, the psyche is not just a result of brain activity, nor is it synonymous with the mind or identified with conscious awareness. It is a living agency with its own sphere of activity that ultimately transcends our merely personal life and experience.[26] This is challenging to grasp because we live in a culture steeped in scientific materialism and, therefore, quite naturally view the world with a Newtonian consciousness that experiences events in terms of cause and effect. In general, we find it much easier to privilege physical events as causes. Psychological events, such as dreams or spontaneous fantasies—which often lack a certain naturalism—seem much more likely to be the effects of those prior physical causes. Furthermore, we tend to experience ourselves as the makers and initiators of those things we encounter in our minds. It seems intuitively obvious that certain thoughts or fantasies take place because we ourselves conjure them in some way.

For Jung, however, the psyche is a function of human experience that is *sui generis*. It acts on us as surely as the physical world acts on us. When you observe the operation of the psyche, you begin to see that it is not merely a reflection of experience in the physical world but an original source of experience in and of itself. To be sure, in the final analysis it is not possible to separate the physical and the psychic, the body and the mind. However, if the mind/body connection means anything, it means that we cannot assume the priority of one of these factors over the other. An understanding of the psyche, asserts Jung, cannot be exhausted with reference to the data of physical, material existence.

The essential element of psychological functioning is the image. More than being simply a picture in the mind, an image is a complex representation of experience. In other words, an image contains within it not only a quantity of information, it also reflects one's feelings about that information, and holds it all together within a form. Psychic images range from the more concrete to the more symbolic.

In a concrete image, the representation is essentially a direct expression of the thing represented, such that the image of the bush in my imagination, for example, is a reflection of the bush that I see before me. A symbolic image, on the other hand, gives expression to something that cannot be contained by the image expressing it. The image of the "bush [that] was blazing, yet it was not consumed," as described in the Book of Exodus, is not a reflection of something in the physical environment. It is not meant to evoke in me simply the idea or concept *bush*. In fact, the meaning I usually attach to the word and image *bush* is, so to speak, suspended. This suspension or extension of meaning gives the image its symbolic aspect. It is a bush that is simultaneously *not* a bush. As I encounter the image of the bush that burns and is not consumed, my imagination is directed beyond the bush, beyond even the fire, to the presence of a "something more" that cannot be adequately expressed in conceptual, non-imagistic, language—in this case, the experience of God. It is exactly this quality that characterizes the Jungian understanding of a symbol: It is the best possible expression for something that cannot be expressed in any other way.[27]

## Directed Thinking and Symbolic Thinking

This understanding of the creative autonomy of the psyche and its manifestation through images is important to keep in mind when considering the nature and value of religious imagery. If I assume that religious images point primarily to physical events, I must either reject them as meaningless and absurd, as do the most dogmatic of scientific materialists, or I must accept them uncritically despite all evidence to the contrary, as do the most dogmatic of religious fundamentalists. If, however, I understand religious images, such as the above example of the burning bush, as being primarily symbolic—that is, as psychic expressions of something inexpressible—then I am able to experience the reality and the truth conveyed by those images without a corresponding sacrifice of reason.

"Whenever we speak of religious contents," wrote Jung, "we move in a world of images that point to something ineffable."[28] It would be helpful to pause for a moment with that statement and unpack it just a bit. The image *points to* this ineffable something. It is not the thing itself, but rather it draws our attention to a phenomenon that defies our capacity to fully circumscribe and conceptualize it. Again, this is the function of the symbol—to give expression to that which ultimately cannot be expressed. Jung goes on to note that even though it is impossible to know how clearly these images represent their "transcendental object," they do not appear to be random or arbitrary.[29] There is a coherence and consistency to religious symbolism that provides compelling evidence that something outside of our conscious awareness is operative and gives rise to such images.

And this is precisely where it gets challenging for many people—*something outside our conscious awareness gives rise to such images.* It is common to speak of an inner life, but it is harder to accept the autonomy of that inner life, to accept that something "inside" us is simultaneously "outside" of the ordinary experience of our own minds. It is truly difficult to grasp conceptually the idea that there are things in our minds that we do not put there. This is because, culturally, we are conditioned to think in terms of directed thought and have very little exposure to the idea and experience of symbolic thinking.

Directed thinking is the working of the intellect in which one takes a quantity of information and operates on it. In directed thinking, the image, concept, or idea thought about is one that has been consciously chosen. Symbolic thinking, on the other hand, is the working of the imagination. Imagination, in the sense that I am using it here, should be understood as an organ of perception in which the symbols and images *autonomously produced by the psyche* are encountered. From this perspective, the activity of the imagination might be conceived of as the *psyche thinking (or dreaming) itself in us and through us.* The contemporary obsession with technological development has the effect of making directed thinking seem more "real" to the modern mind than symbolic thinking.

Technology has become the preferred metaphor for human life in this current age. For example, we conceive of the body as a machine and we think of the mind as a kind of computer. In our everyday language, we speak of experiences as being "hardwired" in our neural connections or we say that we got our "wires crossed" when there is a communication failure. We seek out "life hacks," and sometimes feel we lack the "bandwidth" to deal with the demands of life. Because we feel so comfortable with this metaphor, it is exponentially easier for us to understand directed thinking than it is symbolic thinking. It "makes sense" to picture a system in which data is entered and operations are performed on it producing an actionable result.

However, when technology is the central metaphor and the machine is our guiding image, beings become things, nature becomes a repository of "resources" for human consumption, and people are measured primarily in terms of efficiency and productivity—"human resources" whose value is essentially an economic one. As Marshall McLuhan once provocatively stated, human beings become little more than "the sex organs of the machine world."[30] What is in our psyches is experienced as valuable only in relation to some utilitarian benefit.

A more appropriate metaphor for symbolic thinking would be that of the Tao. This central component of Taoism can be understood, according to Alan Watts, as the underlying essence of life—that which acts of its own accord without the interference of conscious intention, such as the beating of the heart or the baby that forms in the womb of its mother.[31] The Tao can be thought of as an invisible or ineffable yet organizing power at work in things and events. The first line of the *Tao Te Ching* reads, "The tao that can be described is not the eternal Tao."[32] The phrase, "The tao that can be described" echoes the understanding of the symbol that I touched upon earlier: It is a name, or image, that points beyond itself to what "cannot be described." The Tao is that which is "empty, yet it will be inexhaustible" and "infinitely deep, it is the source of all things." In other words, the Tao is the mysterious source from which, though it is empty, all things emerge. One particular virtue of this metaphor is that it moves us from the productivity mindset fostered by the technology metaphor, to a mindset that emphasizes growing and unfolding. That is, we move from the perspective of technical knowledge to that of wisdom.

This is at the heart of what constitutes psychological health from the Jungian point of view. What is important is not only the technical ability to direct one's energy to the tasks of life, but, even more so, the capacity to develop and maintain a meaningful relationship to the ground of one's own being and to the source of energy itself. Attending to the symbols produced by the psyche enlarges and enriches our experience of life. For Jung, a fully lived human life was only possible when infused by the energy of these symbols. "Wisdom," he wrote, "is a return to them."[33]

To include the symbolic in our thinking about psychological experience is to make space in our minds for the unknown and the unknowable, for mystery. This leads us into a realm where science alone cannot guide us, for the etymological root of science is *scire*, meaning "know," and refers to what is known, to knowledge, to certitude and certainty. The symbolic life, on the other hand, is a religious attitude toward life, which, I would suggest, is a giving up of certainties, a knowing through *not-knowing*, and an engagement with mystery.

## The Perception of Experience

Our perception of reality is not the same as the nature of reality. As Jung points out, reality impinges on our senses and is then transposed through the particular activity of the psyche into a psychological image.[34] For example, light waves are translated by the eyes and perceived as colors. Vibrations touch the ears and are translated into sounds. I speak with my friend and the combination of her words and her intonation get translated into a meaning. In order to attend to the experience of reality at all, there must be a filtering out of certain details of experience together with an emphasis on other details. This bracketing out of fragments of experience from the stream of stimuli and events that barrage the organism from moment to moment is essential in being able to "know" anything, in being able to perceive a particular experience as a "thing" separate from other things. As with any perception, the figure of a phenomenon needs to be differentiated from the ground of reality on which it appears.

How that "filtering" occurs depends on several factors, including culture, personal experience, and archetypal dynamics. The implication of this is that every experience, every moment, and every object, carries with it a penumbra of unknown and unknowable aspects. There is a "more" to our experience that cannot be expressed in terms of directed thinking, for we cannot say with certainty how far the limits of that "more" extend.

The psyche is an incredibly powerful organizing faculty of nature. Just as the body "knows" how to organize the activity of cells and sinew in order to heal a wound, so the psyche organizes the chaos of stimuli and information that constantly visits us into an order perceivable by consciousness. It is helpful to reflect on just how much complexity underlies our perception of experience.

Each moment is completely unique. If I stand before a flower right at this moment, I am not the same person who stood before this very flower 30 seconds ago, for now I include the earlier encounter with the flower that had not existed previously. The air, the light, the movement of the people in the houses nearby, the cars passing on the street, the flight of the birds to and from this yard have all, in ways both subtle and dramatic, changed the environment around me in which the new encounter with the flower is taking place. Furthermore, both my mood and my thoughts, and the changes they have undergone, will also have a determining effect on how I receive and experience this moment. "You can never step in the same river twice," said the ancient philosopher Heraclitus. This is not simply a nice philosophical metaphor; it is a factual reality.

Add to all this the dimension of memory. Have I, at some time past, learned the name of this flower, so that I "see" that it is, say, a rose? Or is this my first encounter with this species of flower, unmediated by names and concepts? Memory, in turn, spurs imagination in the form of my associations with roses. For instance, I may harbor a fantasy of presenting a single-stemmed rose to my love, or I may have a childhood memory of being pricked by the thorns of a rose and drawing blood. Finally, all of this activity is conditioned by the culture in which I live. In an earlier age, the sight of the rose may have stimulated an observer to thoughts of Christ's sufferings and wounds, whereas in our culture today I am more apt to see it as an image of romantic love.

This framework of the complexity of experience is summarized by the theologian Raimon Panikkar in the formula $E = e.\ m.\ i.\ r.$, which he explains as follows:

> What we call experience $(E)$ is a combination of personal experience, which is ineffable, unique each time and foreign to repetition $(e)$, conveyed by our memory $(m)$, modeled by our imagination $(i)$, and conditioned by its reception $(r)$ in the cultural context of our time.[35]

Panikkar further points out that all these elements combine in a way such that they are transformed into a new thing—Experience (E). In this form, the various elements are no longer discernible as separate constituents. We can understand this by the analogy of the way that hydrogen and oxygen combine to produce a new thing—water—and thereby lose their individual character as the separate elements of hydrogen and oxygen.

With this formula, Panikkar has given us an image of a core activity of the psyche—the organizing, creative, transformative action of the psyche. The psyche weaves together the disparate elements of raw experience, the unvarnished encounter with reality, and presents them to our consciousness as Experience.

## The Objective and the Subjective Responses

Both directed thinking and symbolic thinking, then, are particular attitudes toward Experience. Each represents a different mode of experiencing the relationship between subject and object. One emphasizes the apparent distinction between subject and object, while the other emphasizes their underlying unity. Broadly speaking, people are apt to prefer one mode over the other, such that these two styles of thinking tend to be reflected in two separate temperaments—that is, two ways of responding to life experience. These two temperaments have been given many names throughout the history of thought, but here I will simply refer to them as the objective and subjective responses to life. The objective response is more at home in the domain of directed thinking, whereas the subjective response partakes of the process of symbolic thinking.

Both attitudes are essential. The realm of the objective response puts the emphasis on the separation of subject and object. This, then, is the realm of shared reality. In this realm, the world exists concretely as the object of one's subjectivity. It is through the objective response that we experience ourselves as separate from the world and from others, which permits us to make distinctions and differentiations between things and between people. This, in turn, allows us to communicate with each other because it enables the experience of a concrete consensual reality that exists separately from any one individual's consciousness.

The subjective response, on the other hand, emphasizes the participation of the subject in and with the object. It recognizes that there is more to the appearances of life and attends to that "more." The subjective response is sensitive to the experience of reality-as-such,[36] which encompasses us and in which we are included. Shared reality is the mutual experience of the world as an object separate from our consciousness. When it is experienced from the more comprehensive perspective of reality-as-such, however, the world is not a separate object because the subjectivity of the individual is included in the notion of "world," and is not a separate consciousness perceiving the world. The encounter with this realm of experience is impossible to communicate because we are *in it*; it is not "in" our minds. This attitude is what allows us to identify with others and with the world, to experience and express compassion and empathy for each other and the underlying unity of all life. At its most developed, this experience is that which is described by mystics throughout the ages and from all traditions as "union with God."

The philosopher Karl Jaspers' word for reality-as-such is "the Comprehensive," of which it is not possible to speak:

> We cannot doubt the existence of mystical experience, nor can we doubt that mystics have always been unable to communicate what is most essential in their experience. The mystic is immersed in the Comprehensive. The communicable partakes of the subject-object dichotomy, and a clear consciousness seeking to penetrate the infinite can never attain the fullness of that source. We can speak only of that which takes on object form. All else is incommunicable.[37]

For the subjective temperament, it is just this background to our ideas and experiences that gives them their true content and meaning. And it is this "incommunicable" background to which the most meaningful of our communications—those that clothe themselves in symbolic dress—point.

Because, as Jaspers says, "a clear consciousness seeking to penetrate the infinite can never attain the fullness of that source," we need to make use of symbols in order to perceive and express these incommunicable depths. The symbol acts as a bridge between the objective and the subjective dimensions of experience. The objective response attends to the communicable, that which "partakes of the subject-object dichotomy." The subjective response attends to the incommunicable in which the subject-object dichotomy has been overcome. Again, both responses are essential. The objective response, on its own, "can never attain the fullness of that source." The subjective response, however, taken on its own, is "unable to communicate what is most essential in the experience." One way to imagine the symbol, then, is as a kind of mask. The front of the mask presents an image that can be perceived and expressed by the objective mind, whereas the subjective mind is responsive to that vast realm that opens out behind the mask—that transcendent mystery that Jaspers calls "the Comprehensive."

## Symbols versus Signs

As I stated previously, we need to make use of symbols. However, it would not be correct to say that we create symbols through conscious intention. Symbols are more a product of "the incommunicable source" than they are creations of the conscious mind. It would be better to say that we receive or encounter a symbolic image. We *meet* the symbol; we do not create it. Were we to create it, it would merely be an expression of something we already know. Such an image would be a reflection of our conscious minds, but would convey little about what is yet unconscious, much less the transcendent and ineffable depths of "the Comprehensive." As I have already noted, Jungian psychology defines the symbol as the best possible expression for something that cannot be expressed in any other way. It is something resonant with overtones of meaning. The symbol, then, cannot be the product of the rational intellect working out a formula to express a concept. It emerges, says Jung, from experience and not from thought.[38] In other words, it emerges from a direct encounter with life, with the individual not simply as an observer but as a full participant.

When an image expresses something already known, Jung calls this a sign. Any image that points to a closed meaning—that is, to an understanding or interpretation that precludes further exploration or reflection, or that is not open to wonder or resonant with meaning— is a sign. When a patient presents a dream to me during an analytic session, for instance, and quickly follows it up with, "Well, I know what that's all about," she is attempting to understand the dream as a sign as opposed to a symbol. "I yelled at my boyfriend last night and I need to apologize," she might say. The image-as-sign is comforting because it is clear. A sign is a signal. It tells you—so it seems—what to do. When you come to a stop sign, there is no ambiguity about what you need to do. You are supposed to stop. You can ignore the signal if you choose, but the meaning is unequivocal. If our interest is in behavioral or technical mastery over life—a desire for a set of instructions about how to act or what to do—we will tend to read images as signs.

## Mastery versus Meaning

Such behavioral or technical mastery in and of one's life, of course, has an important value for the ordering and structuring of life. It is crucial that an individual has the capacity to meet the demands of daily existence. This is a key function of the ego—to make and keep commitments, to be able to make choices, to focus attention on critical duties, and many other tasks requiring the use of the will. Mastery, in and of itself, however, does not lead to the experience of meaning. On the contrary, it is meaning that gives an organizing focus to the concrete tasks of life.

Jungian analyst Edward Edinger gives a simple and eloquent definition of meaning.[39] He describes it as a psychological state that can affirm life. Mastery, by contrast, is not affirmation, but rather the attempt to control life. Put in psychological terms, mastery is a privileging of consciousness at the expense of the unconscious. It is an attempt by the ego to contain the wholeness of what Jungian psychology calls the Self [40] rather than recognizing its proper place *within* that wholeness. By contrast, meaning could be understood as the art of letting oneself be mastered *by* life. It is rooted in the acknowledgment that life, world, and transcendence all exceed our grasp. In the face of the "fullness of the source," the poor power of the ego is no match. Meaning is the experience of being in life, of being related to one's life, of being an integral part of the life process.

It is hard to find precise words for the experience of meaning because it is simultaneously an overcoming of oneself and a coming into oneself. Meaning is not a *thing;* it is not an objectively existing reality somewhere out in the world that can be mechanically acquired or measured, known or named. Rather, it is a quality of our relationship to life. Although we can recognize the experience of meaningfulness, we cannot communicate that experience in its fullness, because some part of the experience touches our deepest subjectivity. We can't even express it to ourselves because we know it, as it were, in a place beyond words. At most, we can attempt to try to convey the quality of the experience by making use of image and metaphor. "I feel so alive," we might say, or, "I feel like a new person," or "Everything just fits."

If we take these expressions of aliveness, newness, or fitting, concretely, they are either nonsensical ("Of course you're not new! You are the same person you were yesterday and the day before!") or totally banal ("Of course you're alive; you're breathing and walking and talking"). But if we understand them in the way they are intended, as pointing to an experience that can't be named directly, we begin to understand their symbolic nature.

"The symbol," Jung writes, "is alive only so long as it is pregnant with meaning."[41] This statement is a resonant one and deserves some extra reflection, for it has a symbolic quality in and of itself. Time and again, when Jung offers a "definition" of the symbol, he resorts to imagistic and suggestive language. Here, he is comparing the vitality of the symbol with the quality of being pregnant. To be sure, we can brush off Jung's use of "pregnant with meaning" as just a turn of phrase, a common usage one might find anywhere. To do this, however, would be to ignore that such a phrase is chosen because of the aptness of the image for the quality of experience it is trying to express. If we let this turn of phrase play on our imaginations, we are rewarded with some surprising meanings and rich associations.

Imagine a pregnant woman. The baby she holds in her womb is a unique, unknown, developing life. Who this baby is and will be is still a mystery, one that stimulates in the imagination of the parents many fantasies of possible futures. Not only do they wonder what their baby will be like, they also wonder what they themselves will be like in relation to this baby. For not only is this new life growing but it is also transforming the life of the mother carrying it, the father anticipating it, and the lives of those connected to this family. Many changes are taking place. Some of these are very apparent, such as the obvious physiological changes, or the awareness of new economic pressures. Some of these changes are, perhaps, less apparent. For, together with the more concrete and practical changes, a profound spiritual and psychological transformation is also taking place. A young woman is becoming a mother, a young man is becoming a father, a brand-new family is coming into existence. New demands will be placed on all the individuals involved. New powers and competencies will need to be developed; old attachments and ways of being will need to be shed. This quality of the new and unknown, of growth and transformation, of hope, fear, and anticipation, as well as the capacity to inspire imagination and forge new relationships, expresses well the power, potential, and emotional intensity that is inherent in the encounter with a truly living symbol.

The symbol is rooted in what Jung calls psychic reality.[42] He distinguishes psychic reality from concrete reality on the one hand,

and from the intellectual, or ideal,[43] realm on the other. Psychic reality partakes of both realms and harmonizes them with each other. It is a definite reality, an effective force in a human life, while yet not being concrete, and it participates in the ideal realm of the mind and imagination, leading to the encounter with what transcends the world, but without thereby becoming insubstantial. Like the baby in the life of a new mother and father, the symbol requires real engagement and responsiveness in the experience of day-to-day living, while at the same time inspiring an abundance of fantasies and feelings, and a reexamination of one's understanding of oneself.

Jung rejects the idea that something is "only psychological"—a view that conflates the psychological with the ideal. In actuality, psychological experience has real effects in the real world and yet reaches beyond the world. The symbol, then, liberates us from both an arid materialism and a sterile idealism. It allows us to stand, as it were, with one foot in each realm. The symbol, in other words, is a "both/and" experience, holding together two perspectives at the same time. It holds together the tension of the real and the ideal, making it, in a sense, real but not real, not real yet real.

## Individual Symbols

Symbols manifest in both individual and collective ways. On an individual level, the dream is the vehicle through which symbols can be recognized most clearly because the images experienced in dreams often lack the kind of naturalism that would lead one in the direction of a literal interpretation. However, dreams are not the only source of symbolic experience for an individual. According to Jung, thoughts and feelings, acts and situations, and even inanimate objects can express patterns of symbolic activity.[44]

Because the patterns that manifest in these various ways are masked by our everyday actions and encounters, their symbolic nature can be more difficult to discern. This is one reason why a Jungian approach remains rooted in dream material, for dreams will often reveal the symbolic configuration hidden within everyday experiences.

An example will make this aspect of the symbol clearer. A man suddenly gets the idea that he wants a new truck. He does not usually drive a truck and knows he can't really afford one, but still the idea of a new truck persists. What distinguishes this idea from other similar thoughts that come and go is that it affects him deeply. It grips him and will not let him go. Furthermore, there is a strong taboo quality to this idea; he feels that there is something wrong with it, that it would involve some kind of transgression. When he examines the idea rationally, he cannot produce any valid reasons for buying a truck, but this knowledge does nothing to calm the powerful desire he feels. This inner conflict is painful and distracting.

On the one hand he cannot just accept the idea and simply go buy a truck, but on the other hand, he cannot banish the idea or the desire and simply decide not to get the truck. He wants it and he doesn't want it. Like a modern-day Hamlet, he finds himself wrestling with a decision, unable to bring himself to act.

This man, an analysand with whom I worked, grew up with a father who suffered from a mental illness. The messages about masculinity that he had received growing up were mixed and confused. He remembered his father as a loving, nurturing presence, and yet would also recount episodes in which his father would ridicule and shame any display of feeling or vulnerability on his part. Around the time of puberty, his father's symptoms worsened, leaving the young boy essentially on his own to make his way into adulthood.

Not surprisingly, expressions of longing for guidance and direction were common in our work together. "I just want someone who will tell me what I should do," he would often lament. Intelligent and intellectually curious, this man's search for a father figure led him to seek out mentors in the world of books and ideas. But his greatest cries of longing were for the world of practical action. "I wish I had someone who could teach me to fish, someone I could go camping with." These statements, symbolic in themselves, found their most intense expression in his sudden and surprising desire for a truck.

For such an individual, who has been wounded in his early relationship with his father, it is important that the therapeutic work proceed simultaneously in relation to both its personal and its archetypal levels. Not only has this man been wounded in his relationship with his actual, personal father, but his relationship to the *archetypal father* has been injured as well. According to Jungian analyst

Mario Jacoby, the relationship to the archetypal father is concerned with "the motivations having to do with exploration and the pride associated with competence and assertive power."[45] It was in the development of this core need that my analysand had experienced a significant disruption.

The symbol of the truck is an image that gives succinct and powerful expression to this essential sphere of life activity. This man is in need of a means of carrying himself through the world with strength and "assertive power." He longs for a mentor who can teach him, building up his competence and self-reliance. In other words, he needs a vehicle that can connect him with a healthy sense of his own masculinity, and he yearns to connect with an energy that would give him "drive" and forward momentum in life.

It is the symbol that mediates such an energy to the individual. To connect to a particular energy means to experience the reality of the symbol. This is essential. To experience it, however, does not mean to literalize it. It does not mean that my analysand *should* buy the truck. Rather, it means that it is not enough for him to work out intellectually or conceptually what the image of the truck means. Instead, he has to enter into the image with all of his emotions and sensations. It means, for instance, really feeling himself sitting in the cab of the truck, imagining what it would look and feel like and how he feels while sitting behind the wheel and driving down the road. Establishing an embodied relationship to the symbol is the crucial task. Once that relationship is in place, it is no longer important whether he buys the truck or not. The issue has shifted to a different plane.

In my analysand's case, the compulsive desire for the truck eventually dissolved. He learned to feel his need at a deeper level and did not have to literalize it by buying a truck he could not afford. His focus naturally shifted to practicing more assertive forms of communication, with no direction on my part that he do so. As it turned out, several months later it became clear that having a truck would be helpful for a number of projects he and his wife had undertaken on their home. At that point, however, the purchase of the truck was not simply the fulfillment of an unconscious emotional need; it was something that met a practical need. He was able to make the purchase in a responsible and measured way, one that fit in his family's budget and was made in full collaboration with his wife. Because of the psychological work he had done, buying the truck could now be a kind of ritual marker for something he had already gained within himself and not just a substitute for its lack. The actual truck could now serve as a reminder for his original, internal experience.

## Collective Symbols

Every person's life produces individual symbols like this that give expression to the particular movements and developments of her psyche. Beyond and behind these more individual symbols are those that give expression to the movements and developments of whole cultures and of the archetypal depths of human existence. These shared or collective symbols have emerged over millennia. They are the symbols with which human beings have been engaged, and by which they have been affected, for countless generations. For Jung, these collective expressions were the most important symbols because they could connect a person to the larger perspective of a shared humanity over and above her merely personal experience. It is in the great religious traditions of the world in which these collective symbols are primarily encountered.[46]

Differentiating between individual and collective symbols is admittedly a somewhat arbitrary exercise and should not be understood or applied too literally or rigidly. For example, the truck symbol discussed earlier is clearly an individual symbol, but for my analysand it pointed to, and connected him with, the underlying archetypal dimension. These two levels of symbolic expression, then, can be thought of as being part of the same continuum. Another way to imagine the relationship between them is to picture the individual symbol as being nested within the context of collective symbols. However this relationship is conceived, it is the nature of the symbol— whether individual or collective—that it points beyond itself and beyond our merely personal lives to something yet unknown, something ineffable.

The idea that collective symbols are more important than individual symbols will likely sound backward to many people. After all, in a highly individualistic culture, anything that limits or circumscribes the individual tends to be viewed with suspicion. One newspaper columnist recently gave voice to this position: "Adopting the answers thousands of full-time ponderers have come up with over thousands of years feels like squandering … freedom."[47] This view, however, frames the issue in terms of a false dichotomy—either one maintains an intellectual or personal freedom, or one "adopts" someone else's "answers." It fails to see that a million individual freedoms that exist without some relation to each other is just a chaos. It is our collective symbols that provide that frame of relationship.

The main point here is not whether the images of any one particular religion are factually and literally true, and it is certainly not a question of adopting one set of "answers" over and above another set. The main point is that our individual existences are rooted in a collective cultural and historical soil out of which they grow. None of us is simply dropped into this world as a completely new thing unrelated to all that has come before. Each life is part of a larger cycle of life—a family and cultural history—that ultimately includes all of human development. This means that each individual bears some relationship to the collective symbols of her cultural heritage regardless of her conscious, personal engagement with those symbols or the religion that is their home.

Edward Edinger uses the Christian image of crucifixion as an illustration of this idea. He notes that regardless of one's *personal* feeling about the symbol of crucifixion, it is a central image in the history of Western civilization—one that has been profoundly potent for a large segment of the human community for millennia.[48] It is reasonable to assume that some understanding of this symbol and its potential meanings would be helpful in facilitating a more complete relationship of the individual to humanity in general and to the depths of the human condition. This fact, of course, is not limited to the collective symbols of the Christian tradition but is true of those found in any of the great religious traditions. Put succinctly, collective symbols are not about *my* life, *my* individual experience, or *my* personal self; rather, they speak of *human* life, of the existential encounter with life itself.

For many people, it seems apparent that the images and stories of the world's religions are simply not true. Images such as a Garden of Eden or a Virgin Birth are seen to be allegorical at best, sheer nonsense at worst. What could such ancient and outgrown superstitions have to do with modern individuals living in the contemporary world? For many others, the value of these collective symbols is self-evident. It is the "unknownness" and the openness of the symbol that is a questionable idea. To call these religious statements *symbols* is a kind of heresy. They are what they say they are. They are concrete and literal truths.

Both of these positions make the mistake of understanding the symbol as being meant as a statement of fact—one that is either demonstrably false or one that is unquestionably true. For one side, the statements of religion seem to be mere inventions of the human mind; for the other, divine revelations. Jung, for his part, felt that such images were "spontaneous manifestations" of the psyche that have proven to be particularly apt expressions of certain experiences that have been reflected on, wrestled with, elaborated on, and developed by human consciousness over the course of centuries. In this sense, they were indeed revelations, in that they revealed important truths about the human psyche and its relationship with its own ineffable depths. He rejected the idea that religious symbols were intentionally fabricated by human beings.[49] A consciously produced symbol could not have such far-reaching effects on the collective psyche of humankind. Such an invented image could only express what was already known and, therefore, would ultimately be too restrictive to convey the full range of the thought it was meant to communicate. A truly living symbol always means more than it seems to say.

## A Function of Relationship

The very nature of the symbol makes it difficult to define or describe. A symbol is more than just a particularly elaborate or esoteric image, and it is so much more than simply an idea expressed in image form. It is, rather, the expression of a field of psychic energy.[50] As I noted earlier, this field can manifest through images, thoughts, feelings, behaviors, situations, and objects. A symbol, then, might be thought of as the expression of a unit of life energy. It is for this reason that Edinger suggested that it was important to approach a symbol as a living thing.[51] Put another way, a symbol is not something to be interpreted, but rather something with which one enters into a relationship. Through the encounter with symbols, our psychological system is infused with a vitalizing energy that supports and furthers our engagement with life. When an individual is in a conscious relationship with the symbolic dimension, life is meaningful and abounding with the energy of purpose.

Jung sums up all that has been said about symbols in this chapter in succinct fashion in a quote from his seminar titled "The Psychology of Kundalini Yoga":

> A symbol, then, is a living Gestalt, or form—the sum total of a highly complex set of facts which our intellect cannot master conceptually, and which therefore cannot be expressed in any other way than by the use of an image.[52]

The symbol could be imagined as a kind of horizon. It points to what is not yet but could be. It reminds us of a wholeness that is absent but yet always present. It draws our gaze past the boundaries of our merely personal existence to the transpersonal depths of our being. Returning again to Jung's quote, it is "the sum total of a highly complex set of facts which our intellect cannot master." This means, of course, that the symbol expresses *more than we can know*. It is too big for the intellect alone, as it cannot be reduced to a unit of knowledge. We encounter the symbol, but never grasp it, just as we do not "know" a spectacular sunset. We stand before it and are moved by it.

At the same time, the symbol allows us to "know" what, ultimately, cannot be known. It allows us, in other words, to know but not know. We know in the sense of "being related to" what is symbolized, but we do not know in the sense of "possessing definitive knowledge." As long as the symbol remains open to the reality to which it points, it conveys this knowing, this relationship with the unknowable. The symbol is the means by which one can be related to a more comprehensive reality. But when the symbol is taken as a sign, when it becomes "closed," then the communication of that larger reality is foreclosed. The symbol itself is not the larger reality but the means of its mediation to our consciousness. However, the symbol cannot contain the whole of what it symbolizes, which always finally outstrips any attempt at expression.

Although it is the best possible expression of this reality, yet it remains a partial and imperfect one.

We encounter here something of a paradox. We need the symbol to act as a container for that more comprehensive reality to which we belong and which we cannot express without it. What is transcendent or ineffable must find expression in form in order for us to be consciously related to it. At the same time, that reality cannot be held by the container of the symbol because it is what Rudolf Otto calls "a sheer overplus."[53] It exceeds all forms and containers. Symbols connect us to wholeness, but they themselves are partial. This is true, for example, of that primary symbol from almost every religion that is used to express the ineffable reality of life—the symbol of God. It is well understood by theologians that the experience called *God* always exceeds whatever can be said about God. Modern theology understands that the images, language, and symbols of religion are ultimately human utterances about God and are therefore limited—no matter how fully they bring an individual into connection with the limitless reality expressed by the idea of God.[54]

The function of the symbol, then, is not to explain, or define, or describe. It is not the definitive answer to some question. A symbol, rather, is a function of relationship between our human consciousness and that which is symbolized. Without that relationship it is not a symbol but merely a concept, an idea, a sign. I believe that many people feel distant or indifferent to religion today because the images of the religious traditions have become for them just that—concepts and ideas to which they are unable to assent, and which do not function to relate them to an experience of the transcendent. For those individuals, religious images have ceased to be, or have yet to become, true symbols.

A symbol becomes a symbol when it involves us, when it facilitates our participation in the reality to which it points. The encounter with the symbolic dimension, then, does not lead to a life of mere objective evaluation or a kind of disembodied intellectual understanding. It is, rather, direct subjective participation. Because it is a function of relationship, the symbol is something to be lived with, not possessed; something to be contemplated, not studied; something to be nurtured, not mined for its treasures. Our attitude needs to be one of discovery and not interrogation, of love and not merely of logic.

# Chapter 2
# Ritual: The Embodied Symbolic

In the last chapter I noted that the engagement with the symbol establishes a relationship with the reality expressed by it, facilitating a direct subjective participation in that reality. The full implication of this idea is that simply having an awareness of symbols and symbolic material on their own is insufficient. To be a full participant requires an embodied engagement and not just an intellectual understanding. For Jung, the symbolic life is possible only when it includes participation in the "ritual of life."[55] In other words, some ritual engagement is needed for the symbolic life to become actualized in a human life. This means that the experience of the symbol is incomplete if it does not involve both thoughts and feelings, both mind and body. Ritual, then, as I will explore in this chapter, can be thought of as the embodied symbolic.

## Deepest Values

Rituals are windows into the deepest values of a society and reveal the primary centers around which collective life is organized.[56] Even though our contemporary world is no longer consciously oriented around the regular performance of collective rituals, we can still see the activity of this archetypal human impulse throughout modern life, such as in baptisms, weddings, and graduations. The lack of a strong sensibility for the symbolic, however, leads to an ambivalence about ritual experience.

One example of this ambivalence can be clearly seen by looking at present-day culture's relationship to the age-old wedding ritual. For many people today, the wedding ceremony has become something of an empty form. Often, the ceremony itself, which can include such ritual elements as the exchanging of vows and rings, or the stomping on a glass, is included as a brief formality that precedes the much more elaborate and extended reception, which is where the major financial investment is made. I have been to countless weddings in which the highest praise for the ceremony—the ritual moment when the couple is actually married—is about its brevity. A further extreme is the dispensing of the ceremony altogether, a reduction of the ritual to a legal formality, a document signed in the presence of a clerk or Justice of the Peace.

In a great many instances, this foundational act of human life has been reduced to a legal formality and an expensive party. However, as my wife Allison Moir-Smith asks in her book, *Emotionally Engaged: A Bride's Guide to Surviving the "Happiest" Time of Her Life*, which explores the psychological and ritual implications of engagement and marriage:

> How many parties have you attended from which you've gone home with a new husband [or wife] who has the power to make life-and-death decisions for you, a new branch on your family tree, and (possibly) a new last name?[57]

Rituals, in other words, are not mere forms; rather, they hold the potential of a truly transformative power. If you have ever found yourself suddenly moved to tears during a wedding, or seen a bride and groom cry through the recitation of their vows, or felt a renewed closeness and connection to your own spouse as you witness the joining of a new couple, then you have been touched by the ritual power of the wedding ceremony.

The modern rationalistic mindset tends to deny that anything substantial lies behind such social forms. Yet, there is in all of us a kind of ritual instinct. There are moments that seem to need a kind of "making special." Thus it is that we mark birthdays with singing and the giving of gifts; we find ourselves in a church at Easter, or in a synagogue during the High Holy Days, even though we stay away the rest of the year; we dress up in robes and funny hats for graduations; and during times of collective crises such as terrorists attacks or catastrophic natural disasters, we seek community, say prayers (even though we "never" pray), and give voice to our pain through poetry, story, and the sharing of memories and comfort.

## The Consolidation of Consciousness

One very basic purpose of ritual, according to Joseph Campbell, is to "concentrate your mind on the implications of what you are doing."[58] In other words, ritual is a means of becoming conscious, of breaking up the psychic inertia that keeps us operating on "automatic pilot." This, in turn, rescues us from a kind of narcissistic isolation as we recognize the impact of life and the world on us, as well as *our* impact on life and the world. In other words, through the consciousness-raising function of ritual, we are awakened to the full reality of the other with whom we may be engaged, whether it be the Thanksgiving turkey on the dinner table, as in the ritual of saying grace, or another person, as in the observance of wedding or funeral rituals.

Sometimes the other that engages us is our own psyche—the movements, crises, and transformations taking place in the unconscious. Ritual, says Jung, can be a form of "mental hygiene," in that it provides a means of containing powerful psychological experiences such as "passionate conflicts, panics of madness, desperate confusions and depressions."[59] What Jung is talking about here is the capacity of certain rituals to give outlet to powerful affects that would otherwise accumulate a dangerous quantity of psychic energy by being kept out of consciousness.[60]

As an example of this, Jung points to the Catholic practice of confession, in which one gives expression to one's transgressions and receives forgiveness. The function of this ritual, according to the Catholic Church, is to restore one's relationship with God when it has been disrupted through sin. Through confession, one is reconciled to God and given "new life."[61] One potential psychological benefit of a ritual like this—when it is authentically practiced—is that it allows individuals a means of expressing and releasing feelings of guilt and remorse that may be burdening them, restoring not only their relationship with God but also with themselves as well as others from whom they may feel cut off.

This level of ritual effect acts as a kind of psychological release valve and is not limited to only religious rituals. Research has demonstrated that personal and even superstitious rituals can be effective in alleviating troubling emotions. In an article titled "Why

Rituals Work," behavioral scientists Francesca Gino and Michael I. Norton note that "even simple rituals can be extremely effective. Rituals performed after experiencing losses—from loved ones to lotteries—do alleviate grief, and rituals performed before high-pressure tasks—like singing in public—do in fact reduce anxiety and increase people's confidence."[62] One example of this level of ritual can be seen in the celebration of Halloween. This annual reveling in ghosts and demons and death can be understood as the vestige of a collective ritual meant to give expression to disturbing and terrifying experiences in a way that can be borne and metabolized by the individual as well as by the group. Such rituals release pressure on the psyche, preventing "negative" emotional energy from building up and overwhelming consciousness. This is what makes them, in Jung's words, "hygienic."

Just as the daily habit of physical hygiene, such as washing one's hands, can help prevent illness, so the regular practice of "mental hygiene," in the form of ritual, can prevent psychological disturbances. It does not take much for troubling emotions to tip us over into a psychological state that is ruled more by the energy of the emotion than by our own rational willing and decision making. We are never far from slipping into a state of unconsciousness, which, in this instance, does not mean a complete absence of consciousness but rather a state in which emotions and behaviors that are not contained and directed by one's conscious will and intention become dominant, effectively driving one's actions and reactions. At one extreme, unconsciousness can manifest in a kind of "blackout" experience, as when someone flies into a "blind rage" and does and says things he does not recall later. Most of the time, however, this is a *relatively* unconscious experience. We find ourselves saying and doing things we don't want to say or do. And although we are fully aware that we are doing these things, we don't seem to be able to muster the power and energy to stop ourselves.

Even when we are in a state of unconsciousness, we often remain conscious witnesses of our own behaviors. Because of this we may not fully grasp that those behaviors are essentially unconscious. Unconscious energies have taken possession of our will, which can leave us feeling helpless in the face of our own actions. In a very unsettling way, we become bystanders to our own lives.

This is what Jung means when he says, "The unconscious no sooner touches us than *we are it*—we become unconscious to ourselves."[63] For Jung, it is this danger of going unconscious—an age-old fear that lives on in the modern psyche—that has given rise to much of human ritual throughout human history. To this end, a primary function of ritual is as an aid to what Jung calls the "consolidation of consciousness"—that is, an energizing and strengthening of that part of the psyche that can keep the unconscious at bay. Put another way, ritual serves as a means of preserving a right relationship with the transcendent. In the language of depth psychology, the transcendent generally goes by the name I have been using in this section—"the unconscious"—that which transcends consciousness. In religious language the word usually associated with the transcendent is *God*.

Most religious ritual could be said to involve the establishment and maintenance of the individual's or the group's relationship with God. This can be seen, for instance, in the Catholic ritual of confession, which I discussed earlier. Through the performance of this ritual, the individual is reconciled with God. In the Muslim tradition, this dynamic takes the form of a ritual profession of faith in a prayer known as the Shahadah—the first of the five pillars of Islam—that expresses belief in the oneness of God. In Judaism, it can be seen, for instance, in the observance of the Sabbath, which, according to one theologian, is one form of experiencing "the presence of God in the world."[64] In Hinduism, an example of this quality of ritual can be found in the experience of Darshan, which is an experience of theophany, or manifestation of the divine, in which there is a mutual beholding of the deity and the worshipper. The fundamental goal of each of these rituals is to connect, or reconnect, the individual with the divine, to aid the person in remembering or strengthening his relationship with his God.

Relationship properly understood, however, means separation as much as it means connection. One can only be related to an "other" from whom there is some differentiation. The remembering of one's relationship with God, then, can be understood as a simultaneous differentiating of oneself from God. From this understanding, the psychological danger noted previously of becoming unconscious, when translated into religious terms, would be that of falling into an identification with God. This takes one of two forms. The first can be imagined as an identification with the all-powerful, all-knowing God, and the second as an experience of God as an impersonal and unconscious dynamism of nature—a kind of blind life-force.

In the first form, the identification is expressed through an inflated godlikeness on the part of the individual—a "proud self-exaltation" as it is named in the Catechism of the Catholic Church.[65] In the second, it is more like something of a blind submersion in the life process— the individual who never rises beyond mere instinctuality. This latter condition is imaged, for example, as a living out of what is called "*nafs*"[66] in Sufism and "*nefesh habehamit*"[67] in the Kabbalah. Both of these are terms for the "animal soul," the state of being driven by one's impulses and appetites.

Understood psychologically, these forms of being identified with God reflect what is meant by the notion of being unconscious. In one case, the energies of the unconscious have been assimilated to the ego, leading to a kind of megalomania, whereas in the other case, the ego remains, or becomes, submerged in the unconscious, with the result that one is governed primarily by one's impulses. Either way, the unconscious dominates. The process of becoming conscious is a process of differentiation from the unconscious. It should not, however, be understood as an overcoming or elimination of the unconscious, but rather as an awareness of and relationship to the unconscious. It could be said, then, that consciousness *is the relationship* to the unconscious.

Seen in the light of this understanding, consciousness is not something achieved once and held forever after as a possession. It is a state that must be constantly maintained, renewed and, from time to time, regained. The psychological process of becoming conscious and the religious practice of remembering the relationship with God are corresponding metaphors that express the same dynamic. When Jung states that the purpose of religious ritual is for the sake of the "consolidation of consciousness," he is expressing the psychological experience related to what religion expresses as the ritual work of remembering and embodying of one's relationship with God.

## Healing and the Holy

In his book *The Ritual Process,* anthropologist Victor Turner describes a function of ritual that can be understood as a variation of Jung's "consolidation of consciousness." Ritual, according to Turner, not only acts as a barrier to the unconscious but it also brings what is unconscious *into* consciousness. In his studies of the rituals of the Ndemba of Africa, Turner points to their use of the term *kusolola* to describe the action of ritual. This is a word meaning "to make appear, to reveal." Ritual brings so-called hidden forces into consciousness where they can be made subject to purposive action:

> Thus, to name an inauspicious condition is halfway to removing that condition; to embody the invisible action of witches or shades in a visible or tangible symbol is a big step toward remedying it. This is not so far removed from the practice of the modern psychoanalyst.[68]

Considering this understanding of ritual in the case of a modern individual today reveals it to have an important implication for how we might think about healing. A concrete example will help to make this clear.

A woman finds herself feeling unaccountably sad as the end of August approaches. She has always felt a certain wistfulness as summer comes to an end, but the feelings she is having go far beyond that. Often, she feels like crying, gets easily overwhelmed, and has little energy and interest for those activities that she usually enjoys and that she knows make her feel good. She worries that she is becoming depressed and tells me so.

As we talk about her experience, she notes that her end-of-summer blues have been getting much worse for the past few years. Indeed, I remember her going through this same experience the previous year. I also remember the reason for it that she identified at the time. She seems to have forgotten, so I ask, "Is there some experience associated with this time of year that might be triggering these feelings?" Then she remembers.

On Labor Day, seven years before, she discovered a lump in her breast. That same week she was diagnosed with Stage 3 breast cancer and plunged into a year of chemotherapy, radiation, nausea, and depression. In the midst of all this, she contracted a rare infection that almost took her life and required emergency surgery. It was a profoundly traumatic experience.

Quite understandably, this woman wanted to feel better. She wanted to be healed from her trauma. But her experience had brought her in touch with her mortality in a powerful way that altered not only her experience of life but her sense of self, as well. She had come face-to-face with her own death and could not return to a pre-cancer state of innocence.

Healing is often conceived as something like a medical or surgical process: Identify the illness-causing agent and remove it. But the knowledge and experience of mortality is a part of the human condition that cannot be healed. And for this particular woman, her awareness of the frailty of life, borne of her too-intimate encounter with mortality, could not be removed. On that Labor Day, seven years before, she had been forever changed. Every year as the holiday approached, her mood would darken. When she experienced this mood as something that should not be, something she should not feel, something that should be removed, she would be tortured by her suffering.

Jung believed that we are able to bear suffering as long as we have some understanding of why we suffer—that is, when our suffering has meaning. In a very real sense, this woman's experience had initiated her into a knowledge of death. Put another way, she had encountered one of the terrifying and sublime mysteries of human existence, a mystery that has engaged the minds and religious sensibilities of human beings from time immemorial. She had encountered, as it were, a terrifying aspect of God. The power of such an encounter can only be called Holy, in the sense taught by the theologian Rudolf Otto of a *mysterium tremendum et fascinans*[69]—a mystery before which the individual experiences fear and awe. For this woman, Labor Day had been transformed from a relatively inconsequential, end-of-summer, civic holiday into a profoundly significant and personal Holy Day.

One primary human response to the experience of the Holy has been to ritualize it. Today, however, the observance of holidays has been considerably watered down, such that it is hard to sense the Holiness that was once attached to them. By and large, we have forgotten that certain days were set aside not simply as a remembrance or a rest from labor, but for the purpose of participating in the power that the day was meant to represent and was even felt to contain. Still, some semblance of this power continues to be active in many instances. To this day, for example, people who never go to church through the year get dressed up and head to a worship service on Easter morning. Why? It can hardly be out of mere habit or obligation if they only go once a year. I would suggest that some part of them wants to experience the specialness of the day, and the ritual actions of dressing up and entering a crowded church mark this day—spiritually and psychologically—as different from all other days. For these people, something of the Holy still clings to Easter.

In the case of the woman with breast cancer, her experience of discovering the lump and getting her diagnosis gave Labor Day a terrible power. It made it truly a Holy Day. It was not possible for her to rid herself of her knowledge of the closeness of death, her human vulnerability. Some acknowledgment, some ritual was needed to be able to face this day and the powerful feelings that were carried in its wake. For her, the approach of Labor Day weekend brought with it a kind of altered state, one that drew her deep within herself. Rather than fight this experience, she made what I would call a conscious relation-ship with it. She avoided making any social plans with other people, kept her expectations of herself low, and allowed herself a quiet solitude. At one point during the weekend, she went for a big run and reveled in the feeling of her strong and healthy body.

In bringing this meaning to the day, she did not rid herself of her sadness, fear, and grief. She did, however, give herself time and space to be able to understand them and make sense of her experience of them. They were no longer felt to be aberrations or signs of illness or weakness, but were understandable feelings arising from her experience. This gave her ordeal meaning, and that, in itself, was healing.

## Tending the Ancestral Spirits

According to Turner, the Ndembu word for ritual also held the connotation of "obligation," particularly in relation to the ancestral spirits. In this understanding, ritual performs two separate but related functions. On the one hand, ritual acts were understood as a way of fulfilling one's ongoing obligations to the ancestors. On the other hand, ritual was understood as something to be employed when one had *failed* to meet these ancestral obligations. In other words, ritual was a means of healing the disordered condition that resulted from having neglected the spirits of the family or community.

This performance of ritual is obviously rooted in a specific cultural time and place. I am using this example as a lens through which to reflect on the contemporary relationship to ritual to see if it is possible to discern some hints about the value of ritual for us today. One way to think about the notion of the "obligation to the ancestral spirits," then, would be to consider it as what Raimon Panikkar calls a homeomorphic equivalent[70] for the responsibility that we carry for the archetypal, cultural, and familial legacies that we inherit, and that impact our experience of ourselves in the world. From the Jungian perspective, it is crucial that we become conscious of this responsibility. The archetypes, wrote Jung, are those psychic elements that have been "inborn in [us] from the earliest times, and, eternally living, outlasting all generations, still make up the groundwork of the human psyche."[71] The past, in other words, lives on in each human being with a depth and power that is often unrecognized. The full development of our human existence is possible only when we can establish a conscious relationship to these depths.

What in one time and culture is known by the name "ancestral spirits," is rendered in the language of Jungian psychology as "the groundwork of the human psyche." Both of these names point to a similar experience. There is an archetypal order with which we must be in right relation and that must be embodied in some way in our living. That was the depth of experience needed for the woman struggling with the anniversary experience of her breast cancer diagnosis. Because of her experience, a new "spirit" had entered her life, and she was "obliged" to acknowledge and integrate the psychological change that had occurred; otherwise, she would be stuck in an unresolved grief for what had been lost. The "spirits," in other words, make demands on us and we ignore them at our peril.

The practical effect of this idea is that those experiences with which we do not deal in a constructive manner have the potential to enter our lives destructively. A simple example of this would be in the realm of parenting. Without becoming conscious of the "ancestral spirits" in our experience of being parented—that is, the gifts, the mistakes, and the wounds that our own parents and their parents before them, brought to the task—we are likely to fall into old, unconscious, and often dysfunctional intergenerational patterns of parenting. In this case, "tending the ancestral spirits" means knowing the strengths and weaknesses, the vulnerabilities and the fault lines that we carry forward from our parental heritage into our own experience of being a parent. This depth of awareness may not prevent us from making our own mistakes, but it may help us avoid being caught and possessed by the "old ghosts."

## Participation in the Divine Drama

Another function of ritual is to help the individual experience a connection to the transpersonal, to provide a bridge by which the energy of the transpersonal can enter and energize the ego. For Jung, a life in which everything is banal, in which one cannot escape the merely mundane, is a life susceptible to spiritual and psychological illness. There is an irrepressible human need for the experience of transcendence, to transcend what is solely concrete and personal, and to become, in Jung's words, "actors in the divine drama of life."[72]

Traditionally, ritual was just such a divine drama. Participants acted out the story of their god or culture hero and would thereby partake in the energies represented by that story. One common example of this can be seen in the communion ritual that continues to take place weekly in Christian churches around the world. In that ritual, the individual is understood to take the body and the blood of the god into their own bodies, infusing their physical bodies—and, indeed, their very lives—with the divine. Similarly, in a common Hindu ritual called *prasād*,[73] food is first offered to the deity who receives it, investing it with divine energy. The food is then returned as a gift to the worshipper who eats it. In both of these rituals, the worshippers *participate* in the story and life of the god. They do not just listen to the story or learn it as an intellectual exercise. Their whole being is involved.

The aim of rituals such as these, and to a certain extent all rituals, is to release the participants from the experience of the finitude of their individual lives and to connect them with the Life that precedes and succeeds the personal life, the Life that ever renews itself through continual transformations, the Life in which we all live and move and have our being.

It is an objective fact that life extends indefinitely before and beyond an individual span of life, that it is marked by resilience and renewal, that life overcomes death—as when a small, green shoot grows up out of a decaying tree trunk. There is, in other words, an undeniable transcendence to life. There is also something about human consciousness that makes us feel separate from this reality—observers as opposed to participants. Ritual can remind us of our participation in life, of our role in the "divine drama."

But why ritual? Why use religious language such as *gods* or *spirits*? Isn't it possible to reach that kind of awareness through objective, scientific understanding?

The answer to the last question, of course, is yes, though with a slight caveat. The value of science and the scientific method are beyond dispute. However, like all human points of view, it has its limits. In this case, the great value of science—its objectivity—is also its limitation.

Whereas science asks us to stand apart from the world we observe, ritual and religion asks us to enter it. This is why Jung talks about being an actor in the divine drama. To be such an actor is not about adopting a set of beliefs to which we intellectually assent. It is more an act of a willing suspension of disbelief in order to *experience the transcendence of life* and not simply to attempt to understand it. For Jung, words like *God* and *spirit* are to be understood as synonyms for the unconscious, but with a particular advantage over that more clinical term. That advantage is the emotion that they can evoke in the individual. Whether one reacts to the word *God* with feelings of adoration or feelings of disgust, what matters is that a reaction is evoked. One does not simply think about a concept; rather, one enters into a confrontation.[74] Through ritual and the religious language that attends it, then, the whole of the human being becomes involved—body, mind, and soul. In this way, the knowledge of the power and transcendence of the life process does not remain as just an objective and intellectual idea. It becomes personal. It takes on a meaning for the individual in the very living of his life.

## Structure and *Communitas*

It is one of the peculiarities of human consciousness that we are both part of the phenomena of life and that we have the capacity to stand apart from life and observe it. These two qualities of our being lead to such radically different experiences that it seems impossible to reconcile them one to another. There is an inherent dichotomy in the human soul, and it creates a tension that can be felt at both an individual and a collective level.

The individual experience of anxiety, for instance, presents an especially magnified example of the observing aspect of consciousness that can help to illustrate this experience of our inner dichotomy. In anxiety, the mind vigilantly scans situations and environments for signs of potential dangers. At the risk of oversimplification, this can be understood as an attempt to deal with fear and uncertainty through an overemphasis on standing apart and observing. One technique for managing anxiety that has gained support and popularity in recent years has been borrowed from the realm of religion: mindfulness. In the practice of mindfulness, the individual shifts attention from what *might happen* to what *is happening*, from a possible future to the lived present. In other words, managing anxiety involves switching from an exaggerated observing consciousness to one that directly participates in the moment as it exists right now.

On a collective level, this dichotomy can be seen in the difference between the scientific and religious points of view. The scientific perspective emphasizes and encourages standing apart, whereas religious consciousness, particularly in its ritual aspect, seeks a more complete participation with life. As I mentioned, these two perspectives seem irreconcilable. Too often this gets expressed in the terribly misguided form of a war between science and religion. This perceived conflict frequently breaks out into open hostility, and one often feels that for the soldiers in this war it is a battle to the death.

In his book, *Psychological Types*, Jung presents a history of this psychic dichotomy as it has passed through the history of ideas in such iterations as the arguments between nominalism and realism, the energies of the Apollonian and the Dionysian, and William James' distinction of tough-minded and tender-minded individuals.[75] Philosopher Alan Watts, in one of his recorded lectures, humorously refers to this same phenomenon as the division between "prickly" people and "gooey" people.[76] All of these correspond to what, in the previous chapter, I referred to as the objective and subjective responses.

According to Turner, these two qualities of human consciousness are equally necessary. Each quality forms part of a dialectical process by which individuals and societies are renewed and sustained. Turner's terms for these qualities, as experienced on the social level, are *structure* and *communitas*. Structure is more or less self-evident: It is that part of life that is governed and maintained through "language, law, and custom."[77] Communitas is expressed in the dissolving of these structures. The result of this dissolving is that individuals and societies are enabled to experience humanity-as-such—that is, our common participation in and identity with life and with each other. Communitas, then, is the unmediated experience of being.

It is crucial that the dialectic between these two dimensions of life remains open and active. If it does not, the consequence is that each domain becomes the shadow of the other and is acted out in a destructive form:

> Exaggeration of structure may well lead to pathological manifestations of communitas outside or against "the law." Exaggeration of communitas, in certain religious or political movements of the leveling type, may be speedily followed by despotism, overbureaucratization, or other modes of structural rigidification.[78]

Structure is needed to meet the material needs of people, but it is communitas that infuses life with meaning. However, the dissolving process of communitas makes sense only when it functions in relation to some structure. Ritual provides a means for individuals and groups to enter the liminal space of communitas through which they are temporarily delivered from the confines of structure in order to be renewed and reenergized by the freedom that such an experience of communitas allows.

A simple example of this ritual opening to communitas as it applies to the experience of an individual would be the practice of meditation. One purpose of meditation is temporarily to dissolve the structure of directed ego functioning, so that the experience of being can break through. This is achieved through various techniques designed to interrupt the individual's identification with the activity of his own mind. Afterward, the practitioner rises from his cushion to return to the tasks of the day.

Joseph Campbell gives a powerful statement of what he sees as a universal need for such ritual communitas:

> You must have a room, or a certain hour or so a day, where you don't know what was in the newspapers that morning, you don't know who your friends are, you don't know what you owe anybody, you don't know what anybody owes you. This is a place where you can simply experience and bring forth what you are and what you might be. This is the place of creative incubation.[79]

For Campbell, it is an absolute necessity to create a space like this in which one can "bring forth what they are and what they might be." What is implied by his statement is that to do this requires some kind of special act. It is a work that must be performed with consciousness and deliberate intention. It doesn't just happen. In other words, the structure of the ritual is necessary for the experience of communitas or being.

When it is not held by the container of ritual, the attempt to obtain an unmediated experience of being can become dangerous, like a fire that burns out of control. Dissolving tips over into dissolution. This is evident, for instance, in the excessive use of alcohol and drugs. Ritual uses of alcohol and drugs exist in many religious settings, from the Christian communion wine to the Peyote ceremonies of the Native American Church.[80] What is casually today called "partying" is an expression of the impulse to dissolve the inhibiting structures of day-to-day living, as well as to overcome perceived emotional and psychological blocks or stresses. Partying works, but outside of the containment that ritual can provide, it can all too easily become destructive to oneself and others.

This brings us full circle to where we started this chapter—with Campbell's description of the function of ritual as "concentrating one's mind on the implications of what one is doing." The structure of ritual both requires and facilitates consciousness. It thereby allows for a life-giving encounter with the wild edges of living without overturning the order of our everyday lives but refreshing and renewing them instead.

# Chapter 3
## Religion: The Lived Symbolic

So far in this survey of the symbolic life, I have looked at two of its fundamental components: symbol and ritual. In this chapter, I will explore a third element: religion. Properly speaking, religion should not be understood as a component of the symbolic life in the same way as symbol and ritual are, but rather as something like its emergent mode of expression. The term *religion,* however, is a problematic one, for it is one of those words that when we hear it, we tend to think we know what it means. I would venture that each of us, in some way, has some preconceived idea, some more or less fixed image, some more or less stereotyped view that is conjured into consciousness by the word *religion.* It is a word that is overlaid with a multitude of different associations and connotations, either positive or negative, depending on one's background and experience.

Much, of course, depends on the quality and content of one's exposure to and participation in religious ideas and practices. On an individual level, there is the question of whether or not one has ever been active in a religious tradition, and if so, whether that engagement was experienced as helpful or harmful, meaningful or trivial. On a collective level, the issue revolves around the kinds of images and ideas that a person may or may not have encountered about the topic of religion. Religion is a complex subject that has inspired a rich and sometimes confusing profusion of opinions and reflections. It is a generative field of study that spawns many approaches and under-standings, depending in large degree on the temperament of the individuals who study it, ranging from intellectual theological sophistication to contemplative reflection to dogmatic orthodoxy and more. Such a complexity is necessarily obscured when religion is portrayed through the medium of popular culture, which has a huge influence on the way a large number of people will encounter ideas about the nature of religion.

A core task of this chapter, then, will be to articulate clearly an understanding of religion as reflected through the symbolic attitude that I have been developing in this book. To understand religion as a participation in the symbolic means shifting our perspective and seeing religion as a fluid activity instead of a fixed thing. In other words, it means distinguishing between religion and *a religion*. Because it presents itself in a simple and concrete form, it tends to be easier to think in terms of religion as a thing—a set of beliefs, dogmas, or practices that one holds as a possession, or a particular group with which one identifies, such as Christianity or Buddhism. Religion as an activity, conversely, points to a way of attending to and living in relationship with the transcendent. Here, the difference between the objective and subjective responses seems to be determinative.

The objective response tends to emphasize the "thingness" of religion and to see religion as an end; one discovers the truth of a particular religious view, either through some revelation or by being intellectually convinced of the arguments of the religion, then commits oneself to that group and its viewpoint. Much like one's commitment to a political party or a sports team, a more or less final decision is made regarding membership in the group.

Through the lens of the subjective response, religion is a *means* toward an end that cannot ultimately be defined; the doctrines and practices of tradition open for the individual the experience of a transcendent mystery through which truth can be encountered. The objective attitude is inclined to see religion as an answer—right or wrong—to the problems of life, whereas the subjective attitude is more likely to experience religion as a kind of question that one addresses to life. It is a questioning, moreover, that does not seek a final answer, but rather the living experience of wonder. It is a losing of oneself in mystery, a deep participation in life that energizes and enlivens. The subjective response does not seek to understand symbolic experience but to live it. Religion, from this point of view, then, is the "lived symbolic."

## The Irrational Facts of Experience

One implication proceeding from the ideas discussed in the previous section is that any definition of religion depends first of all on the understanding one has of the nature of the self and its relationship to the phenomena of life. Of particular importance is whether that relationship is conceived as having a predominantly rational nature, or whether it has the capacity to maintain an openness to nonrational experience. When the rational is emphasized, the self effectively takes a dominant position in relationship to knowledge and experience. When openness to the nonrational is emphasized, the self takes a subordinate position. For the dominant self, the accent is on the self as knower. Knowledge, in other words, is conceived as something possessed by the individual—*I* know, *I* understand. When the self is subordinate, on the other hand, the accent is on the *experience* of knowing. In this case, knowledge is not a possession, but rather an encounter with an ultimately unknowable other.

Both of these modes of knowing have value and importance, but they lead to very different experiences of meaning. The meaning of a tree, for example, reflects the quality of consciousness that perceives it. To the rational, dominant self, a tree has meaning in relation to its usefulness for something or someone other than itself. A tree gives shade, provides wood for building, and produces oxygen for other beings who, in turn, are understood to be part of a food chain, providing nourishment and energy to other beings. For a subordinate self, open to the experience of the nonrational, the tree is first and foremost a living being, a mystery of life that possesses inherent meaningfulness simply in its very being. Such a self can certainly benefit from the usefulness of the tree, seeking shade, cutting wood, and breathing in oxygen. But it is just as likely to be inclined to feel reverence and responsibility toward the tree, feeding it, tending it, and even defending it against those who perceive only its utility value.

In *The Reenchantment of the World*, Morris Berman shows how the development of scientific consciousness in the sixteenth and seventeenth centuries marked a fundamental shift in the human relationship to life. It was a shift from a more subordinate self, embedded in nature and the experience of life, to a more dominant self, seeking to exert control on nature. During this shift, the focus of human interest began to be more granular, such that expansive and ultimately unanswerable questions, such as, for example, *Why are we here?* were quickly replaced with very different ones along the lines of *How does it work?* This new style of question proved to be not only answerable but also actionable. When you understand how something works, it can be put to use for human ends. "Embedded within the scientific program," writes Berman, "is the concept of manipulation as the very touchstone of truth. To know something is to control it."[81] He refers to this state of mind as "instrumentally rational."

When religion is looked at through this state of mind, it tends to be defined in terms of its "thingness." These definitions focus on religion as "a set of beliefs" or as "the body of persons adhering to a particular set of beliefs." Furthermore, the beliefs are understood to serve a particular function: setting forth "a moral code governing the conduct of human affairs."[82] In other words, these definitions emphasize a view of a dominant self, in both individual and collective forms, that holds in its possession a discrete content—a set of beliefs—with a clear utilitarian value—governing the conduct of human affairs.

Today, the "instrumentally rational" is deeply lodged in the collective psyche. For good or for ill, it is the default lens through which we look at the world. For Jung, however, the overdevelopment of the rational and the devaluation of the nonrational was a primary cause of neurosis, as well as a catastrophic loss of meaning. He believed that the antidote for this danger was religion. To avoid any confusion about what he meant in his use of the word *religion*, however, Jung elaborated with his own very specific and concise definition: "Religion means dependence on and submission to the irrational facts of experience."[83]

It is not difficult to see how Jung's definition of religion stands in direct contrast to the "instrumentally rational" attitude of mind. Instead of manipulation and control, there is dependence and submission. It is a radically different way of relating to life. Rather than advocating a psychological position in which human beings stand apart from life and seek to gain mastery over it, Jung is expressing the necessity of recognizing the sovereignty of the life process and our human participation *within* that process. If, through the scientific program, as Berman suggests, it is nature and the environment that are to be acted upon and changed, then in the religious program, as articulated by Jung, it is one's own self.

Jung is not alone in his understanding of the nature of religion. The Jewish theologian and philosopher Abraham Joshua Heschel expressed a similar view regarding the right relationship to the transcendent, using the religious language of God in place of Jung's more neutral and general psychological language of "the irrational facts of experience." For example, Heschel pointed out the impossibility of possessing knowledge of God "as if He were a fact among facts."[84] A merely rational approach keeps the individual in a state of separation from the object it seeks to understand and is therefore wholly insufficient for the apprehension and experience of the transcendent. "The task," wrote Heschel, "is not to know the unknown but to be penetrated with it; *not to know* but *to be known* to Him, to expose ourselves to Him rather than Him to us."[85]

The same conception of the proper relationship to the transcendent was echoed by philosopher Karl Jaspers when he wrote, "To live by God does not mean to base oneself on calculable knowledge .... Faith is no possession. It confers no secure knowledge, but it gives certainty in the practice of life."[86] Each of these statements is pointing to the same understanding: Religion is not knowledge *about the transcendent*, but rather the experience of and relationship *to the transcendent*.

Because "it confers no secure knowledge," this experience of religion is very difficult to grasp. It is not an idea; it is an experience. It is not a quantity of information; it is a quality of encounter with life. The words and phrases used—*the transcendent, God, the irrational facts of experience*—all point to what is ultimately unknowable. Or, to put it another way, with these words, concrete knowledge about some thing "out there" is not given or gained. Rather, these words guide the individual toward participation in a knowing that is simultaneously within and beyond her.

Such an experience is difficult to grasp because the words and language used do not refer to some object of knowledge. It would be more accurate to imagine them as exclamations in the face of a powerful experience, like a "Wow!" that bursts forth from the mouth of someone standing in awe before a spectacular sunset. "Oh my God!" we suddenly call out when something joyful, or surprising, or terrifying, or sad comes into our awareness. The words used, then, are expressions of that which cannot be translated into the field of consciousness except by way of symbols. And since there is no object to which these words and symbols refer—no discrete thing that can ultimately come under the control of reason to be possessed in the form of "calculable knowledge"—then the symbols and images of the religions cannot be understood as literal statements. They are, as one author puts it, but "hints and clues from the 'other shore.'"[87]

## The *Numinosum*

An understanding of religion based on an orientation to the "other shore" is one that is infused with the power of the *numinous*. This is a term that was introduced by the theologian Rudolf Otto to designate a nonrational experience that is "felt as objective and outside the self."[88] This concept was very influential on Jung's thought and formed a central component of another of his key definitions of religion. Religion, he wrote, is:

> a careful and scrupulous observation of what Rudolf Otto aptly termed the 'numinosum,' that is, a dynamic existence or effect, not caused by an arbitrary act of will. On the contrary, it seizes and controls the human subject, which is always rather its victim than its creator.[89]

For Otto, the experience of the numinous was an essential component of any authentic religious experience: "There is no religion in which it does not live as the real innermost core, and without it no religion would be worthy of the name."[90]

It is hard today to feel into the idea and experience of the numinous. Our rational bias discourages us from thinking in terms of "a dynamic existence" that "seizes" an individual, making her its "victim." Instead, the meaning of powerful experiences tends to be reflected solely through a physical or biological lens. An individual looking through this lens would be more inclined to pathologize such experiences, as it would lead her to assume, for example, that the nervousness she feels, and that carries with it the sense of ominous foreboding, is the result of some malfunctioning of the body's activity due to an unlucky genetic predisposition or an imbalance in the endocrine system. These days we do not speak, for instance, of "fear and trembling" in the face of the divine. Instead, we tend to prefer the reductive language of anxiety, which we believe has the virtue of asserting a primarily physiological, and therefore rational, basis for certain troubling experiences.[91]

It has become increasingly the norm through the late twentieth and early twenty-first centuries to treat the normal occurrence of virtually all difficult emotions as medical conditions in need of treatment.[92] To get a feel for the nature of the numinous as it manifests in everyday life, then, it will be easiest to make use of a couple of simple examples from the uplifting end of the spectrum of human experience. The *numinosum* is a quality of experience that is most often felt to be present in extraordinary and spiritual occurrences, but as the following examples show, it can also lend an extraordinary and spiritual quality to ordinary and everyday events.

I looked at one such example in Chapter 1, in the description of the symbolic power that attends the birth of a baby. There are very few life events that provoke as great a range of emotional experiences as childbirth. Hope, joy, fear, possibility, doubt, worry—all of these and more accompany the birth of a child. To witness the whole process of pregnancy and birth is to be overcome with a feeling of awe that is inspired by the miracle of life. New parents are utterly and forever changed and must find a way to metabolize a new and often unexpected set of feelings and expectations they may discover in themselves. In a very real sense, the full sweep of life is experienced in a moment. A new father, holding his tiny daughter, may begin to dream of what it will be like to dance with her at her wedding. A new mother may wonder if she can protect the son asleep at her breast from encountering the struggles and pain that come with living in the world.

Another vivid example is the experience of falling in love. To fall in love is to be overpowered by love. It is never the result of careful deliberation, but rather overtakes us suddenly for good or for ill. This can also be a dangerously disruptive experience, as it doesn't always happen when and where and with whom it should, as the statistics on infidelity make plain.[93] In this way, the divine energy of love can certainly become an occasion for fear and trembling. The experience of being in love is also a paradoxical one, making us feel happy and sad at the same time. We feel the joy of hope and potential, and the fear of loss and hurt. Somewhere deep in our being a new love terrifies us because we sense, however unconsciously, that it must culminate in letting go—in loss—even if that letting go is not until the end of our lives with the death of one of the partners. In other words, the numinous quality of falling in love brings us into contact with the full existential sweep and emotional drama of life. Again, as in the experience of new birth, we experience the whole of life in a moment.

These examples are ordinary life moments in which we touch the wonder, power, and mystery of life—that is, the numinous. If we follow Jung's definition of religion, which we have seen consists of both "a careful and scrupulous observation of the *numinosum*" as well as "dependence on and submission to the irrational facts of experience," we can begin to understand that what he is pointing to is the need for turning toward such experiences and opening to the transformations that they are working in us, and through us. In other words, religion means a deepening of our encounter with life.

This definition of religion is a challenge to and a rejection of the ideas championed by Freud and others—that religion is something like a comforting illusion, a childish fantasy, an infantile wish-fulfillment of a longing for the protection of a strong and benevolent father, or an opiate for the masses. Rather than comfort and illusion, religion is a means of experiencing the full range of life, not turning away from it. Understood as an engagement with the numinous, religion is, to paraphrase the Buddhist philosopher Keiji Nishitani, an exposure of the individual to the full existential realities of human life.[94]

## Religion versus Creed

The modern connotation of the word *religion* tends to reflect the "thingness" of religion—that is, its institutional forms that are expressed through such things as a specific set of beliefs or membership in a particular group. This is what the word implies, for instance, in the phrase *spiritual but not religious*, which has become a commonplace way for increasing numbers of people to label their relationship to religion. The implication of this phrase is that religion is an institutional encrustation to which many people feel unable to assent, despite, or because of, their sensitivity to the spiritual.

In his writings on religion, Jung makes a similar distinction between a personal, subjective relationship to the transcendent and the collective expression of dogma and belief. For Jung, however, it is the word *religion* that more accurately and appropriately describes the personal dimension. The word that he prefers to use to designate the collective expression is *creed*. Creeds are those structures that grow out of and are built up around what Jung refers to as "original religious experience."[95] They function as both a means of remembering that original experience, as well as a channel for the re-experiencing of it. The emergence of a creed, then, facilitates the participation of large numbers of people in the religious mysteries that were their inspiration and from which they were initially derived. Over time, however, these structures can tend to become habitual thought forms, gradually emptied of their original power and mystery, and increasingly attenuated from their transcendent source. The collective form gradually eclipses the subjective response such that the creed may become more of a barrier against religious experience than an opening to it.

The spiritual but not religious response can be understood as one solution to this development—an attempt to return to the power of the original spiritual core that seems to be cut off by the hardening of the shell of the collective creed. A fundamental problem with this response, though, is that it has the effect of amplifying the split between personal religious experience and the shared forms of its expression. The spiritual but not religious sensibility rightly perceives that an exclusively collective approach to religion all-too-easily becomes a closed and rigid system aimed at its own preservation and disconnected from its original depths. By the same token, however, when religion is only an individual experience, it becomes diffuse and unrelated, a merely private affair divorced from the social realm and thus incapable of providing a meeting ground for the encounter between self and other.

Jung's distinction between religion and creed also at times can seem to perpetuate this same split between the individual and collective forms of religious expression. Properly understood, Jung's intention was not to reject the institutions of religion, but to recover a feeling for the original, numinous experience at their heart. More precisely, Jung wanted to understand that human faculty that was both capable of and, simultaneously, in need of the experience of the numinous and transcendent.

Religion and creed are not by necessity opposed to each other. The creeds that developed out of the experience of the numinous originally held symbolic value, acting as a means for directing attention toward the mystery of the transcendent. As such, writes Jung, they are capable of facilitating religious experience for countless people for millennia. However, when the split between religion and creed, between personal experience and collective form, becomes too polarized, the result is an exaggerated focus on the literal truth, or lack thereof, of religious statements. In other words, the question about religion gets framed as one of belief in its *contents*.

This either/or point of view severs the connection and the interplay between the rational and nonrational functions of consciousness. Symbols are interpreted as concepts, and religion as a primitive and superstitious proto-science attempting to make concrete and factual statements about life and the world, along the order of, say, physics or biology. For Jung, the way beyond this split is through recognition of the symbolic character of religious forms. Once we can grasp the symbolic nature of religious statements, we become aware of "the unfathomable wisdom that is in them," and begin to appreciate our debt "to the institution which has not only conserved them, but developed them dogmatically."[96]

And this, of course, is one of the supreme values of the many creeds—they are the repositories of unfathomable wisdom. They hold and preserve what no individual could discover, much less produce, in a single lifetime—the collective wisdom of the human encounter with life. The loss of these spiritual treasuries would be a catastrophic one.

## Religiosity, Religiology, and Religionism

Jung's distinction between religion and creed provides a helpful model for beginning to think about the different components of religious experience. It remains problematic, however, because it too easily lends itself to oppositional thinking with religion conceptualized as something opposed to creed, and individual experience as something opposed to collective tradition. On one side exists the living spirit of religion; on the other side is the dead form of belief.

A somewhat more differentiated understanding of the dimensions of religion can be found in the writings of theologian Raimon Panikkar, whose work offers a remarkable balance of theological illumination and psychological grounding. Panikkar presents a model of religion that provides a way beyond the oppositional trap. He suggests that the fullness of religious experience includes three distinct, though interrelated, aspects, which he labels as religiosity, religiology, and religionism.[97]

*Religiosity* can be understood as that faculty that enables the individual to have an experience of the transcendent. It corresponds to what would typically be called spirituality. It is that aspect that is expressed by an openness to and responsiveness toward the numinous. The term *religiology* indicates the human endeavor to reflect on life and on one's beliefs, as well as the broader study of religion through science, philosophy, and theology. This is the rational dimension—the *logos* of religion—through which human beings take up an intellectual and imaginative relationship to their experiences, reflecting on the implications of those experiences. The third aspect is the sociological dimension of religion, which Panikkar calls *religionism*. This is the dimension that includes membership in a specific group that adheres, at various levels of openness, to a particular set of beliefs, such as, for instance, Buddhism or Islam. This is also the dimension that corresponds most closely with Jung's notion of creed.

Panikkar's model is a protection against any tendency to be lulled into an overly simplified or one-dimensional idea of what is indicated by the word *religion*. It is a reminder, rather, that we are dealing with a field of human activity containing a rich complexity. Together, these three domains reflect the wholeness of religious experience that begins with the opening to the experience of the transcendent (religiosity), is continued through the reflection on that experience (religiology), and which is then lived out through a disciplined engagement with the forms through which that experience is expressed (religionism).

Religion in its fullness reflects all three of these elements without being reduced to or identified with any one of them on its own. Religion is not just one individual's private spiritual experience; it is not just a collection of ideas and beliefs to be accepted or rejected; and it is not simply a particular tradition or group to which one chooses to belong. Rather, religion involves the whole of our being in relationship to the self, each other, and the universe in which we find ourselves. It is, then, the lived experience of all three of these aspects as they interact, deepening and mutually informing and transforming each other, and transforming us, at the same time, as we engage with them.

## The Awakening of Faith

The perspectives outlined in this chapter lead to an understanding of religion that could be described as follows: Religion is the means by which an individual orients herself in relationship to life with all its transcendent breadth and depth. It proceeds through engagement with symbolic forms that mediate numinous experience and, at the same time, enable the communication and transmission of that experience.

Panikkar's model of the three dimensions of religion makes it clear that this is an activity that requires the full participation of the individual with all of her faculties—feelings as well as thoughts, body as well as mind, imagination as well as will. Jung is in complete agreement with this. The experience of that aspect of life to which religious symbolism and ritual point cannot be gained through a passive reception of some doctrine or the intellectual understanding of some point of theology. Rather, one must commit one's whole being to the experiment. It is through such a commitment of the fullness of one's being that religion becomes the "lived symbolic" and, thus, expressive of its true transformative potential.

It is this transformative power of religion that, for Jung, was the essential quality. Careful observation of the numinous on its own was not enough, nor was dependence on and submission to the irrational.

The circle is not closed until the individual allows herself to be transformed by her experience. Religion, then, is not an act, nor is it merely a practice. True religion emerges out of the experience of transformation. For Jung, as I have noted, the term *religion* most properly refers to the inner experience of the individual and not to the outer form of her activity. In particular, it describes "a consciousness which has been *altered by the experience of the numinosum.*"[98]

One of the primary ways that this change manifests is in the felt experience of having a solid foundation that holds beneath and despite of the vicissitudes of life. Earlier in this chapter, I quoted Karl Jaspers expressing just this experience: Faith "confers no secure knowledge, but it gives certainty in the practice of life." This quality of possessing an underlying foundation was vividly expressed in the dream of an analysand:

> *I have found or created a way of surfing on waves that are close to the beach. There is a platform under the water to catch you if you fall when it feels like you will crash into the beach. At first I think, "This is a cheat." Then I ask myself, "Am I enjoying this?" I realize that I am.*

This man's dream was the culmination of several surfing dreams that featured the danger of crashing onto the beach or being knocked down by rough waves. He associated the appearance of the platform as being related to both his ongoing meditation practice and to our analytic work together through which he experienced a much-needed affirmation and support of his spiritual life.

This emergence of a solid foundation correlates with what theologian Henry Cantwell Smith, using religious language, calls the awakening of faith. He suggests that it is the task of religion—here meaning the religious tradition or creed—to awaken faith. In other words, through the symbols, stories, rituals, and teachings of a religion, the individual's personal encounter with the transcendent is awakened. For Smith, faith is understood to be deeper and more personal than religion. It is "a quiet confidence and joy which enable one to feel at home in the universe."[99] Or, as the dream of my analysand phrased it: "*'Am I enjoying this?' I realize that I am.*"

As noted earlier, Jung felt that too often this trajectory was reversed—the original numinous experience hardened into a dogma and became fixed into an institution, which he called a creed. Smith, on the other hand, is suggesting the possibility that through the creed an authentic numinous experience can be enkindled in the individual. Religion, understood as the lived symbolic, then, is the organizing structure that is formed from and expresses our encounter with the *numinosum* and that can simultaneously open us to the possibility of that encounter. Approached in this spirit, it becomes that which facilitates our living in relationship to the transcendent, or numinous, realm.

# Part 2

# Why Do We Need
# a Symbolic Life?

# Chapter 4
## The State of Religion

Since the time of the Enlightenment beginning in the late sixteenth century, there has been no shortage of voices declaring the decline and ultimate demise of religion.[100] In recent years, these voices have been energized by several studies showing a steady rise in the number of people unaffiliated with a religion. The interpretation most often made from the information in these studies is that there is a kind of infectious dissatisfaction with religion that is leading to a mass exodus from religious institutions and that it is gaining momentum. It is frequently considered a foregone conclusion when these studies are reported that such trends will continue in a more or less linear fashion and will lead to the inevitable dissolution of religion. Many celebrate this possibility as a triumph of human reason, with humanity finally outgrowing its attachment to "childish superstitions," whereas others see it as a sign of the decline of civilization and a descent into moral anarchy.

Looking strictly—and somewhat superficially—at the numbers, it is understandable that many people would be led to suppose that religion is disappearing. The religious imagination, however, stretches back into the prehistoric mists of human existence and shows no end to its ability to produce forms through which it expresses itself. Given this prodigious generativity, it might be prudent to recognize that religion is a much more durable aspect of the human soul than we often tend to consider.

The ebb and flow of religious consciousness and observance is nothing new. Indeed, it is one of the central themes of religion itself and appears in the scriptures and stories of almost every tradition. It is the archetypal theme of the descent from a golden age of enlightenment and wisdom to a fallen state of humanity, and it can be found in various forms throughout the world's religious systems. It is found in ancient Greece in Hesiod's description of the five ages of man, descending from a golden age to an iron age, and again in Hinduism, with its account of the four great Yugas or epochs of human existence that mark a gradual degradation of wisdom, knowledge, and spiritual awareness. It resounds again and again in the accounts of the prophets of the Hebrew Bible, each of whom, in some way, is called to exhort the nation of Israel to return to its covenant with God, from which it repeatedly drifts away.

On a historical level, we can trace this theme, for instance, throughout the development of Christianity, which is often marked by new movements that arise following periods of religious decay, such as the emergence of Pietism in Germany in the seventeenth century or the so-called Great Awakening in eighteenth century America.[101] In more recent times, the death and overcoming of religion was yet again considered a foregone conclusion during the great social changes that took place in the 1960s, as Karen Armstrong notes in her book *The Case for God*. The wave of secularism that rolled through during that time seemed to be the ultimate fulfillment of the spirit that flowered during the Enlightenment. And yet, it never materialized. According to Armstrong, "It was ... premature to speak of the death of religion, and this became evident in the late 1970s, when confidence in the imminent arrival of the Secular City was shattered by a dramatic religious resurgence."[102] This time, the resurgence took the form of powerful fundamentalist expressions of religion on a worldwide scale, including the Islamic Revolution in Iran and the emergence of the Moral Majority in the United States.

Personally, I am as skeptical of the modern prophetic voices uttering the old belief that religion will eventually be overcome as I am of those religious voices that see signs of the fulfillment of apocalyptic prophecy in the conditions of modern life. Still, it is important to recognize that there does seem to be some profound shift in the human religious experience that is currently taking place.

The experience of a transcendent dimension of existence has never been an easy one, it would seem, for the vast majority of human beings. About 2,500 years ago, the ancient Greek philosopher Heraclitus said, "What is divine escapes men's notice because of their incredulity."[103] Today, that difficulty is only exacerbated by the fact that we live in a globalized world, more aware than ever of the diversity and complexity of the many forms that the human response to transcendence can take. It becomes increasingly difficult to hold to the idea that any one tradition can have an exclusive claim to truth in the face of such diversity. But then, one might reasonably wonder, what relationship, if any, does a particular tradition have with the truth?

For Jung, this question was answered in terms of a religion's ability to provide an adequate means for an individual to gain access to the deeper experience for which it is the mediator. Whatever decline religion experienced, Jung believed, was because of its failure to do this very thing. He noted that the institutions of religion in the modern era had become increasingly unable to provide for their adherents an *experience of the numinous*.[104] They had ceased, in other words, to provide a genuine initiation into religious experience and instead merely moralized about it:

> [T]heologians fail to see that it is not a matter of proving the existence of the light, but of blind people who do not know that their eyes could see. It is high time we realized that it is pointless to praise the light and preach it if nobody can see it. It is much more needful to teach people the art of seeing.[105]

It is this failure to teach people the art of seeing, I would suggest, that is primarily reflected in the studies reporting on the decline of religious affiliation. It is to an examination of these studies that I now turn.

## The Rise of the "Nones"

A recent study published by the Pew Research Center titled "The U.S. Religious Landscape Study" documents the decline in religious activity among certain segments of the U.S. population.[106] The factors measured to assess religious engagement included such things as belief in God, the practice of daily prayer, attendance at religious services on a regular basis, and a tendency to describe religion as important. The study shows a great deal of stability in religious life in the United States in that those who identify themselves as affiliated with a specific religious tradition are as observant as they ever were. However, the study also finds that the overall percentage of people so affiliated has shrunk by a moderate amount, from 83 percent of the population in 2007 to 77 percent in 2015—a decline of 6 percent over 8 years, or roughly 20 million people. This decline is driven, in large part, by those people who, under the category "religious affiliation," answered "none," and who are therefore known colloquially as the "Nones." During this time period, the percentage of "Nones" grew by a corresponding amount, from 16 to 23 percent.

This study further notes that not only are the "Nones" unaffiliated but they are also becoming less religious in general. Only 61 percent of "Nones" said that they believe in God in the 2015 survey, down from 70 percent in 2007. When all the numbers are combined, they show that only 50 percent of adults in the United States attend religious services at least once a month (down from 54 percent in 2007) and only 53 percent say that religion is very important to them (down from 56 percent in 2007).

The initial interpretation that springs to mind in the face of these numbers is that people are "losing their religion," to paraphrase the R.E.M. song, at a faster and faster pace. However, as author and Congregational minister Lillian Daniel points out, the group of "Nones" is not a monolithic group with one set of reasons and motivations.[107] Many, it is true, are leaving religion for myriad reasons, but it is also the case that many people in this category have never been introduced to religion in the first place.

The Pew Study notes that the rise in percentage of "Nones" is driven by people entering into young adulthood, the so-called Millennial generation. According to Daniel, this is a group that very often has not been exposed to a religious tradition. Among the causes for this is the fact that their parents had left and rejected religion at an earlier time, and also, as I will discuss shortly, because of the paradoxical effect of the increase in religious diversity, both within families and in the larger communities in which people have grown up. In contrast to the Millennials, Americans of the older generations— the Silent Generation, the Baby Boomers, and Generation X—are "by and large, about as religious today as when the Religious Landscape Study was first conducted in 2007."[108]

Surprisingly, the survey also indicates that despite the decline in religious observance, Americans are becoming *more* spiritual, with a 7 percent rise in the number of people who "feel a deep sense of spiritual peace and well-being" at least weekly (up from 52 percent in 2007 to 59 percent in 2014), as well as a sense of wonder about the universe (from 39 percent to 46 percent). On the face of it, Americans would seem to be becoming more and more "spiritual but not religious."

It is not all bad news for the religions, however, as another recent survey from Pew has shown that the overall percentage of "Nones" worldwide is projected to decline over the next few decades as the population of the world increases.[109] Although the absolute number of religiously unaffiliated is expected to continue to grow, so too will that of the religiously affiliated, and at a higher rate, such that the relative percentage of "Nones" begins to shrink.

Religion may be going through some kind of transformation on a global scale, but it is not facing an existential crisis. Even so, there does seem to be something of a convulsion going on in the religious depths of the collective psyche, leaving many people today feeling disoriented and unrooted.

## The Four Functions of Religion

As I noted in Chapter 3, religion is a complex human activity with several different aspects. There, I discussed Jung's distinction between religion and creed as well as Panikkar's three dimensions of religion— religiosity, religiology, and religionism. Here, I want to introduce one more framework through which to reflect on the state of religion today. This is a configuration put forward by Joseph Campbell in several of his works, including his exhaustive series on the mythologies of humankind, *The Masks of God*.[110] In this schema, Campbell delineates what he sees as the four functions of mythology, which he identifies as the mystical, the cosmological, the sociological, and the pedagogical, which he also refers to as the psychological. Like concentric circles, each of these functions describes an increasingly focused field of activity, proceeding from the ineffable vastness of the mystical dimension down to the psychological specificity of the individual.

Although Campbell speaks of myth, it is clear throughout his work that when he uses the word *mythology*, he is referring to the religious dimension of life, as when he writes, "Myth is the secret opening through which the inexhaustible energies of the cosmos pour into human cultural manifestation."[111] In this way, Campbell's understanding of mythology correlates to what I have been describing as a participation in the symbolic dimension.[112] His four-function model, then, is a helpful one for understanding the different ways that religious forms and expressions mediate an experience of the transcendent to the different domains of human life. Looking at each of these functions in turn will provide a useful structure for identifying some of the ways that contemporary life presents a challenge for an adequate realization of this mediation.

Each function represents a relationship with the different dimensions of life. The first of these is the mystical function. When this is operating, religion serves the purpose of "eliciting and supporting a sense of awe before the mystery of being."[113] This is the central purpose of religious life, as it is the one that undergirds and "vitalizes" all the other functions that follow. The second is the cosmological function, the purpose of which is "to render a cosmology, an image of the universe."[114] This image guides the relationship that human beings form with the environment in which they live, for good or for ill. The task of the next—the sociological function—is "to support the current social order, to integrate the individual organically with his group."[115] The final level is what Campbell calls the pedagogical or psychological function, the role of which is "to initiate the individual into the order of his own psyche, guiding him toward his own spiritual enrichment and realization."[116]

In the remainder of this chapter, I will work through the four functions in reverse order and consider how well the current religious landscape is able to fulfill or not each of these essential life tasks. Each of these domains poses challenges for contemporary religious life, some greater than others.

## The Psychological Function of Religion

What does it mean to live a human life? How do we make the passage from child to adolescent to adult to elder? Who do we become in the process and what is it that will facilitate the optimum unfolding of our potentials and personality? These are the questions at the heart of the psychological function of religion, the purpose of which, as I noted above, is "to initiate the individual into the order of his own psyche."

The key word here is *initiate*. This indicates that the process is not random or arbitrary but has a particular focus and intentionality to it. Who I become and how I understand the meaning and purpose of life has everything to do with those things that I experience as the central values of my life. Whether I am aware of it or not, such central values possess a god-like power. The values that form the core of my response to life, whether conscious or unconscious, have a compelling quality and create a psychological field by which all experience is evaluated and interpreted. Those values, then, are not merely a set of preferences or even principles. They are those entities that I experience as lending value and worth to my being and to my life.[117] It is crucial, therefore, that I am able to form some conscious awareness of and relationship to these central values so that I am not unconsciously driven by them. This is the work associated with the psychological function of religion.

The essence of a religious outlook is that it involves an investment of oneself in a center of value that lies outside the ego personality. Through this, one is initiated into a particular relationship with life and with the cosmos. At its best, this initiation can lead to an awakening of what Jung calls "the creative meaning and potentialities of adult existence."[118] Such an awakening, however, cannot happen if one's highest value is too narrow and limited to support the full unfolding of one's potential. A refusal to allow oneself to be limited at all, on the other hand, means that the central value is likely to be so diffuse that the effective result is a center occupied by nothing substantial at all. These two dangers of the psychological level are the twin hazards of idolatry on the one hand and relativism on the other.

In *Stages of Faith*, James Fowler defines *idolatry* as "the profoundly serious business of committing oneself or betting one's life on *finite centers of value and power* as the source of one's … confirmation of worth and meaning."[119] Even a quick look at the preoccupations of our contemporary culture offers insight regarding the life values into which people today are initiated and which are expected to provide the basis of a meaningful life in our time. At the top of the list are those things that constitute what Fowler calls a "low civil religion," including youth, material success, and social status.[120]

One finite value that is especially dominant in the world today is our addiction to technology, which includes the fever for the technological mastery of life. The primary measure of meaning of this realm of being is productivity and achievement. The incredible technological advances in so many areas of life that the human race has witnessed over the last 200 years has led us to believe that there is little in our world that cannot be changed for the better through the application of technology, including the human being. But this belief leads us to experience ourselves as manipulatable objects— mechanisms that we can simply tinker with to make ourselves "function better." Through this mindset we become *things* that are either efficient or inefficient, and no longer living, growing *beings*. The focus on the technical, with its language of equations and algorithms, forecloses the experience of the imaginal—the wandering, symbolic, poetic imagination that senses the unseen. We become, in other words, that which Jung warned of almost 100 years ago: "the standardized, mass produced, 'normal' human being demanded by the machine age."[121]

On the other end of the spectrum lies the danger of relativism. This results from an insufficient investment in any central value, such that there is no framework of commitment through which experience can evaluated. The relativist seeks to always keep his options open, like an eternal bachelor ever playing the field. However, this eventually puts enormous pressure on the individual to invent from day-to-day, and even moment-to-moment, what it is that constitutes meaning and purpose. Under these conditions, one tends to follow whatever gives off the strongest signal, which is usually filtered through the prism of desire.

Leading with desire is an exercise in attempting to feed the spirit with what Emily Dickinson calls "fickle food upon a shifting plate." Satisfactions are fleeting and mercurial. What satisfies today will not satisfy tomorrow as it is not the particular thing that is sought—the material object, the new experience, the sexual partner—but rather the excitement generated by the thing we want to possess. This is the model of human being as consumer and it leads to the conflation of meaning with novelty and to the restless pursuit of stimulation and entertainment.

A lived human life gains meaning and definition in relation to the specific commitments we make, be they relational, vocational, or spiritual. These are the vehicles in which our lives gain their content and character. It is through our commitments that life becomes a work, in the sense of a creative opus, with a focus and a center that give meaning, coherence, and depth to our experiences. Without this focus, events can seem to be disconnected and isolated happenings, with only an accidental relation to our overall life story. In this way, the values that occupy the center of our lives determine the horizon against which we come to know and understand our own story and its relation to life as a whole.

Operating at the psychological level, religion has the capacity to initiate the individual into a conscious relationship with a set of lasting values that provides a sure and stable foundation for creative growth and development. Grounded in transcendent values, we are then less susceptible to unconsciously living by values derived solely from the collective culture, on the one hand, or the shifting winds of our own impulsive desires, on the other. Both of these "default" modes of living stand ready to fill the vacuum that forms when this aspect of our being is left untended.

## The Sociological Function of Religion

According to Campbell, the sociological function of religion performs two primary tasks. First, it lends support to the social order as it is currently structured and, second, it enables the individual to be functionally integrated with his group. At the social level, then, religion gives coherence to a particular cultural group and to the individual's connection with that group. In a homogeneous culture, or at least one that is perceived to be homogeneous, this dimension of religious experience is essentially imperceptible in its operation. However, in our increasingly multicultural, multireligious, and heterogeneous world, it is on the level of religion's social function where many of the most challenging disunities are felt.

In a recent review of several studies, religious researcher and reporter Daniel Cox found an inverse correlation between cultural and religious diversity and the frequency of religious observance.[122] Perhaps somewhat surprisingly, the increase of religious diversity that has taken place in recent decades in many cities and communities in the United States has been accompanied by a decrease in religious participation.

In his report, Cox draws out the differences between people from religiously diverse social settings and those from more religiously homogeneous settings. Of those people whose social networks were more diverse, 63 percent said they seldom or never went to religious services. This is almost double the percentage reported by those whose social networks were made up of people who share the same religion. Cox suggests that exposure to religious diversity ultimately undermines any claim regarding the experience of consensus on the subject of religion—a fact which may weaken an individual's motivation to participate in a specific tradition. He observes:

> The practical effect of rising religious diversity is to expose Americans to ideas and views that could challenge their religious beliefs. A recent survey found that 77 percent of Americans are acquainted with someone who is nonreligious, 61 percent know someone who is Jewish, and 38 percent know someone who is Muslim.[123]

A concomitant result of this growing religious diversity is a parallel increase in interfaith marriages, which show a similar effect on religious engagement. Children of these mixed-religion marriages, it turns out, are less likely to be exposed to religion growing up than those who come from marriages between partners with a shared religious heritage. Whereas 60 percent of children from families with religiously similar backgrounds attend religious services regularly, only 40 percent of children from religiously diverse families do so. Furthermore, as Cox notes, "Americans raised in mixed religious households are also less likely to have prayed regularly with their family and to have attended Sunday school,"[124] two of the main factors used by the Pew Research Center's Religious Landscape Study to measure a person's religiosity.

These statistics are in line with the observation from the Pew Study regarding the religious activity of the Millennial generation who, it was noted there, is far less likely to be affiliated with a religious tradition than that generation's older counterparts. Because Millennials have grown up in a much more globally connected and multicultural world than the generations before them, the correlation between Christianity and American identity has become for them significantly eroded. For this younger cohort there is no longer an inherent pressure to conform to this particular set of religious social norms—that is, the legacy of America's Christian heritage. Cox ends his review with this provocative statement: "Religious diversity might not represent a dramatic threat to religion, but it may represent another small hole in an already sinking ship."[125]

*

For his part, Jung tended to be fairly dismissive of the social aspect of religion and to speak of the social and the spiritual as if they were mutually exclusive realms of experience. In 1957, he observed that the majority of people who regularly attended religious institutions did so out of "force of habit," driven primarily by social convention, and generally had little interest in the substance of their religion.[126] As it turns out, this observation is supported by recent evidence from a study reported by the Public Religion Research Institute.[127] In that study, people were asked to respond to a survey about their personal religious participation. When the survey was conducted by phone— that is, when people were required to report on their religious activity directly to another person—the respondents over-reported such things as weekly attendance in church. When the same questions were asked anonymously online, people reported significantly lower levels of church attendance. This difference in participants answers points to the presence of a social expectation to be seen as religiously engaged. As one author of the study wrote, "The existence of religious participation inflation demonstrates that church attendance remains a strong social norm in the U.S."[128]

Jung correctly felt that such social considerations in and of themselves were not sufficient for giving an individual any true spiritual foundation. However, in dismissing the value of social norms in religious practice, he failed to give adequate recognition to the spiritual significance of our social lives. Indeed, many scholars argue that religion is primarily about how we relate to one another—that it is, at its core, a practice of ethical action toward our fellow beings.[129] Others point to the value of the collective practice of religion as a counterbalance to our culture of narcissism, against which it "rubs like sandpaper."[130]

As social beings, it is essential that our religious life speaks to the interpersonal context of our lives. Today, that means the experience of living in a highly connected, globalized world rich in the complexities of cultural and religious diversity. As the reports on the relation between the increase in diversity and the decline in religious engagement clearly imply, it is impossible today to live with the illusion that an exclusive truth inheres in any one particular religious tradition. Each tradition, it is true, asserts the truth and uniqueness of its particular revelation. The challenge posed by the realities of contemporary social life is for the traditions to be able to do so in the full knowledge and acknowledgment of the reality and truth of *other* revelations at the same time.

Any religion that cannot conceptualize and contain the reality of religious plurality, in some form or other, is too narrow to be of spiritual value for the world in which we currently live and is unlikely to be able to survive. The alternative is to take refuge in exclusivism— the belief in the exclusive truth and value of one's own tradition. Such an approach requires the rejection of all alternate symbolic representations of transcendence. This leads, necessarily, to the dehumanization of the adherents of those alternate systems.

For Diana Eck, the head of the Pluralism Project at Harvard Divinity School, the way beyond this new danger of the social function of religion is to take a pluralist approach. This involves encountering the differences of the various religions, engaging with them, and affirming the distinctiveness of each specific tradition, even as one maintains an engagement with, and commitment to, one's own chosen spiritual path.[131] If religion is to fulfill its function of providing a shared context for our collective life in this diverse world and of relating us as individuals to that collective life, a pluralist sensibility will be fundamental to achieving this most crucial of tasks.

## The Cosmological Function of Religion

Just as the individual needs to be related to his group, so too do both the individual and the group need some way of conceiving their relationship to the larger world and beyond. What is the nature of the universe and what is our place in that universe? These are the questions that speak to the cosmological function of religion.

For Campbell, whatever cosmological image a religion or mythological system produces must "correspond ... to the actual experience, knowledge, and mentality of the culture folk involved."[132] In other words, such a cosmological image must harmonize its picture of the universe with that of the scientific knowledge of the time. Cosmology, however, does not just describe the physical reality of the universe; it also encompasses the *quality* of that reality—that is, its story. Human beings do not just seek answers to questions about the composition of things and their typical processes, we also want to understand how we are related to those things, what their meaning is for us. We are driven not only to ask "What" and "How" but also "Why." Is the nature of the universe cold and empty or is it welcoming and reliable? Is it random, operating by chance, or is it ordered and predictable?

In many ways, it is the cosmological dimension that we most often think of as being at the heart of religion's decline. The public battle between science and religion, especially when it is mired in debates such as those between evolution and creationism, is taking place on this level of mythological understanding. Both sides in this battle are fighting over their vision of the nature of the universe.

On the one hand, it seems clear that the old myths and religious stories have been unable to keep up with the exponential growth of understanding about the nature of the universe that has come from the scientific world.[133] The vision offered by physics at times seems more vast and mysterious, more awe-inspiring and astonishing, frankly, than anything found in the Book of Genesis.[134] From the conception of dark matter, to the question of the holographic nature of the universe, to the mind-blowing photographs taken by the Hubble telescope, today's physics tests the limits of the human imagination. Religion ignores these developments to its detriment. A great deal of work has been done in some corners of contemporary Christian theology to reconcile a theological understanding of the world with the scientific one.[135] This shows, for the most part, that the religious world understands that it cannot expect a literal interpretation of its creation stories to be able to withstand the challenge coming from the world of science, despite the exertions of the fundamentalist corners of the various traditions.

On the other hand, though the sciences present an epic vision of the vastness of the universe, they do little to address that fundamental human question of "Why." As awesome as its vision is, a scientific perspective alone cannot supply the soul food that a truly living myth can provide. As one writer frames this dilemma:

> You scientists have this stupendous story of the universe. …
> But so long as you persist in understanding it solely in a quantitative mode you fail to hear its music. That's what the spiritual traditions can provide.[136]

I believe that the evolution versus creationism debate rages on because each side offers an incomplete solution to the crucial need for a functional and meaningful cosmology. The creationists defend their position by dismissing a vast body of knowledge about the nature of the universe as it actually is and how it came into being. As such, they ask us to close our minds to some of the most astonishing facts about the cosmos of which we are a part. The other side, by contrast, neglects the critical and vitalizing importance that *meaning* has for human life. They rightly insist on attention to facts, but limit the factual to the physical, not understanding that there are psychological and spiritual facts that have a completely different nature. This category of facts takes the form of story and symbol. These are what help us to live meaningfully and not just practically.

Both aspects of life, the meaningful and the practical, are essential. A truly whole cosmology must reflect the wholeness of our being—body, mind, and soul. It must be one that addresses not only the "What" and the "How" of the universe, but the "Why" as well. One suspects that only some as yet unrealized reconciliation between the practical and the spiritual, the scientific and the religious, will allow for the development of the kind of truly comprehensive cosmology that is needed for these times in which we live.

## The Mystical Function of Religion

The various functions that I have been exploring in this chapter are not discrete entities; rather, they are rooted in the experience of the numinous. In Campbell's schema, this experience corresponds to the mystical function of religion, which he describes as the function that undergirds and vitalizes all the others. For Campbell, the mystical function is primary, serving the purpose, as quoted earlier, of "eliciting and supporting a sense of awe before the mystery of being." The quality and nature of this aspect of religious experience is what lends a specifically religious character to all the other functions.

For Jung, much of the decline in the effectiveness of institutional religion was due to the atrophy of its ability to mediate the experience of the *numinosum*. Professions of "religious sentimentality" had replaced authentic experiences of the "living mystery" with the result that religion's capacity to provide psychological grounding or moral direction to the individual had become entirely ineffective.

It was not only Jung as a psychologist who was making this point. The Jewish theologian Abraham Joshua Heschel makes a powerful statement of exactly this idea:

Religion declined not because it was refuted, but because it became irrelevant, dull, oppressive, insipid.

When faith is completely replaced by creed, worship by discipline, love by habit; when the crisis of today is ignored because of the splendor of the past; when faith becomes an heirloom rather than a living fountain; when religion speaks only in the name of authority rather than with the voice of compassion—its message becomes meaningless.[137]

Religions, first and foremost, are human responses to the transcendent. The experience of what Jung calls the *numinosum* is a powerful one that calls forth a response from the human being in the nature of an attempt to capture and express it in some form. This expression, in turn, allows the individual, or the group, to remember, connect with, and experience some resonance of that original experience. There is certainly nothing unusual about this impulse to capture a powerful moment in some expressive form. This is the impulse that gives rise to art, poetry, and music. It is also expressed in the observance of civic rituals and traditions, such as parades, town fairs, and other festivals. Such is the impulse that is active in religion.

But the human expression remains just that, a human expression. It is not the original experience, but a means of recalling that experience to the hearts and minds of groups and individuals. The religious form functions as a means of (re)connecting one to the transcendent only as long as it inspires those hearts and minds to gaze beyond it. In other words, the purpose of the symbol (or story, or song) is to align the being of the adherent with the energy that gives rise to the particular symbol. As soon as the focus becomes fixed on the form of expression—when the religious image becomes, as Heschel writes, "an heirloom rather than a living fountain"—it is then no longer transparent to transcendence and becomes a barrier rather than an opening to the numinous.

This latter situation creates a vicious circle that leads to a degraded understanding and devaluation of the symbolic. When the form of religious expression becomes prioritized over the numinous experience that infuses it—that is, when the symbol is conflated with that which it symbolizes—it separates the individual from the experience and empties the symbol of its effectiveness. Like a battery that can no longer carry a charge, the symbol is experienced as arbitrary and irrelevant, something superfluous and easily discarded. Because of this the numinous can no longer be perceived in its fullness. It loses its power and becomes no more than a concept. In other words, the numinous is reduced to an idea and identified in people's minds with its expression, such that it is a mere name, becoming ever more opaque to the original experience that inspired it.

This process of symbol degradation is apparent, for instance, even in regard to that most central symbol of religion: God. Raimon Panikkar reminds us that the word *God* does not posit a thing or a being; rather, it is "an untranslatable symbol ... a word we employ in order to understand what is at one and the same time a mystery, a place of freedom, and a kingdom of the infinite."[138] Each of the descriptors Panikkar uses here expresses something that cannot be circumscribed. Each one points to something that is beyond our power to even imagine. As a symbol, the word *God* is meant to catapult the spiritual imagination into a realm beyond our powers of conception, a realm of mystery, freedom, and infinitude. Such an experience could be called a state of transcendent arrest—a stopping or overcoming of the conceptual mind through an experience that "humbles and at the same time exalts us, circumscribes and extends us beyond ourselves."[139]

For too many people, however, the word *God* has come to be identified with a being, like the bearded old man of Michelangelo's Sistine Chapel. This being does not inspire a sense of freedom but is instead associated with a set of rigid behavioral expectations and rules. Although it may have been that the image of an old man in the sky once inspired a sense of awe, today, with our knowledge of the vastness of the universe, such a figure just seems puny, even comical. We do not experience such a God as a window to the infinite, but rather as a door that locks us into a more concretized imagination that cannot rise beyond the human and the mundane. Given this state of affairs, many people today have naturally and understandably rejected the symbol *God*. The symbol is no longer understood as a symbol, pointing beyond itself, but is seen to be an attempt to express a concrete content of dubious merit.

It is one of the contentions of this book that the sense of the symbolic can be vitally and authentically recovered, even in the case of symbols that have generally become closed or degraded. More often, however, the process unfolds in a more unconscious way.

The fact that symbols can become degraded, weakening their capacity for mediating the experience of the transcendent, does not mean that the human drive for transcendence becomes any less active. According to James Fowler, when religious symbols have been emptied of the sacred, the result is a "vacuum of meaning" which is very often filled by "a resurgence of interest in all kinds of occult and spiritualistic phenomena."[140]

Fowler's assertion is, in fact, confirmed by the recent work of Clay Routledge, a professor of psychology at North Dakota State University, who has found that a lack of religious belief is frequently filled by some other belief of a paranormal nature. The lack of religion in a person's life, says Routledge, is concomitant with a felt sense of lack of meaning. In turn, this spurs in the individual the desire and search for meaning. For a certain percentage of people, this search leads them to "empirically unsupported ideas about U.F.O.'s."[141]

Routledge theorizes that such paranormal beliefs stem from the same impulses and sensibilities as those who hold religious beliefs— that is, the feeling that we are not alone in the universe, and the hope that there is some potentially benevolent force in the universe that might rescue the human race from possible extinction. That these views "do not explicitly invoke the supernatural and are couched in scientific and technological jargon," he writes, may make them "more palatable to those who reject the metaphysics of more traditional religious systems."[142]

This understanding of the phenomena of UFOs is remarkably similar to that expressed by Jung in 1959 when he wrote a short book titled *Flying Saucers: A Modern Myth of Things Seen in the Sky*. In that book, Jung suggested that UFOs are projections of an underlying archetype, an inborn longing for salvation from the "heavens," which in former times took the personified form of a god or gods. "It is characteristic of our time," wrote Jung, "that the archetype ... should now take the form of an object, a technological construction."[143] In the studies by Routledge and his colleagues, this insight of Jung's—and by extension, his theory of the archetypal nature of the religious function of the psyche—is given valuable empirical support.

There is little doubt that the state of religion today is in a great deal of flux and transformation. Many people believe that we live, or should be living, in a post-religious world. And although there is much that is ugly in religion—much that is oppressive, violent, and distorted—there is also much that remains that is life-giving and even necessary for human fulfillment, both spiritual and psychological.

Throughout his career, Jung was accused of being a mystic. It was a designation that he chafed against, preferring to be considered a man of science. But Jung's work was prescient in its understanding that the scientific, rational formulation of life was inadequate and insufficient to the everyday needs of human beings. As important as it is to develop an understanding of life, it is that much more important that we are able to live it and experience it, in all its ineffable depth. A great deal of Jung's work, it could be said, was directed to the recovery of the mystical function of religion. He believed that we needed a means for being open to the "original experience" of the numinous and transcendent that had been obscured by a degraded sense of the symbolic. Ultimately, it is experience, he wrote, that is of primary importance:

> Everything about this psychology is, in the deepest sense, experience; the entire theory, even where it puts on the most abstract airs, is the direct outcome of something ex-perienced.[144]

It is this focus on experience—his insistence on a living encounter with the numinous and not just an intellectual formulation of it—that makes Jung's work "mystical." It is also the reason why, I believe, that the so-called mystical dimension of Jung's work should be reassessed and embraced as the valuable and beneficial factor that, in fact, it is. For it is the experiential, "mystical" experience that is healing and transformative. Science is confirming this through much of the work emerging, for instance, from the interaction of neuroscience and psychoanalysis. This work focuses on the therapeutic effect of nonverbal, implicit emotional (that is, nonrational) communication in the interpersonal exchange between therapist and patient.[145] It is confirmed, as well, in the world of religion, by Raimon Panikkar, who notes the emergence of a longing for the experiential, as opposed to the doctrinal, dimension of religion.[146] He sees the "mystical" approach gaining strength over the more doctrinal aspects of the faith. This is what makes an understanding of the religious function of the psyche so crucial, for it is through the religious function that we can engage with full participation in the experience of life. The loss of access to the mystical is not just of academic concern; it represents a dangerous development not only in the spiritual domain but in our psychological lives as well.

# Chapter 5
# Loss of Symbols

It is not a matter of indifference if our religious traditions begin to fail in fulfilling the vitally important functions they are meant to fulfill. Our relation to the universe, to the social world, and to ourselves, together with the experience of awe before the transcendent mystery of life, are profoundly important human imperatives necessary for our physical, emotional, psychological, and spiritual health.

The question of our relationship to life is no simple matter, as evidenced by the fact that human beings have wrestled with the meaning of this relationship since there have been human beings capable of the act of reflection. Our comparatively short human life is simply not enough time for us to fashion from scratch an understanding of human life, its meaningfulness (or lack thereof), and the forms through which we can best engage it.

The religious traditions are treasure houses of hard-won wisdom. The symbols and stories of the religions provide containers for our conscious minds to engage with and connect to essential and timeless truths. The loss of connection to this wisdom is potentially catastrophic and exerts a pressure on the human being that is impossible to endure. What is no longer held and contained by the symbols of our religious traditions falls heavily on our own frail psyches.

## Creative Autonomy of the Unconscious

The religious perspective begins in the understanding that the human being must frequently contend with a power that is greater than the rational mind's capacity to contain and control. This way of thinking is anathema to the spirit of rationalism that dominates modern life. We like to think of ourselves as rational beings— technocratic and even-tempered masters of the universe. It does not take much effort, however, to see behind this façade of our modern self-image and to recognize that there is a vast amount both within us and without us that we do not understand and cannot control.

The language that Jung uses to speak of this power that confronts us is psychological language. When he refers to it, he does so most often by using the concept of the unconscious. Psychological language has the virtue of presenting things in a form that is more generally accessible today than the old mythological language, but it is also quite problematic in that it tends to be understood and interpreted reductively. When we hear psychological language, we are prone to hear it in terms of categories that are already familiar to us, in particular those of the conscious mind or of some physical, bodily process. A psychological event is assumed to be something similar to our conscious experience—that is, a product of our thoughts, or the way that our thoughts are affected by our behaviors and the choices we make. Alternatively, the psychological is seen as a secondary effect of the activity of either our brains or our bodies—the firing of neurons or the activation of the nervous system. The implication of both of these assumptions, of course, is that there is a more basic and understandable (and therefore more controllable) cause to which psychological activity can be reduced.

Throughout his work, Jung is at pains to communicate that the unconscious means something unknown, even unknowable. Furthermore, this unknown factor has its own autonomy. The unconscious is not merely some reliquary of the artifacts of thought and feeling that were once conscious but have become rejected and repressed. Rather, it is an autonomous, creative, active faculty of the human psyche that is not subject to the control of the conscious mind. It is, in fact, the source from which the conscious mind proceeds. For Jung, psychological language is not meant to be a form of biological language, but more like a meeting ground of the biological and the mythological.[147] Indeed, he repeatedly makes the point that the term *unconscious* is but the modern dress for the experience of an agency that would formerly have been personified as gods or spirits. Far from being something like an inert void, the unconscious is that self-moving power within the psyche which we do not control, but to which we can only respond and relate. For Jung, everything hinges on how we relate to this power:

> Whenever, therefore, in an excess of affect, in an emotionally excessive situation, I come up against a paradoxical fact or happening, I am in the last resort encountering an aspect of God, which I cannot judge logically and cannot conquer because it is stronger than me.[148]

Such an experience is an encounter with a numinous energy, in the face of which the power of the ego is no match. Therefore, as Jung continues, "I cannot 'conquer' a *numinosum*, I can only open myself to it, let myself be overpowered by it, trusting in its meaning."[149]

## Containers for the *Numinosum*

The question that immediately arises is How? How does one open oneself to the *numinosum* and let oneself be overpowered by the Holy? Clearly, Jung is not suggesting letting oneself be torn apart and destroyed. On the contrary, he is asserting the importance of finding some means of allowing this "stronger than me" power to manifest in a way that allows the individual not only to endure it but even to be strengthened by it.

Jung's understanding of the power of and proper relation to the *numinosum* is rooted in his own experience of "emotionally excessive situations." His entire psychological opus grows out of what is famously called his "confrontation with the unconscious," which is described in the autobiographical book *Memories, Dreams, Reflections*. During that period of his life, Jung, beginning in his late 30s and continuing on into his 40s, was beset by the kind of "excess of affect" that he describes in the quote above. He wrote about the critical necessity for him of finding images inside of his emotions as a way of containing them and calming himself. He stated that had he not been able to do so, "I might have been torn to pieces by them."[150]

Jung's personal experience helped him understand the importance of creating or, more precisely, discovering vessels in which the powerful energies of the unconscious can be channeled and contained. Without such symbolic containment, the individual is either in danger of being "torn to pieces" or forced to split off the dangerous emotional energy.

The danger of being torn to pieces means the possibility that the ego—the seat of our disposable psychological energy that can be directed by an act of conscious will to organizing and fulfilling the daily tasks of life—becomes overwhelmed and flooded by unconscious material. A symbol acts like a grounding wire that can safely redirect unbearable emotion. When this is lacking, the "circuits" of the body and the conscious mind can become dangerously overloaded. Under these conditions, a person lives in a state of unbearable emotional arousal and feels unable to function. This is the experience, for instance, of someone tormented by anxiety and who finds it impossible to tolerate being out in public, or who is immobilized by depression such that it takes a herculean effort for her just to get out of bed. Sometimes the overwhelming experience is the seemingly impossible task of metabolizing a profoundly disturbing life experience, as in the case of the woman in Chapter 2 whose breast cancer diagnosis tore away the veil of innocence that had protected her from the experience of her mortality.

The other alternative—splitting off the emotion—is probably a more common response today to the lack of a functioning symbolic container. In this case, splitting off involves some sort of suppression or repression of the emotion, often through various mechanisms of denial or distraction. Alcohol and drugs, work and entertainment, sex and consumerism are all ways that we use to split off our emotions. This can be effective, in a manner of speaking, but it often comes with potentially destructive consequences, such as addiction, crippling debt, broken relationships, or one of the many stress-related illnesses that have reached epidemic proportions in the United States today.[151]

A further problem is that splitting off emotion is not a one-time solution but must be constantly maintained through reinforcement and rehearsal of the means of suppression. The effect of this over time is that even the simplest and most basic experiences of one's inner life become intolerable because of the threat that they could be accompanied by some previously split-off experience. I recently heard an example of this kind of situation from a mother who had taken her daughter on a road trip to look at colleges. As they drove in the car, the girl insisted on having the radio on at all times, filling every moment of silence. The mother, who had been hoping to have extended time to connect to her daughter on a more intimate level, became quite frustrated. When she asked why it was so important for her daughter to have the radio continuously playing, the girl replied that she needed constant stimulation in order not to "get stuck in her own head." It is a stark statement of someone who is terrified of being confronted with her own mind because she lacks the necessary capacity for reflection that could help her manage the potential emotions such an encounter might awaken in her.

What makes the splitting off of emotion so dangerous is that it does not eliminate the difficult emotional experience. It simply cuts it off from consciousness and therefore from the possibility of bringing in one's reflective capacities to bear upon it. In other words, one is no longer able to think about what is being felt. It begins to run its own course without the participation of the rational capacities of the individual. As a result, it gains energy and power in the unconscious and often emerges in distorted and destructive forms.

*

The experience of the *numinosum*, though it is potentially life-giving, is fraught with dangers. Certain experiences cannot be psychologically metabolized through an act of will, particularly those episodes that bring us into close contact with the frailty of our bodies and our minds—mortality, mental illness, the encounter with evil, the shadow of hatred, the sublimity of love, the experience of grief. Such experiences are very often beyond our powers to assimilate without help. One of the main functions of religious symbols is to guide the soul through such heightened and dangerous times. The symbol, as Jung once wrote, "is used against the perils of the soul."[152] This is why we should not celebrate if these age-old symbols cease to function. Neither should we imagine that we have transcended the supposed "superstition" of religious belief. The presence of symbols allows us to face what would be difficult, if not impossible, to face without them. They provide crucial spiritual and psychological protection, the loss of which, Jung warns, invites potential consequences that should not underestimated:

> That is what people don't know: that they are exposed, naked
> to the unconscious when they can no longer use the old ways,
> particularly since nowadays they don't even understand what
> they mean.[153]

It is hard for us today to sufficiently grasp the implications of losing these symbolic vessels that can receive and channel the contents of the unconscious. What exactly are the contents of the unconscious and how are they experienced? And just what does it mean to be exposed to the unconscious?

We are deeply stained by the rationalistic spirit of our age, by the belief that "where there is a will there is a way." We do not recognize that such a supposedly positive belief also carries a dark shadow. The consequence of this belief is particularly evident, for instance, in the therapeutic encounter. Patients in therapy often express shame at not being able to effect this or that change through the use of willpower. When a person believes that she should be able to "pull herself up by her own bootstraps," it is felt as particularly painful and shameful when she discovers that she cannot. But the truth is that to believe that we should be able to change and do anything to dramatically alter our lives, our bodies, or our relationships through willpower alone, is to ascribe divine powers to the human being. Paradoxically, this not only has the effect of cutting us off from our human nature but also from the experience of divinity, as well.

The contents of the unconscious are those things that are *not* subject to our will. They refer to any powerful experience that we cannot master, do not initiate, and that often seems to run counter to our willing. When I find myself, for instance, caught in a mood I cannot shake, overtaken by a reaction I cannot manage, or going down the rabbit-hole of thought or fantasy that obsesses or embarrasses me, I am encountering the activity of the unconscious.

Recall Jung's statement quoted earlier: "I cannot 'conquer' a *numinosum*, I can only open myself to it, let myself be overpowered by it, trusting in its meaning." As I have noted, the attempt to "conquer the *numinosum*" often takes the form of splitting off one's psychological experience, which has the effect of lending it a potentially destructive energy that threatens to overwhelm the individual. Regardless of our belief in our status as rational beings, it seems to be the case that with certain particularly powerful experiences, the choice is either to "*let oneself be overpowered by them*," as Jung suggests, or to be overpowered by them against one's will. This may appear to be a subtle difference, but it is an important one. To let oneself be overpowered is to participate in the experience, to join with the energies at work, as opposed to resisting them. This participation gives the experience a creative and constructive form. Very often this choice hinges on the presence of an effective symbol through which the encounter with the numinous energies can be properly mediated.

One function of religion, writes Edward Edinger in his book *Ego and Archetype,* is to make visible and mediate the "transpersonal categories of existence" to the individual.[154] When there is no symbol in which these powerful experiences can be contained and expressed, those same experiences fall back upon the ego and get enacted through our personal lives. Under these conditions, it becomes exceedingly difficult to perceive the archetypal dimension of these experiences. The result is that the transpersonal begins to overload the personal. This is a psychologically perilous situation because when the transpersonal cannot be located by the individual, "the ego is likely to think of itself as everything or as nothing."[155] For this reason, Edinger states that "*Religion is the best collective protection available against both inflation and alienation* ... It is quite doubtful if collective human life can survive for any period without some common shared sense of awareness of these transpersonal categories."[156]

This danger—of the lack of an adequate container for the transpersonal—is a common theme that can appear in various guises in the dreams that people present in analysis. It often appears, for example, as the image of a house that is in peril of being damaged or destroyed by some outside force, such as a flood, a tidal wave, a storm, or a falling tree. For Jungian psychology, dreams are a kind of showing forth of the psychological reality of the individual that makes use of the language of metaphor and symbol. The image of the house under threat, then, offers a vivid portrayal of the destructive power that builds up in those aspects of psychological life that have been kept too much outside of the structures that we build up for ourselves and in which we attempt to "house" our lives. In this case, it is the impersonal or transpersonal dimension, as represented by the forces of nature—flood, tidal wave, storm, and tree—that threaten from without.

Another frequent image that shows up is that of a suitcase or bag that cannot hold everything that the person is trying to pack in it. This image is often paired with one of rushing to get to an airport before one's flight leaves and being unable to get there, in part because of the struggle with the suitcase. Here, the container (the suitcase) is simply too small, too restricted. Whereas a person can always add an addition onto a house or rearrange its interior to create space for something new to be incorporated, the capacity of a suitcase is fixed and what one can carry in it is severely limited. Something always has to be left out. This constellation of images suggests that it is just such limitations that prevent one from "taking flight"—that is, being able to periodically transcend the everyday, or to get where one needs to go.

At other times, there is no vessel or structure at all. This is the particular danger that Edinger warns of above. At such times it is the person herself, either through the body or the psychological structure of the ego, who becomes the container for the transpersonal energies. This is what Jung means when he speaks of being "naked to the unconscious" and it was exactly the situation I found myself in at a relatively recent period of my life, a situation that was expressed very powerfully in one of my own dreams.

## A Personal Illustration

When I was in my mid-forties, I experienced a very impressive dream following a series of extremely difficult life events that had culminated in the death of my sister who succumbed to the ravages of ALS two-and-a-half years after her initial diagnosis. We were very close, and her loss was devastating. It was a period of my life that thrust me fully and forcefully into the stage of midlife—a transition, I soon learned, that would require a complete reorientation of my relationship to life and to the people who shared it with me.

The dream that visited me at that time, I believe, illustrates very clearly the consequences that result from the conflation of the transpersonal with the personal, and so I will discuss it here, along with some of the psychological background. In the first part of the dream:

*I am standing with my wife in front of what looks like a large bowl or vessel. There is a red light swirling inside it. Suddenly, the light rises up out of the vessel and forms a ball of energy up near the ceiling. And then a large beam of energy shoots out of the light and into the top of my head. I scream in pain and fear.*

The dream presents an image of an energy that can no longer be contained by the structure that was formerly able to hold it. Lacking this structure, the energy streams powerfully and violently into my body through the top of my head.

As I explained above, this dream appeared just as I was coming out of one of the worst times of my life, a time of deep and profound grief. For me, grief was a constant companion. It seemed to me like one long altered state of consciousness, a time of being possessed by the unavoidable awareness of the tragic dimension of life. The cruelty of a disease like ALS, the discovery of pain as a necessary consequence of loving another human being, the permanence of loss, and my helplessness in the face of all of these realities had shaken all the certainties I'd had about myself and my relationship to life. I had a hard time feeling that anything really mattered. I began to question the ambition I had always felt in my work. My still developing faith, which had started to become an important part of my life, now felt empty and foreign to me. Most disturbingly, I began to question my value as a husband and a father, two roles that had always been fundamental to my self-image.

It was just as the cloud of grief began to lift and I was attempting to resume my former engagement with life that I had this powerful dream experience. I didn't recognize it at the time, but its appearance signaled that my struggles were not so much coming to an end as entering a new stage. With a troubling synchronicity, this dream of an energy painfully shooting into my head heralded a period of my own difficult illness, one that was marked by debilitating headaches that often left me bedridden.

I had always made a virtue of possessing an exceeding self-reliance, overlooking the fact that such an attitude can be as much a defense against vulnerability and intimacy as it is a strength of character. Now, during the worst times of my illness, as I lay in bed, I found myself utterly dependent on the care of others in a way I had never experienced before. Day after day, for several weeks, my wife appeared at my bedside to nurse me through my pain or to bring me something to eat or drink. Many times my kids would crawl in beside me to read to me or to simply snuggle up with me and comfort me.

Often I found myself puzzling over this. Why? Why did they keep showing up? Why did they continue to be so kind and patient and loving with me? I could do nothing for them. Why did they keep doing so much for me? It slowly dawned on me that the answer was very simple: Love. This sounds obvious, of course, but for me, at that time, it was a revelation.

I have come to regard that time of my illness and dependence as an extended lesson in receiving love. As I emerged from that time, I discovered in myself a new openness to the world around me. A sense of the sacredness of life and a compassion for the secret struggles that dwell in every heart deepened and took root in me. My interest in and energy for work returned, and my engagement with my faith was renewed.

For me, the passage from the loss and breakdown of one state of psychological organization (the vessel) to the coalescing of a new state was a successful one. But what exactly, it would be reasonable to ask, was the nature of these "vessels"? Of what were they composed? The dream imaged an energy rising up out of a large bowl. It is as if, once that energy had become active, the vessel was revealed to be inadequate, perhaps too shallow, to contain it. What was it in my life that proved to be so inadequate for encountering the powerful experiences (the energy) that were visited upon me during those difficult years?

The energies of life are made manifest in relation to different fields of experience, chief among these being our relationships, our work—particularly creative work—and the communities in which they are embedded. In my own case, however, it was not these aspects of life from which the outgrown vessel of my dream was composed. After this time of illness had passed, my marriage and my work were just what they had been before, at least as far as their forms were concerned. Even the communities in which I was invested, both personal and professional, remained intact. I was still married to the same woman, still working as an analyst, and still attending the same church. What had begun to change was something much more basic, much more fundamental. The vessel, I would suggest, consisted of the sense of meaning that undergirded all of these dimensions of my life. Or, to put it another way, the vessel was composed of the story that made all the other aspects of life possible.

My unconscious belief, forged early in childhood, that life was something that had to be muscled through on one's own, had become too small of a framework, too shallow of a story, to include in it the relationships I had developed over the years with my wife, my kids, and many others, including myself and my own creative depths. This was particularly so in light of the painful realities I had come to know all too well—that life is precious and short and that love costs nothing less than everything. The image of the energy pouring into my head was a graphic depiction of my attempt to absorb these lessons through an outworn paradigm, to master life through will and ego alone. My physical illness symbolized, in a concrete way, the dangers of this attempt, while at the same time opening the way beyond it.

I needed a new vessel, a new story, one based on interdependence, mutuality, cooperation, and compassion—in short, on love. It was the second half of my dream that provided the symbol that made the development of this new story, this new vessel, both possible and clear. In this part of the dream:

> *I am walking through the streets. I look in a store and see the owner and a customer engaged in a transaction. I realize that this transaction itself is Jesus. Everywhere I look I can see Jesus in all the interactions and transactions of the world.*

Here, the dynamic agency of the dream has been transformed from the free-floating and unnamed energy of the first part, and revealed as the specific quality of "all the interactions and transactions of the world," to which the dream gives the name *Jesus*. In other words, the undifferentiated archetypal energy is given a symbolic container, a defined story. I noted earlier that the lack of such a symbol puts extreme psychological pressure on the relatively frail ego that attempts to contain the infinity of the transpersonal in the finite capacities of the personal life. This is like trying to capture the ocean in a bottle. One vital function of a symbol is that it forges together multiple meanings in a kind of shorthand image. At the same time, it provides a medium through which the individual can come into relationship with the powerful and ineffable forces with which she is confronted.

In my case, this particular dream made use of a symbol—Jesus— that already had some value and meaning for me. This familiarity allowed me to make sense of all that I was going through, bring order to my inner chaos, and find meaning in my despair. On the other side, the context of my personal circumstances together with the specific emphasis the image was given in the dream brought new depth and levels of understanding to my experience of the symbol of Jesus.

This is clearly not a literal or dogmatic representation of Jesus. In the dream, that name is given, not to the figure of a person, but rather to the quality of the transaction between the store owner and the customer. Jesus is the symbolic expression for the nature of all the interactions of the world. That is, the complex of ideas associated with the image of Jesus are to be understood as representing the ultimate nature of the transactions and interactions between people. Or, put yet another way: Jesus is the best possible expression (for me, at least, and in these particular circumstances) for the nature of the experience of human encounter and exchange.

For me, the dream expressed the critical importance of shifting from a position of relentless self-reliance to one of mutuality, interdependence, and love. Having an adequate understanding of and a sensitivity for the religious experience represented by the figure of Jesus is essential for an understanding of a dream like this. One of the central elements of Jesus' ministry, of course, is the message of love.

("Love one another. As I have loved you, so you must love one another.") Indeed, for the Christian, love is understood to be the very nature of God. The image of Jesus, then, is a particularly apt dream symbol that gives expression to my own developing awareness of the importance of love and the necessity of interdependence.

Because the image of Jesus has symbolic value, it is actually expressive of multiple facets of meaning at one and the same time. In addition to the central meaning of love, it also points to the purposeful nature of my suffering, that it was not just arbitrary or unlucky, but meaningful, if I could understand it deeply enough. Furthermore, it suggests that even the most common moments of everyday life can be resonant with significance and even divinity—something known to every poet. All these and more are the undertones and overtones that reverberate when the particular note, Jesus, sounds as part of the dream's music.

This encounter with the dream Jesus has come to give my experience of this particular religious symbol, and of Christianity as a whole, a much more personal and psychological relevance than it previously had. Of course, dreaming of Jesus does not necessarily mean that one is, or even should be, a Christian, any more than dreaming of Krishna would mean that someone is therefore Hindu. The point of sharing my story—the dream and my experience of it—is to assert the indispensable value of what I have been calling containers for the *numinosum;* it is not to suggest that Christianity has any more priority or validity than any other tradition. The human psyche needs symbolic containers with which to meet and metabolize the archetypal and transpersonal energies of life, but they certainly do not have to be Christian symbols. They do, however, have to be real.

## The Reality of the Symbol

Earlier I said that a symbol is not just some arbitrarily and casually chosen or produced image. When I say here that a symbol needs to be real, then, I mean several things. First, it needs to be a living possibility for the particular individual. This does not mean belief. A living image is one that evokes in the person any response other than indifference or mere aesthetic enjoyment. Curiosity, confusion, inspiration, irritation, attraction, and even anger all point to the living symbolic possibility inherent in an image. When the writer Anne Lamott, struggling with alcoholism and seeking her higher power, was visited by an image of Jesus, her first response was, "I would rather die!"[157] In spite of this reaction, she eventually would go on to write powerfully and honestly about her personal engagement with Christianity. Hers is an example of how even when a symbol is alive for a person, that does not mean that it will be easy to accept, or that it will even, initially, be palatable.

Lamott's experience points to a second quality that marks a symbol as real, one that is closely related to the first: The symbol is not consciously chosen. Of course, the conscious mind may play a role in the decision to engage with a particular image, but the initiative lies outside of conscious awareness. A symbolic image can speak to us, disturb us, challenge us, insinuate itself into our consciousness, force itself upon us, flirt with us, or announce its presence dramatically in dreams, visions, or fantasies. But it is the symbol that initiates the movement. Consciousness responds. There is nothing magical about this. We have all had the experience of, say, flipping mindlessly through a magazine and suddenly stopping when something—an image or a phrase—catches our eye. We may not know why we have stopped, but something has captured our attention. In the same way, symbols exert a kind of gravity that activates and pulls in our attention. If we want to give a rational-sounding explanation to this, we might say that something in our prior life experience has primed us to respond to a particular image or symbol. The truth, however, is that the experience is as often as not felt to be related to what has *not yet* been lived, to the realm of our becoming, a kind of call from our future self.

Finally, a symbol is real when it is specific. There is no image, for instance, of "divinity" as such. Rather, divinity manifests in a concrete and specific image to which we apply the conceptual idea "divinity" after the fact. Vishnu reclining on the primal serpent Shesha, the pillar of fire that guides the Israelites through the wilderness, the sacred mountain described by the Oglala Sioux holy man Black Elk—the divine is perceived by means of the specific form through which it shines forth. Likewise, in Jungian terms, no one ever dreams of the Self. *The Self* is a technical term applied secondarily to an experience of a specific image with a particularly noteworthy value, whether it appears in a representational form, such as the figure of the Buddha, for instance, or in a more abstract form, such as a mandala.

The specificity of the symbolic image makes it possible to encounter the transpersonal dynamism as a psychological entity, a separate "Other" to which we can take up a relation and which we can come to know, as it were, from a safe distance. To have such a relationship, Jung wrote, "frees instinct and the biological sphere as a whole from the pressure of unconscious contents. Absence of symbolism, however, overloads the sphere of instinct."[158] What he means is that without the vessel of the symbol, it is the body, the nervous system, and the emotions that are left to be the containers for the undifferentiated energies of the archetypal and transpersonal domains. This was the danger I had found myself in as all my old certainties had fallen apart, the situation that called forth my dream.

It is important to remember here that the language of and about symbols is always figurative, poetic, and metaphorical. Words such as *container, structure,* and *vessel* are all images employed to circumscribe a quality and function of the symbol. One always has to be cautious about reifying these descriptors into concrete "things." The temptation to apply an image in a technical, mechanical, or literal manner always hovers near. Such a move would result in the loss of its symbolic nature. The structures that "break down" are not discrete things, but rather the *matrix of meaning* with which the specific images and situations are infused. Put simply, a symbol is a story and human beings need stories in order to live.

## People without Stories

From the very start of our psychological existence, we are, in a sense, besieged from within by our own imaginations. The fantasy production of earliest childhood is not yet subject to the inhibiting power of directed thinking. Although our rational capacities may increase with age, this underlying imaginative production never ceases.

At its highest form it is productive of great art and beauty, but it is also capable of spinning images of dread and destruction. Throughout our lives we are always at the mercy of the terrors of the psyche.

This is not an exaggeration. A minimum of reflection will confirm it. We have all had the experiences of nightmares that cause us to be startled awake in a sweat with a heart racing from fear. Perhaps you are one of those who are visited by terrible images of their loved ones suffering bodily harm in a traffic accident, or at the hands of some sinister figure, when they are late getting home. Or maybe you occasionally disturb yourself with the violence of your imagination at those times when you are taken over by feelings of anger or rage. Certainly, anyone who has suffered from debilitating bouts of depression or anxiety that come on without really understanding why, or without a recognizable trigger, knows full well the terrors of the unconscious.

Symbols and stories bring order and, therefore, meaning to the contents and experiences of this prodigious fantasy production. They also serve to provide a measure of inoculation against the worst of these contents. Stories, particularly religious and mythological stories, because of the breadth of the horizon they convey, offer anchors for the unrestrained imagination. A story is an Archimedean point from which to view one's relation to one's own selfhood, to others, and to the cosmos as one conceives it. At the same time as it provides objective distance from these dimensions of life, a story also furnishes a means of participation in and with them.

Even more than the utility of a fact, stories fulfill the requirements of the imagination because, although facts are invaluable for answering the questions of "What" and "How," stories give us a "Why" with which we can live. According to the Jungian analyst James Hillman, story is an essential element of psychological health:

> From my perspective as depth psychologist, I see that those who have a connection with story are in better shape and have a better prognosis than those to whom story must be introduced. ... To have "story-awareness" is per se psychologically therapeutic. It is good for soul.[159]

Traditionally, it has been the religions that have provided the sustaining and containing stories of a culture. It is certainly true that there is a danger that such culturally conditioned stories can become rigid and oppressively doctrinal systems that threaten the individual imagination, leaving no room for the discovery of one's own right relation to the larger culture. However, a lack of any framework of meaning through which to make the encounter with life leaves the individual exposed to a chaos of emotions and experiences that are impossible to metabolize on one's own. Such an unmediated encounter with existence can overwhelm the unprotected psyche.

In so many ways in our predominantly rational and secular culture, we have become a people without stories. As such, we lack sufficient psychological and spiritual resources with which to meet the "perils of the soul," which today go by medico-psychological names— anxiety, depression, compulsion, addiction, and the like. These terms have become our new stories, the substitutes our culture employs in place of the more expansive stories of myth and religion. These new stories have the serious drawback of reinforcing the experience of the individual's mind/body/psyche as the container for the potentially overpowering archetypal energies of life. For this reason, they are inadequate to the task of giving any meaningful foundation to the individual.

## Treatment for the Human Soul

In my own experience, the connection to the symbolic dimension, expressed by the image of Jesus as the transactions of life, gave my time of illness and emptiness meaning. It allowed me to experience my suffering as linked to a new and emerging story of the importance of love and interdependence, which had the effect of revitalizing all aspects of my life. Had I taken the struggles of this time of my life merely as symptoms of depression, which I was encouraged to do by many knowledgeable and well-meaning people, it is a good probability that I would have missed what I've come to understand as the initiatory significance of this experience.

I do not mean to suggest in any way that depression is not real. But as a story with the power to summon and direct psychological energy and potential into the difficult adventure of life, it is limited at best and completely ineffective at worst. Today, we are quick to give the name depression to a whole host of psychological states and to treat them solely as a medical concern, an illness to be cured. This attitude obscures the possibilities of spiritual and psychological growth that a depressive experience may be signaling. The medical paradigm on its own is too narrow a horizon against which to understand our lives. It leaves us as passive players, a kind of biological machinery in need of technological interventions. The great value of religious and mythological symbolism is that it helps us see our personal struggles against a much broader and more comprehensive background of the age-old human drama, the archetypal level of existence. This is a treatment for the human soul.

If depression is conceived solely within the framework of medicine, then treating it as an illness makes perfect sense. A combination of cognitive behavioral therapy and antidepressants are then indicated and prescribed. While it is true that many patients are helped by this approach, at least temporarily,[160] many others feel that this form of treatment is at best only partially effective. Still others seem to become even more entrenched in their depressive symptoms, almost to the point where they seem to be defending their symptoms against the treatment itself. It seems, perhaps, that this may be a case of our too-rational and all-too-human desire to "conquer the *numinosum*."

If, however, we are also able to conceive of depression from the framework of the religious function of the psyche, then it can be understood as something like a night sea journey, a wandering in the wilderness, or a dark night of the soul, initiating the individual into a new and wider experience of herself. It is not that this makes the experience of depression any less painful or difficult—it is not a path of denial—but it does bring to it a meaning that allows it to be borne. This is what Jung means when he talks about letting ourselves be overpowered by the numinous. To be overpowered means that we open our narrow perspective to a larger, transpersonal, or "divine" dimension. In Jungian terms, this is the realization of the Self.

If the goal of the medical approach is to "conquer the *numinosum*," then the goal of what I am calling the religious approach is, paraphrasing Jung, to open ourselves to it, to let ourselves be overpowered by it, and to trust in its meaning. For this, the symbol is needed, which allows the individual to be "overpowered" without being destroyed. The symbol is the container that enables us to integrate these powerful experiences into our lives.

As a psychotherapist, Jung found that his patients' concerns were as much spiritual as medical. It was not just the alleviation of symptoms that they were seeking, but also a sense of meaning in their lives, a way to live in the world with hope and purpose. It was not just a matter of, say, helping someone resolve her anxiety so that she could go back to the business of life—work, family, and community obligations—but of helping the person to an orientation for her life that brought a new and vital matrix of meaning to these core domains. It was a matter of helping someone discover her story, her "Why," so that she could re-enter life more fully. In the next chapter, I will discuss in more detail the devastating consequences that can result when such a "Why" is missing.

# Chapter 6
## Religion and Psyche

It cannot be denied that our current age is a distracted one. The technological boom that we have been living in for the last century or so has proceeded so rapidly that it has been impossible for human beings to establish an adequate relationship to all the changes it has wrought. Philosophical, spiritual, and ethical questions require time and space for reflection, and this is just what our technologies have made increasingly scarce.

### The Human Machine

There can be no doubt that our advancing technology has been incredibly successful in improving the ease and comfort, as well as extending the life spans, of a great number of people on this planet. However, it is also true that that very success can simultaneously be a barrier against an encounter with our deepest selves and can keep us from facing our own souls.

For Jung, the incursion of technology into our homes meant that we could never escape the time-bound concreteness and banality of ordinary life in order to experience the timelessness of the symbolic life. Writing during the first half of the twentieth century, he spoke of the disruptive effects in the way such things as radios, televisions, and telephones reach not only into our homes but into our very consciousness.[161] One can only wonder what he might make of a world in which not only the homes but also the pockets of every single person are filled with all of these devices rolled into one and carried about everywhere we go.

Earlier, I noted that in a technological world the machine becomes the guiding metaphor for how we think about our human nature. When this is the case, it follows that the way we imagine healing with respect to psychological distress is going to be affected by this worldview. In particular, we are more likely to see healing in terms of a repairing of the human machine. If, however, the root of suffering, as I suggested at the end of the last chapter, is meaning and not mechanics—the "Why" and not the "What"—then our technological outlook may at times be doing more harm than good.

## Reasons for Living

For Jung, the conceptualization of the human being as a machine was anathema. He was emphatic that the decline of religious consciousness and the rise of the mechanistic view of human nature resulted in an increase in psychological suffering. However, as he pointed out in his book, *Modern Man in Search of a Soul*,[162] he had no statistical evidence to back up this assertion. That evidence is now available to us.

In 2000, the *American Journal of Psychiatry* published a study seeking to determine which factors were the most effective in preventing suicide attempts in people with depression. The authors of the study looked at such things as the number of recent stressors in a person's life and the scores obtained on objective measures of the severity of one's depression. They found that none of these factors were as predictive of suicidal behavior as were the presence or absence of "reasons for living."[163] In other words, it was not the "What" that was the critical feature of depression; it was the "Why."

Among the reasons for living identified in the research were such things as feelings of responsibility toward family, the presence of survival and coping skills, and moral objections to suicide. These factors, the authors state, show "apparent influences from culture, religion, and sociopolitical attitudes."[164] Individuals who were more likely to attempt suicide showed higher measures for such things as hopelessness, subjective depression, and suicidal ideation, all of which were inversely correlated to the possession of reasons for living. In other words, those who showed the presence of reasons for living experienced less hopelessness, perceived their depression as less severe, and had less suicidal ideation than those who identified fewer or weaker reasons for living. The authors conclude that "during a depressive episode, *the subjective perception of stressful life events* may be more germane to suicidal expression than the objective quantity of such events."[165] The results of this study strongly suggest that it is not simply what happens to us that is the determining factor regarding the effect it has in our lives. It is whether we have adequate internal structures to contain, absorb, and make sense of what happens to us.

More recently, an article published in the *Journal of Psychiatric Research* in 2016 reviewed several studies measuring the presence of reasons for living. That review affirmed the finding that the presence of such reasons, particularly "moral objections to suicide" and "survival and coping beliefs," were protective factors against both suicidal ideation and suicide attempts.[166]

Those familiar with the writings of Viktor Frankl will hear in these results echoes of his influential work on the essential value of meaning in the endurance of suffering. As he writes in his classic work, *Man's Search for Meaning*: "In some way, suffering ceases to be suffering at the moment it finds a meaning, such as the meaning of a sacrifice."[167] Jung, too, gives meaning central importance in his work. It is meaning, writes Jung, that is healing. "Meaninglessness," he says, "inhibits fullness of life and is therefore equivalent to illness. Meaning makes a great many things endurable—perhaps everything."[168]

## The Protective Effect of Religion

Another study, also published by the *American Journal of Psychiatry* in 2004,[169] points to related findings, homing in on one particular area of reasons for living. In this report, titled "Religious Affiliation and Suicide Attempt," researchers looked at the effect of religious engagement on suicidal thoughts and behaviors. The study reviews some of the findings of previous studies on this subject, as well as presents new data from the authors' own research.

In general, the authors of this review found that studies of religious commitment show that it tends to have a protective effect against suicide. One of the studies they looked at had been done across 25 different countries. It showed that the protective effects of religion were not due to any specific tradition or denomination, but rather were the result of "strong religious commitment to basic life-preserving values, beliefs, and practices that reduce rates of suicide."[170]

In the authors' own research, they found that individuals with some form of religious affiliation were less likely to have had a history of suicide attempts, one of the main predictors of future attempts. The religiously unaffiliated not only had a significantly higher rate of past suicide attempts, as well as more first-degree relatives who had attempted suicide, they also tended to be less often married, were less likely to have children, and had less overall contact with family. All these factors correlate with what the research I discussed in the previous section identified as important reasons for living. The authors concluded that "religion may provide a positive force that counteracts suicidal ideation in the face of depression, hopelessness, and stressful events," while "lack of affiliation may be a risk factor for suicidal acts."[171]

Significantly, those without religious affiliation also showed greater levels of aggression, impulsivity, and substance abuse. As the authors note, "suicidal behavior is related to aggressive and impulsive traits, and anger predicts future suicidal behavior in adolescent boys."[172] Past studies have shown that a strong religious attitude is correlated with lower hostility, anger, and aggressiveness, a finding that was borne out by the authors' own research. One such study, for example, looking at twin samples, found that a religious upbringing moderated inborn genetic factors around what psychiatry calls *disinhibition,* which is manifested in such things as disregard for social conventions, impulsivity, and poor risk assessment.

From the point of view that I have been developing in this book, this facet of the study confirms the idea developed in the previous chapter that religious symbols act as grounding wires for the powerful energies of the unconscious. Aggression and impulsivity are powerful archetypal dynamics that can cause an overloading of the circuits of the mind/body system. They need some kind of containment, some way of humanizing the raw material of the psyche, in order to be expressed in one's life in an effective and nondestructive way. As this study points out, religion is one such vessel of containment and means of humanization.

## Therapy for the Disorders of the Soul

In the light of these studies, perhaps we can begin to understand why Jung felt that a religious outlook was the bedrock of psychological health, and why he once made the claim that "every one" of his patients in the second half of life became ill *because* they had lost this foundation:

> Among all my patients in the second half of life—that is to say, over thirty-five—there has not been one whose problem in the last resort was not that of finding a religious outlook on life. It is safe to say that every one of them fell ill because he had lost what the living religions of every age have given to their followers, and none of them has been really healed who did not regain his religious outlook.[173]

It is a difficult thing to live a human life, as the innumerable chorus of philosophers, theologians, psychologists, political activists, artists, and poets throughout history attest. "In the deepest heart of all us there is a corner in which the ultimate mystery of things works sadly," wrote William James, as he contemplated the question "Is life worth living?" in his essay of the same name.[174] We are desperately in need of some framework that organizes the chaos of life events and crises into a cohesive, meaningful whole, shoring up our resilience and endurance, so that we can achieve what Paul Tillich called the "courage to be."[175]

"All religions," wrote Jung, "are therapies for the sorrows and disorders of the soul." This is not so much because religions provide moral precepts for living, but because through their symbols and stories they can help us to develop "an attitude which tries with charity and forbearance to accept even the humblest things in one's own nature."[176] It is on the basis of this humble self-acceptance, Jung believed, that the evolution of both individual consciousness and the collective culture becomes possible.

This is a radical idea! The "sorrows and disorders of the soul" are tended, not through some program of moral or behavioral perfection, but through "humble self-acceptance." A truly religious attitude, Jung is suggesting, looks with empathy and compassion on the reality of the human condition, which inevitably includes incompleteness, imperfection, and suffering. These are the torments that bring people into analysis and therapy, of which they hope to be cured. But any cure ultimately comes from finding a meaningful context for these existential realities in our lives. Suffering is unavoidable in a human life and yet, if we lack the means for bearing and understanding our sufferings, we are either broken by it, as the studies about suicide cited above attest, or we seek ever more anxiously to find ways to avoid it. Given the proper means—a living symbol, a meaningful story, a religious outlook—our suffering can be turned from something destructive into something creative and transformative. In other words, suffering becomes a doorway to greater consciousness, and when we can establish a conscious relationship to it, new depths of our being are awakened.

The experience of suffering is a spiritual problem. It throws us into an encounter with life that calls up the question of "Why"—that is, the need for meaning. Any exclusively biological or rational approach to psychotherapy (a word which, as Thomas Moore has taught us, literally means "care of the soul"[177]) will be inadequate to the task. Jung is adamant on this point, noting that the experience of suffering takes us beyond the boundaries of normal, everyday experience. While we are still within the purview of the normal and everyday, common sense and reason are of unquestionable value. However, once we cross over into the frontier of suffering, common sense and reason reach the limits of their helpfulness. Here, it is not reason that heals but meaning. Suffering suffused with meaning becomes creative. It deepens our relationship to life and calls forth a response from within us that holds redemptive and transformative potential, often beyond the limits of our personal lives. It is with this understanding that Jung speaks of conveying to his patients a healing fiction—a story with the capacity to grip the mind and heart of the sufferer, and through which his mental and emotional pain can give way to renewal and aliveness.[178]

Thus, out of the confusion of suffering comes the coherence of meaning. For we are people who need a story to live, a *mythos*. When we possess such a story—one that gives orientation to our lives—the experience of life becomes something filled with potential and possibility.

## The Question of Meaning

The question of meaning, as Edward Edinger reminds us in *Ego and Archetype*, is not directed toward some monolithic and objective "meaning of life." Rather, it is a personal and subjective question more aptly rendered as "What is the meaning of *my* life?"[179] In other words, it is not a search for a quantity of information that defines what human life is, but rather the working out of one's own relationship *to* life. It is a question, then, that is intimately related to the experience of identity: "Who am I and how can I live in the world?"

Edinger notes that the waning of religion leaves the inner life without an expression that is generally and collectively approved. While he is right about this assertion, he tends to frame the issue in a binary fashion. He writes of the issue as one of seeking meaning in objectivity—material existence, political life, scientific knowledge— versus one of seeking meaning in subjectivity—"the unique, not-to-be-duplicated" experience of the individual "which is not susceptible to an objective, statistical approach."[180] It would probably be more complete to frame the issue as the need for the individual to find a meaningful relationship between one's unique subjective experience and its encounter with life in the objective world.

A key aspect of Jungian analysis is facilitating just this relationship, which, in fact, stretches in two directions. On the one hand, the individual is in need of being meaningfully related to collective consciousness, which is the specific time and place with its particular norms and expectations in which a person lives. On the other hand, there is the necessity of relating to the collective unconscious, which is the universal experience of being human, the archetypal and existential needs and concerns that stretch back to time immemorial. Both of these realms are objective realities that confront the individual and they are often in conflict with one another, a fact which presents the individual with a difficult problem to resolve. This problem cannot be solved on a merely cognitive or behavioral level; rather, it requires the mediation of the symbol.

Only the symbolic level is effective here because only a spontaneous image that encompasses and expresses the archetypal human experience made manifest in the particularities of an individual life as it is confronted with the concerns of the present zeitgeist, has the power to touch the mind, heart, and body—that is, the wholeness of the individual—all at once. But just here lies the dilemma of our time. The experience of the symbol is an important healing factor in the psyche, but today we do not have the understanding needed to perceive, or even simply receive, the symbol. If something presents itself to us spontaneously, we either treat it dismissively—"It's only a dream" or "That's just your imagination"—or as something pathological, such as a delusion, a hallucination, or some form of magical or wishful thinking.

As I have said several times, the experience of the unconscious is very hard to grasp, in part because we keep trying to translate it into the terms of consciousness. The true nature of reality, however, is always more than what we can know, more than what we can think. "Life is life," wrote Raimon Panikkar, "and not necessarily thinking."[181] The full contact with the deepest level of reality, he goes on, occurs "without the mediation of consciousness."[182] This is precisely, I believe, what Jung refers to as immediate or original religious experience, the experience of the numinous before conceptualization within the categories of consciousness.

The question and the challenge, then, is how the individual can be assisted in developing the perceptual capacity for the reception of this kind of experience, which is central to establishing the life-affirming state of meaning. This is a primary function of religious activity. However, it is not simply a matter of "prescribing religion." I am not making the case for a particular tradition, or even a traditional religious system. What is needed is that symbolic field by which the individual is affected and which conveys to him a healing or life-giving quality.

That said, because the religious traditions of the world contain and represent the store of collective human wisdom, they provide a kind of horizon against which an individual's personal experience can be perceived and understood. To this end, they *can* act as guides that lead us more profoundly into our own individual experience. At the same time, the collective nature of the religions guards against the dangers of an excess of individuality. Individual experience must always be reconciled with collective experience both past and present. As Jung warns, "That which is *only* individual has an isolating effect, and the sick person will never be healed by becoming a mere individualist. He would still be neurotically unrelated and estranged from his social group."[183]

If we are objective enough, we can recognize that a totally pure and separate individuality is a dubious idea. We do not come to these ultimate questions of meaning as blank slates. Each of us has our own conceptualization of what the symbol *God* means and to what kind of reality it points. So much of what gets stirred up in us by the symbol *God,* or by any other common symbol, derives from the environment in which we grew up—our culture, our family, our peers, as well as our own personal temperament and experiences. Accordingly, whether such a symbol calls up negative or positive connotations and responses depends in no small measure on the quality of ideas and understandings to which we have been exposed. At this time in human history, as at other times past, the symbol *God* stirs up strong feelings in both directions. It is hard to find anyone who is truly neutral in response to this idea. For all these reasons, it is important to become conscious of our images, concepts, and beliefs about religious ideas and symbols, as well as their social, cultural, and familial roots, so that these do not become barriers against the possibility of actual life experience in all its ineffable potential.

## The Chosen God

There is no need to seek out numinous experiences; they are always present and active. Our task is merely to take up an adequate relation to them, to bring some coherence to our encounters with them, and to consciously and constructively decide which energies we want to cultivate. Although we may not "know God" in the form that we imagine is suggested by religion, nevertheless the activity to which this symbol has always given expression continues to be present. We need some symbolic form through which we can meet this power.

Until relatively recently in human history that symbolic form was given with the particular cultural circumstances in which one found oneself. One simply lived within the religious tradition of one's ancestors. In today's globalized world, we find before us a bewildering array of religious forms from which we imagine we might choose the best fit. At the same time, the very possibility of such a choice seems to suggest an arbitrariness or even unreality to the object of religion, that is, to God. Can we really choose our own god? Doesn't that very idea undercut the claim of any god to be God?

These questions, in fact, reveal an unconscious religious bias. They are rooted in a strictly monotheistic understanding of religion. To those of us with Judeo-Christian roots, whether or not we have any conscious relationship with our religious history, it is difficult to grasp the idea of "choosing" our God. It is, however, a well-established idea in the Hindu tradition, in which there is the notion of the *ishtadevata*, the "chosen god."[184] Hinduism, being a polytheistic tradition, is very comfortable with the idea of different paths to God. Different human beings with their different temperaments respond to the ineffable reality of life in different ways. One's *ishtadevata* reflects one facet of God and is one name among many possible names, but the one that best conveys to the individual the experience of the divine. It is a "choice," but one that is chosen because it is the one that is *already* experienced as possessing efficacy for that person.

With the idea of a "chosen god," we come very close to a psychological approach to religion. The concept of the *ishtadevata* would correspond to what Jung calls the *god-image*, the psychological experience of God, which is to be distinguished from the metaphysical reality (or unreality) of God. In this context, "choice" should not be understood as something arbitrary. It is not the kind of choice meant by our contemporary consumerist perspective, in which, for instance, I can freely choose from a catalog of images depending on which is the "best deal" for me.

Here, "choice" should be understood more as something like assent. We do not close our eyes and arbitrarily pick a god-image, but rather, we choose to respond to—to assent to—the image that calls to us, that affects us, or even the one that challenges us. It is an investment of oneself, akin to how we might pick a life partner. There are billions of people in the world, but only a few present themselves as potential relationships, and fewer still that inspire our exclusive attention and devotion. Ideally, when we choose a partner, we assent to a commitment whose possibility we already experience internally.

Such a choice gets us in the game, so to speak. It gives us a means to engage energies and experiences that would be overwhelming and even unbearable for us without it. And if it is a real and not an arbitrary image, if it is one that is transparent to transcendence and inspires our investment—whether that is an investment of devotion or of struggle— it opens the way for a dialogue with Reality, a relationship with and to life.

Jung conceived of this dialogue as being between the conscious and the unconscious aspects of the psyche. But whether we prefer to cast this relationship in psychological language or in religious language, it reveals itself as true when it involves our whole being—our feelings as well as our thoughts, our bodies as well as our minds, our spirits as well as our psyches.

Our "chosen god" may be given a religious name, such as *God,* or it may be given a psychological name, such as *Self.* Either way, we have to hold the name lightly, knowing that it is but a finger pointing at the moon and not the moon itself. From this perspective, we can see that all our god-images are psychological constructs that enable to us to engage in a meaningful dialogue with the depths of our own being. Jung called this dialogue a *religio*.[185]

For most of us living at this time in our collective history, the return to a premodern literalism of religious symbolism or to the provincialism of a self-enclosed faith tradition is impossible. However, the need to find channels to the depth of experience and the coherence of life that these modes have always provided to our human existence remains. As Jung remarked, "We moderns are faced with the necessity of rediscovering the life of the spirit; we must experience it anew for ourselves. It is the only way in which to break the spell that binds us to the cycle of biological events."[186] The life of the spirit is the means by which we are helped to remember that we are not simply mechanisms but living beings with living souls.

Symbols are one of the means by which life energy pours into us, giving meaning to our day-to-day existence. They are also the means through which we can give ourselves *to* life—they provide containers for our emotional and psychological investments and commitments. The lack of such symbols, as we have seen, leads to devastating consequences. To this end, it is incumbent upon psychology to remember that the religious traditions have been, and continue to be, the repositories of humanity's most potent symbols, in that they house images replete with resonance, authenticity, and vitality.

# Chapter 7
## The Role of Religion

What is made abundantly clear in the studies on suicide and religious affiliation is that religious questions are not just abstract and theoretical considerations far removed from the everyday reality of our lives. In a very real way, they have life and death importance. Whether we address these questions or not, and how we wrestle with them and answer them for ourselves, has a direct impact on the breadth of what we are able to live and the depth with which we are able to live it. The question of God is not a search for information about some distant being or general principle. It is a question about *our* being and the nature of our relationship to life.

Many people, of course, will not recognize themselves at all in that previous statement. They are not religious, do not think one way or another about religion or God, and get along just fine without either. Regarding the act of reflecting on life and its meaning, a large percentage of this group will range from indifferent to hostile. "Just Do It" is more than just a marketing tagline; it is part of the American cultural mythos—the belief in what might be called the productivity-minded *homo economicus*. From the perspective of this worldview, introspection does not have any obvious and tangible "deliverables." Because of this, tending to one's inner life is often seen as something morbid, a reflection of self-absorbed "navel gazing" indulged in by people who never get anything done. It is probably safe to surmise that a good number of the "don't think, just do" people live comfortably and happily within the current myth of our culture—having a job, having a family, and getting pleasure where one can. There is certainly nothing wrong with this, so long as it can sustain one's energy for and engagement in life. A difficult truth, however, is that of this group, many, unbeknownst even to themselves, will only be temporary residents. As Jung explains:

In our time, there are millions of people who have lost faith in any kind of religion. Such people do not understand their religion any longer. While life runs smoothly without religion, the loss remains as good as unnoticed. But when suffering comes, it is another matter. That is when people begin to seek a way out and to reflect about the meaning of life and its bewildering and painful experiences.[187]

There are two points in this quote to which I want to pay particular attention. The first, of course, is the experience of suffering as an opening to the religious dimension of life. "Why" is the operative question that gets activated during such times. As we saw in the previous chapter, the need for adequate "reasons for living" is crucial. I will speak more about the role of religion in the face of suffering below.

The second point I want to highlight here is Jung's statement that those who have lost faith in religion "do not understand their religion any longer." There is a suggestion here that the problem is not so much religion itself as it is our ability to relate to it. We are a postmodern people living in a pluralistic world. The form of relationship to the religious dimensions of life that functioned for premodern peoples living in more exclusive and homogeneous groups will not function for us today. It is, of course, the contention of this book that there is a path to understanding available to us that can re-establish that relationship and allow the life-giving capacity of religion to flow again in ways conducive to the needs of contemporary people. The first step, however, is to formulate an adequate understanding of the role of religion, to begin to differentiate it from other domains of life, and to develop, as far as is possible, an appreciation of the unique value and relevance of the religious outlook.

The public discourse about religion has been, and continues to be, far too simplistic and shallow to help us adequately understand the role of religion in our lives. The tone, tenor, and content of this discourse—from both its proponents and its critics—have all but drained religion of its symbolic power. In the next section of this book, I will be talking about how one can cultivate the capacity for symbolic experience. However, before we are able to begin that task, it will be necessary to recover some understanding of the depth and complexity of the function of religion. Although I cannot address the full scope of this question here, in the remainder of this chapter I will try to identify a few key aspects of the role of religion in a human life.

## Endurance of Suffering

The experience of suffering is a certainty in every human life, and it calls forward a felt need for the religious dimension. Pain, loss, illness, violence, injustice, the struggle for survival—all of these and more can be moments when our sense of being in control of our lives is ripped away. We are exposed to the contingencies of life, naked before the *mysterium tremendum*. At this point, as Jung expressed in the previous quote, "people begin to seek a way out and to reflect about the meaning of life and its bewildering and painful experiences."

In my work as an analyst, every single person that I sit with has, in some way, had to wrestle with the fragility of human existence, the brevity of human life, or the recognition of the potential for brutality in their fellow human beings. This experience is certainly not limited to people in analysis; one cannot be a conscious human being and not be touched by the suffering inherent in this human life.

I believe that this is why Jung says that "people begin to seek a way out"—a way out of suffering and the sense of meaninglessness and arbitrariness that it evokes. People seek something that can give them the nerve to confront the seeming indifference of life. One of the primary functions of religion has been to provide a way out of raw suffering and into meaning—from Buddhism's teaching of suffering and the cessation of suffering, to Christianity's symbol of the suffering of Jesus leading to resurrection and new life, to the manifestation of *Al-lāh* in Islam as *al-Rahmān*, the Compassionate, the God who shares in and has pity for the sufferings (pathos) of humanity.[188]

Suffering, of course, is not only the result of our personal experiences of pain and loss but it can also be experienced in the encounter with the darker aspects of our own archetypal nature. Having lived through the cataclysmic events of two world wars, Jung was acutely sensitive to the fragility of human rationality and civility. He knew how close beneath the surface of civilization the forces of chaos dwelt. For him, the unfathomable destruction unleashed by war was a clear sign that our belief in the power of *homo rationalis* was naive at best and dangerous at worst.

As I write these words, the disturbing events in Charlottesville, Virginia, in August of 2017 are still powerfully reverberating across the United States and beyond. An organized hate rally, in which a crowd of white nationalists marched with torches and paraded with Nazi flags and symbols, erupted in violence and murder. These radical groups that espouse racist ideas and traffic in hate have been emboldened by the casually racist rhetoric of Donald Trump, whose behavior and discourse as President of the United States daily undermines and effectively abandons the norms and standards of the conduct of government. These norms are not simply niceties. They are meant to support and maintain the ideals and values of the Constitution by putting the individual citizen in touch with principles beyond the personal preferences of any one person. It is yet to be seen whether this rupture of norms will prove to be a permanent development, but it is a recent and egregious example of the destructive potential that lurks behind the thin veneer of civilization.

The breach of these membranes of civilization is painful and results in intense spiritual and existential suffering. This is so because we come face to face with the monstrous potentials of our own human nature. Most of us, perhaps, do not feel capable of the kind of brutality we often witness from a safe distance on the news, and yet at some level we are all implicated. From time to time, it even breaks into our own lives—a moment of road rage when we scream at other drivers or intentionally cut them off; a moment when we "lose it" and yell at our spouse or children, and maybe even strike out at them; a moment of getting swept up in an affair that leaves a broken marriage and devastated family in its wake; a moment of drunkenness that ends in a car wreck in which people are injured or killed. These are examples of the kinds of experiences that can happen in anyone's life. None of us is immune to the darkness that is part of the human soul.

Our naive belief in our own rational nature has made us forget or deny this "danger from within," which from the earliest times was understood and, as far as was possible, defended against by the practice of religion and ritual.[189] Through the religious response, suffering is potentially contained and comforted; in addition to this, it can become an opening to an experience of the divine itself, an enlargement of the spirit. Through our suffering we are confronted with a difficult aspect of the mystery of life. At the same time, we encounter the ground from which true compassion for our fellow sufferers can spring, which is at the same time a deepened understanding of our own humanity.

## A Widening of Vision

It seems to be a fundamental aspect of our human nature to reflect on life and our place in the universe and to ask "Why." Like the title of Gauguin's famous painting, we seem compelled to ask, "Where Do We Come From? What Are We? Where Are We Going?" These are questions that necessarily direct our attention beyond ourselves and our concrete biological existence. When we begin to ask these questions, we have entered the realm of religion.

To be sure, we can answer these questions in a very concrete way. We could simply declare, as Richard Dawkins does, that "we are machines for propagating DNA. ... It is every living object's sole reason for living."[190] This is one answer and it is apparently satisfying to a great many people, but for the rest of us it does little to satisfy the soaring imagination and the human spirit. For Jung, the psyche had its own anatomy, just like the human body, and that anatomy was composed of archetypal realities that expressed themselves in symbols. Religious symbols, in particular, reflect this psychic anatomy because they are collective symbols that have been shaped and elaborated by the human imagination for millennia. When we are able to form some relationship to and understanding of these symbols, they infuse our lives with a felt sense of meaning.

Mere existence is not enough. This is made clear in the studies on suicide and religion. We are beings that need a *meaningful* existence. As Panikkar reminds us, the unfolding of our humanity is not a merely biological unfolding.[191] It is not something that simply happens on its own, nor is it something we can make happen by our own efforts. We need the guidance of others. We must be initiated into a fully human life.

There is nothing unusual in this. We encounter such guidance throughout our lives—in child-rearing, in education, and in apprenticeships and training of all kinds. Most of the time, we need a living human being to provide this guidance, though it is certainly the case that the creative works and collective traditions left by past generations are essential aspects of any direction or instruction. This wisdom of our forebears can be a sufficient, and under certain circumstances, even a superior substitute for living mentors.

The religious traditions, of course, are one such repository of wisdom, and part of their role is to initiate men and women into a wider, "fully human" life. Panikkar uses the Greek terms for life—*bios* and *zoê*—to describe the direction of this initiation. He writes, "Initiation begins with the step from *bios* to *zoê*, from pure physical-chemical biology to humanly conscious life."[192] This echoes Jung's position, quoted at the end of the previous chapter, in which he describes the necessity of recovering a spiritual understanding of life in order to "break the spell that binds us to the cycle of biological events." The process of moving from *bios* to *zoê*, from mere existence to meaningful existence is an ever-deepening and developing one as we experience a widening of our vision of the self-in-the-world, as well as our sense of the self-with-others.[193]

This widening of vision is possible because religion helps give order and structure to life. By providing a center that lies outside the everyday concerns of living—the conflicting demands and desires of our days, as well as the often competing, archetypal energies that impinge upon us—religion exercises an ordering influence on our lives. This is in accord with Jung's description of the Self as a center and circumference that relativizes the position of the ego. From this perspective, religion can be understood as a kind of gravity field that helps us center our lives in ultimate values and not merely passing ones.

## The Subversion of Values

It is certainly true that religion as it is actually practiced does not always, or maybe even often, live up to its purpose and potential. Religion is a human activity performed by human beings with all of their human tendencies and imperfections. We have to dig deeper than the initial surface impression if we are to gain a true understanding of the role religion is meant to perform. A good source of this deeper understanding, of course, is to turn to the insights of those who have lived a religious life and who have done the long and patient work of reflecting on religious matters and their function in human life.

Some of the harshest critics of religion are, in fact, deeply religious people. Here I would recall the words of Abraham Joshua Heschel, quoted earlier in Chapter 4, in which he lays the blame for religion's "defeats" at the feet of religion itself: "Religion declined not because it was refuted, but because it became irrelevant, dull, oppressive, insipid." For Heschel, a mystic, theologian, and rabbi from a family of rabbis, the purpose of religion does not consist in satisfying needs, but in "fanning discontent." Speaking from the perspective of the Jewish faith, he states:

> The aim of Jewish piety lies not in futile efforts toward the satisfaction of needs in which one chances to indulge and which cannot otherwise be fulfilled, but in the maintenance and fanning of the discontent with our aspirations and achievements, in the maintenance and fanning of a craving that knows no satisfaction.[194]

This quote reveals one of the essential roles that religion is meant to fulfill: to take our common and accepted values and subvert them. It challenges our collective assumptions and finds our usual aspirations and desires wanting. Often, because of this tendency, people judge religion to be repressive and restrictive, a means of exercising oppressive control over the hearts and minds of its adherents and desiring to do so over non-adherents. And it is true that there are elements within the religious world whose mode of expression is just this kind of repression and condemnation. We see this today in the

United States from those who interpret the subversion of social norms in terms of a "war" against the prevailing culture.

At first glance, the quote above from Heschel might seem to belong to this category. Is it really true that all our efforts toward the satisfaction of our needs are futile? Is Heschel right when he states that we only "chance" to indulge our needs, and that ultimately, they cannot be fulfilled? Is there anything inherently wrong in seeking the satisfactions of such things as position, wealth, sex, or fame? Where do these things fit in the economy of the spirit?

A closer reading, however, finds that there is no condemnation of the "satisfaction of needs," no denouncing of our "aspirations and achievements." Heschel is not issuing a moral injunction against the pursuit of desire; he is suggesting that there is a deeper and greater value in discontent, in dissatisfaction, and in longing. It is not that seeking satisfaction is wrong; it's just that it is fleeting. He is reminding us that satisfaction—as a goal in itself, as an end—is ephemeral and "futile."

This perspective presents a challenge to the idea, championed by such luminaries as Freud, that religion is an infantile wish fulfillment of a longing for protection by a strong and benevolent father. According to this line of thinking, religion is a way of taking refuge in a comforting illusion, of never growing up, and of remaining a kind of dependent child. In contradistinction to this view, Heschel's suggestion is for a fanning of discontent and a "craving that knows no satisfaction." The religious attitude, according to this view, is not one of resting in the comfort of an illusion. Rather, it is the *difficult work* of seeking truth by examining the way that we see and understand the world. For Heschel, religion and love of God meant compassion and action. It meant being affected by the suffering of those around us and doing something about it. He lived this out in his own life with his participation in the Civil Rights movement, marching with Martin Luther King Jr.

Heschel believed that we should not defend ourselves from the human predicament with its experience of suffering:

I would say about individuals, an individual dies when he ceases to be surprised. I am surprised every morning that I see the sunshine again. When I see an act of evil, I'm not accommodated. I don't accommodate myself to the violence that goes on everywhere; I'm still surprised. That's why I'm against it, why I can hope against it. We must learn how to be surprised. Not to adjust ourselves. I am the most maladjusted person in society.[195]

Religion is a means by which we are brought into relationship with ultimate values. It can inspire devotion and commitment because through it, the ultimate values that it expresses are bestowed on one's personal existence. Fowler points out in regard to the things we value as having ultimate worth, that we do so because we feel that they lend worth to our lives when we are in relationship with them. We have a need, in other words, to be in relationship with those powers that have the capacity to "undergird 'more being.'"[196] The values to which we are related and by which we order our lives, in other words, hold profound psychological and spiritual import.

Too often, however, the values that the culture affirms seem to diminish our sense of being. Consumerism cannot support a healthy sense of self because its engine is lack and inadequacy. That is the task of most marketing campaigns, to heighten this sense of lack and to create and amplify a feeling of being inadequate, which in turn is meant to drive consumption. But as economist E. F. Schumacher points out, to make "the cultivation and expansion of needs"[197] the primary driver of our economic system is the very antithesis of wisdom, which, in turn, is most often concerned with the *overcoming* of desire, described in different ways in the great religious traditions of the world.

As I noted at the outset of this book, Jung was unequivocal about the fact that people have a fundamental need to be connected to something bigger than themselves and that they need to rise above the "grinding mill" of merely economic existence, in which they are what he called "nothing but." Using Panikkar's terms from earlier, we could say that consumerist living is an amplification of *bios* existence that never opens out to *zoê*. This creates a sickness of meaning. Questions like "Is this all there is?" and "What's the point?" are regular visitors in the analytic setting.

In my analytic work, I have frequently observed this need for the transcendence of the banal, the need to lose oneself, to break out of a constant and mundane self-consciousness with its focus on life's errands and obligations. This longed-for state is akin to what the psychologist Mihaly Csikszentmihalyi calls the state of *flow,* which is associated with the experience of more presence and aliveness in one's being.[198] The theological word for this experience would be *zōopoiēsis,* which means "a making alive; vivification."[199] The New Testament passage "whoever loses their life will preserve it" (Luke 17:33b) expresses a fundamental psychological truth. But, if this losing of oneself cannot be done constructively, it will be carried out destructively.

The longing to break out of the "nothing but" experience heightens the need for novelty and sensation—we seek the way out through addiction, sex, entertainment, virtual reality, thrill seeking, shopping—anything to experience a heightened state of being. Even war, writes Jung, becomes a welcome diversion, as it involves people in something with a significance beyond their own daily lives.[200]

The inevitability of hedonic adaptation, the tendency to become desensitized to stimulation and the need for greater and greater "hits" means that this process of seeking sensation must constantly pursue greater and greater levels of stimulation. Positive Psychology calls this the hedonic treadmill. It is a central role of religion to connect us to a center of values that can help us step off just such a treadmill. As Schumacher writes:

> The exclusion of wisdom from economics, science and technology was something which we could perhaps get away with for a little while, as long as we were relatively unsuccessful; but now that we have become very successful, the problem of spiritual and moral truth moves into the central position.[201]

## A Source of Life

Quickly reviewing the psychological qualities that I have
^suggested so far that religion supports, sustains, and, even at times,
produces, we can list such things as resilience, compassion,
imagination, security, and, of course, meaning. I noted also that
religion can provide a sense of order to life—a frame through which
life's activities and events are given coherence. It is important, however,
not to get too reductive here. I am not suggesting that religion is *for
the sake* of these psychological benefits. That would be to apply a
utilitarian perspective to the phenomenon that we are looking at. In
examining the role of religion, I am not trying to extract the essential
(psychology) from the accidental (religion). I am not making the case
that the *goal* of religion is to produce these psychological effects.

These qualities are certainly concomitant with the experience of
religion (or can be), but we should be careful of dissecting the body of
religion lest we kill the whole for the sake of the parts. If there is such
a thing as "a goal" to religion, we would be hard pressed, I think, to
find a better articulation of it than Jung's own:

> No matter what the world thinks about religious experience,
> the one who has it possesses the great treasure of a thing that
> has provided him with a source of life, meaning and beauty
> and that has given a new splendor to the world and to
> mankind. He has pistis* and peace.[202]

Again, I am not necessarily talking about a specific religion, nor even
more generally about any of the great world religions, though,
unquestionably, these can be and are for many people the kind of life-
giving treasure of which Jung writes.

For his part, Jung could not find his treasure inside the Christian
religion that was his heritage, sensitive as he was to the riches that it

---

* *Pistis* is the Greek New Testament word for faith. Jung understands this word as meaning
the possession of a trust and confidence in life and living that emerges from the experience
of the numinous. For a more in-depth discussion of *pistis,* see the section titled "A
Consecration of Oneself" in Chapter 11.

contained. Jung lived out the fate of what he called the "Modern Man in Search of a Soul," the individual for whom the mythic wholeness of life had been ruptured and needed to be restored.

The modern worldview initiated by the Scientific Revolution, writes Morris Berman, was "grounded in a sharp distinction between fact and value." Science's mastery of differentiation, precision, and dissection make possible the technical understanding and manipulation of much of life, but it cannot give direction with regard to life's purpose and meaning. Science, in other words, tells us "How" but not "Why." We now have a better understanding of how we, as a planet and a species, emerge out of this expanding universe, but it is no longer so clear *why* we are here. In Berman's words, "Medieval man was given a purposeful position in the universe; it did not require an act of will on his part. Modern man, on the other hand, is enjoined to find his own purposes."[203]

It is just this that constitutes the rupture of the mythic coherence of life.

For Jung, the profound consequence of this loss of mythic wholeness was brought home to him in 1925 when he visited the Pueblo Indians of Taos, New Mexico. His experience among the Pueblo peoples is instructive. It was his first extended interaction with a non-European culture, and he was deeply impressed by the people, principally their chief, Ochwiay Biano, also known as Mountain Lake. Jung spoke of the Pueblo as a people who possessed a dignity and composure that he found admirable. He relates that at one point during his visit, he was given the privilege of learning about some of their religious beliefs and practices, in particular, their sacred relationship with the sun.

Jung was told that the daily ritual practices of the Pueblo peoples was intended to help their father, the sun, make his journey across the sky. Furthermore, he learned that this was done not just for the village and its people, but for the whole world. This experience and understanding struck Jung deeply. He saw clearly how the sense of dignity that he had noted was rooted in this understanding of the meaning of their lives. It gave the Pueblo peoples a sense of their place in the universe and made their lives "cosmologically meaningful."[204] For Jung, this revelation sowed serious doubts for him about the meaningfulness of modern life. He wrote, "If we set this against our own self-justifications, the meaning of our own lives as it is formulated by our reason, we cannot help but see our poverty."[205]

This problem of the mythic engagement with life seems to have lodged itself firmly in Jung's soul. He wrote that he envied the Pueblo the meaningfulness of their lives and the power of their beliefs. He longed to find a myth of his own in which he could center his life. Later that same year, while on a journey through Africa, he had an experience during which, as he describes in *Memories, Dreams, Reflections*, his own personal myth suddenly became clear to him. It happened in a moment as he came across the magnificent view of a broad, sweeping savanna. Looking out he could see herds of countless animals grazing and moving, and he felt a numinous sense of having come upon something like the original creation of the world.

His description of the event is rapturous. The sight gave him the feeling that he was the first human to come across this scene, to suddenly and truly know that the world existed. "There the cosmic meaning of consciousness became overwhelmingly clear to me," he wrote.[206] He spoke of realizing in that moment that without the contribution of human consciousness the world would exist in a state of unconscious nonbeing. Through the gift of consciousness, human beings become co-creators of the world. For Jung, this realization meant nothing less than the knowledge that, through consciousness, "man found his indispensable place in the great process of being."[207] This experience would come to infuse his work for the rest of his life.

It is clear that, in finding his own personal myth—the myth of the cosmic meaning of consciousness—Jung's life became "cosmologically meaningful," just as he had found the Pueblo peoples' lives to be. In this myth, Jung found that which, for him, revitalized and renewed all the old religious symbols. He had found his treasure, his source of life, and it was one that would allow living water to flow again from the hardened rock of tradition.

One of the primary aims of Jungian analytic work is to facilitate, as far as possible, just such a recovery of the mythic coherence of life.

In discovering our own personal myths, and in reclaiming a religious sense of life, we, too, can find that foundation, that source of life that can bring us *pistis* and peace.

# Part 3
# How to Cultivate a Symbolic Life

# Chapter 8
## What Jung Teaches

Throughout this book I have been articulating an approach to religion that reflects a meeting place of the psychology of the individual and the wisdom of the collective religious traditions. Each, I would argue, needs the other. On the one hand, the traditional religions have lost a great deal of their power to inspire the engagement of people today. They seem ever more remote from the modern experience of the individual. On the other hand, our contemporary culture has lost its capacity to understand and engage religion in a meaningful way. As such, the individual is cut off from a potent support for living. As Karen Armstrong points out, collectively we have lost the "knack" for doing religion and placed all of the blame on religion for that deficiency.[208]

As I understand it, Jung's notion of a personal myth—yet another formulation for the idea of the symbolic life—is one way we can avoid the pitfall of creating a false dichotomy, pitting individual experience against collective tradition. Jung's own personal myth, for instance, did not arise in a vacuum. He struggled with his own Christian heritage and he was deeply engaged in a study of the mythologies of the world. He also dug deep into his own psychology, both his experiences of the world outside and of the world within. This wrestling with the traditions and beliefs of humanity and with his own psyche is the background and preliminary work that prepared the ground for the emergence of his own personal myth.

Likewise, for us today, there is still a great deal to be gained by an engagement with the religious traditions. By this I do not necessarily mean that one should become a believer or an adherent of a particular faith. It is not simply a matter of choosing a religion to belong to and naively following it. What I am suggesting is that there is wisdom and guidance available within the traditions that it would be virtually impossible, and possibly even dangerous, to attempt to discover and generate on one's own power and initiative. "Human thought cannot conceive any system or final truth which would give [a person] what he needs in order to live," says Jung.[209] The development of the symbolic life is not like formulating a business plan or setting a personal goal that one implements and methodically works toward. It is nothing less than a profound encounter with the existential realities of living. It is to possess an experiential knowing, that is, the capacity to recognize the truth communicated by the particular symbolic commitments that claim us.

Our personal myth may or may not be aligned with a particular tradition. Still, some reconciliation with one or more collective forms of religious expression is likely to be a necessary element. Recall Jung's warning, quoted earlier in Chapter 6: "That which is *only* individual has an isolating effect, and the sick person will never be healed by becoming a mere individualist. He would still be neurotically unrelated and estranged from his social group."

All of this points to the fact that it is important, even essential, to develop a perspective toward religion that is religious but not religious. It is no longer possible to be wholly contained within the exclusive embrace of a collective religious tradition that purports to be the "one true faith." The relationship of each of us to the universe, to the world, to each other, and to our own interior depths is exponentially more complex than what would have been experienced by an individual at the time when the great religions were first coming into existence and being elaborated. No single worldview has the power to hold the complexity of the modern world together. At the same time, as I have noted, a purely individual approach to the problems of existence is inevitably going to be alienating and too superficial to support us.

If neither the collective traditions nor the individual approach alone is enough for the development of the religious life, we must then find some third way in which these two essential components of human life are expressed and held in a generative relationship to each other. In this section I will explore some ways through which we might begin to cultivate a living symbolic ground for our lives. In what follows, I will not be suggesting a method for doing so or laying out concrete techniques. There are countless resources available for such things as working with dreams, active imagination, prayer, or meditation, and the reader is encouraged to explore this ever-expanding literature. Rather, I want to examine some of the underlying principles associated with the "How" of the symbolic life and the means by which it can be cultivated.

## Qualities of Experience

Religion, as understood through this third way that I am suggesting, is not a possession but rather a relationship. As such, we should be cautious about how much we imagine is in our power to manifest with respect to this way of experiencing life. For Jung, the crucial elements of a fully realized human life are "faith, hope, love, and insight." He calls these the "four highest achievements of human effort."[210] What is striking about these so-called achievements is that they are really qualities of experience as opposed to the attainments of the human will. They are not produced through effort or technical mastery; instead, they emerge out of our engagement with life. In other words, they are independent of our will. They cannot be made, but rather happen *to* us. For this reason, Jung calls them "gifts of grace."

This is not to suggest that there is nothing we can do toward the "achievement" of these vital qualities of experience. The whole apparatus of ritual, liturgy, and community found in the various religious traditions informs us that, even though we do not create these qualities of experience, still we can draw closer, so to speak, to the stream of living water from which these human achievements may flow.

Still, Jung cautions us against thinking in terms of methods. The very word *method* tempts us into thinking and acting in terms of a technical application of a sequence of actions, as if those actions themselves will be the cause of a particular effect. The problem with the reliance on such a technical approach is that *the state of the individual* tends to be excluded from consideration. This leads, furthermore, to the individual holding himself back from the procedure he is applying. This adherence to objectivity is appropriate to the scientific method but is insufficient and ineffective for the psychological or religious approach to experience.

In the symbolic life, we are not separate from the effect that we are trying to achieve. Our hearts, minds, feelings, and imaginations are all implicated in our personal engagement with life. The full achievement of a religious outlook will not be achieved by the application of something outside and separate from ourselves. It requires the commitment of our whole being.

Once again, we are back to the problem of what we mean when we talk about "our whole being." As I have stated, it is extremely difficult to hold the idea that our whole being includes aspects of ourselves that don't feel like us, or don't match the image we have of ourselves, together with aspects of ourselves that we don't yet know about. In other words, it is difficult to remember our unconscious nature.

The symbolic life is a profound encounter with an inner "Other," felt as being completely different from our ego-consciousness while, at the same time, experienced as the deepest part of ourselves. This is important to keep in mind as we enter into this discussion of the "How" of the symbolic life. We should expect that what we encounter and discover will be a challenge, not only to how we see ourselves, but also to how we think we "should" see ourselves, or perhaps allow ourselves to be seen by others. In taking on this venture, we must be willing to suspend what we think we know about ourselves—for instance, that we are "religious" or "not religious"—and open ourselves to the living dimension of immediate experience to learn what it has to teach us.

It can be scary to challenge our assumptions in this way. What we think we know about our relationship to the religious dimension can be completely upended. Jung makes this clear in a statement from what is known as his *Visions Seminars*, in which he says, "The religious attitude, it is quite different, and above all it is not conscious. You can profess whatever you like consciously while your unconscious attitude is totally different."[211]

## Religion

One of the ways Jung taught that we could draw closer to the living stream of the spirit was, quite simply, by an engagement with an existing religious tradition. Each tradition, whether it was the Catholic Church or a Tibetan Buddhist sect, could be a home to the human soul. Furthermore, there were some people, Jung believed, for whom a particular tradition was the most suitable place to meet the needs of their souls. One of the first tasks, then, would be to discover the nature of one's religious life as it currently exists, to see if any resonance with an established religious tradition might, indeed, already exist.

This is not so much a process of choosing a tradition because it feels most congenial to one's current understanding of oneself. It is, rather, a listening for that which "speaks the language" of our deepest being, even if we find it disagreeable. Only by exposing ourselves to the particular thought, language, wisdom, and value system of the religious traditions can we develop an adequate empathic understanding capable of recognizing the way each one reflects transcendence and renders it accessible to the individual.

In exploring these symbolic and religious systems, one is not trying to discern factual truth but rather personal resonance. Do such ideas feel meaningful? Do they make one's life feel more complete or more satisfactory? These are the appropriate criteria to bring to such an exploration. Through this kind of engagement, one can then begin to notice the response that emerges from within:

> If you should find, for instance, an ineradicable tendency to believe in God or immortality, do not allow yourself to be disturbed by the blather of so-called freethinkers. And if you find an equally resistant tendency to deny all religious ideas do not hesitate: deny them and see how that influences your general welfare and your state of mental or spiritual nutrition.[212]

Again, this is not to be understood as indulging in mild curiosity, or in simply declaring oneself to be a Taoist after reading through the *Tao Te Ching* or a book by Alan Watts. It is a serious engagement in which one truly wrestles with the demands and challenges, the symbols and ideas that one encounters. Approaching this question from the perspective of psychological health, Jung took the position that individuals needed to discover if their religious tradition worked for them, if it could truly help them to confront and resolve the difficulties and demands of life.

Jung also believed that if a person truly "belonged" to a tradition— even if he was resistant to it—it was potentially dangerous to be alienated from it, for such alienation could lead to neurosis. A person who is unable to recognize that there is a spiritual dimension to human life, who responds to the fundamental questions of that life with shallow or conventionally acceptable answers, who cannot raise his eyes above the horizon of the daily grind and the merely personal is much more likely to experience, at some point in his life, a state of discontent, or even neurotic suffering.

Jung cites the case of a young woman who had suffered for years from anxiety. His initial impression of her was that she was very intelligent but somewhat superficial. Her grandfather had been a Zaddik, a revered spiritual leader from a Hasidic community, but her parents had drifted away from the faith and raised her essentially without it. For Jung, this spiritual heritage was an essential part of her nature, but because she had no religious ideas or framework through which it could be adequately expressed, her life could only be lived on the basis of a "mistake"—that is, that her intellect alone could furnish for her an adequate foundation for living. The result was an anxiety neurosis, which Jung interpreted as an experience of the fear of God. He reports that he confronted her very directly with this idea. He told her that she had forsaken her grandfather's legacy and therefore her God. "You belong to holy people," he told her, "and what do you live? No wonder that you fear God, that you suffer from the fear of God."[213]

Whatever we may feel about Jung's therapeutic style here, something in the young woman found his interpretation resonant and she was able to accept this idea. "Suddenly," relates Jung, "her life had a meaning, and she could live again; her whole neurosis went by the board."[214]

In my own experience, the embrace of religion, in those cases in which it meaningfully occurs, is rarely as sudden as it apparently was in the case of Jung's patient. It is more often a slow, sometimes wary, approach, full of starts and stops, curiosity and doubt, advances and retreats. But when a person begins to feel there is "something there," something that seems to fit, it can have as powerful an effect as Jung describes in the case of his patient.

Often people cannot describe why they find engaging with religion meaningful. It is not a question settled at the level of intellectual and conceptual knowing. It is a matter of the heart, of an experiential and intuitive knowing. The symbols of religion, as I have said, make possible a simultaneous conceptualizing of an aspect of life together with an immediacy and a "re-experiencing" of it. Thus, not just the intellect, but the whole of the individual—body, mind, and soul—is engaged. The religious symbol, then, brings one closer to an experience of transcendence than any concept on its own can hope to achieve.

It was because of this possibility that Jung directed many of his patients toward the tradition of their ancestors. He recognized that if there was a fit between the psychological need of the individual and the symbolic content of the religious tradition, engaging that particular religious form could have curative effects. In other words, if someone could find "symbolic knowing" within a religious system, it could lead him to psychological and spiritual health.

## Dreams

Very often, of course, the journey of the religious life cannot be made by traveling the worn paths of traditional religion but must make its way through the untracked wilderness of one's own self. For Jung, this was a much more harrowing passage to make. Religious symbols act as buffers against the potentially overwhelming power of the numinous. Without them, one is "naked to the unconscious," as I discussed in Chapter 5.

The loss of symbolic containers is no trifling matter. When collective religious symbols lose their power to mediate the energies that once had been invested in and expressed through them, those energies fall back upon the human psyche and live on in the unconscious. What Jung discovered in his work with his patients was that the psyche spontaneously produces symbols that show remarkable similarity to the collective images and symbols of religion and mythology. These symbols appear in the nightly dreams of ordinary people. They show themselves not only in images derived from particular traditions, such as figures of Jesus or the Buddha, but more often in images that show a thematic parallel to similar motifs widely encountered in the images that populate the religions of the world. Examples of archetypal themes appearing in dreams include such things as threshold guardians (perhaps appearing in the form of a bouncer at a club); a journey to the underworld (descending into a strange basement to find something that was lost); a cataclysmic flood (a tidal wave that threatens the dreamer's house); the end of the world (a nuclear explosion); and countless more.

Most impressive to Jung were the many mandala symbols that appeared in the dreams brought to him by his patients. The figure of the mandala is a universal symbol found in various forms in many different religious traditions, including Hinduism, Buddhism, Christianity, Judaism, and Islam. It is an image that presents in the form of a circle or quaternity. The mandala image often carries a numinous quality and conveys in its form a sense of wholeness. In the context of the psychology of the individual, it serves an organizing and stabilizing function in the psyche. In his study of the mandala symbol as it appeared in the mythological and religious systems of the world, Jung determined that this type of symbol, in its collective form, represented the immanence of God, the experience of God radiating in and through creation. This led him to conclude that such a symbol, spontaneously appearing in the dreams of modern people, had an analogous meaning. Where the collective mandala symbol pointed to the God apparent in creation, the individual dream mandala indicated an experience of "*the God within.*"[215]

It was statements like this that caused Jung's detractors—both the religious and the ardently nonreligious—to label him a mystic. And, indeed, he himself conceded that the notion of a "God within" was a mystical one, but one that was unavoidable given the psychological material—the images and symbols—regularly presented to him by his patients. Jung's position, however, was to point out that the same dynamics that once were, and still are, expressed in religious symbolism, have psychological reality, whatever other reality they may or may not express. In other words, the benefits of spiritual experience are accessible to each person through the activity of the psyche. For this reason, Jung once declared, "All dreams reveal spiritual experiences."[216]

Whatever else God may be, it is a living experience that confronts us in a powerful way. Even when we find ourselves unable to forge a relationship with an established religion, the experience of God nevertheless remains present in our own psychological lives. The dream—approached experientially and not just intellectually—provides a potential link for the modern individual to the age-old experience of God. This link between psychological experience and religious experience is one of the major themes of Jung's work. In fact, there is a remarkable parallel between Jung's description of the experience of God and that of the unconscious as it manifests in the dream. He suggests that both are experiences of something that expresses a will that runs counter to our own. About God, Jung said:

> To this day God is the name by which I designate all things which cross my willful path violently and recklessly, all things which upset my subjective views, plans and intentions, and change the course of my life for better or for worse.[217]

Similarly, about the unconscious he says:

> Since the meaning of most dreams is not in accord with the tendencies of the conscious mind but shows peculiar deviations, we must assume that the unconscious, the matrix of dreams, has an independent function. This is what I call the autonomy of the unconscious. *The dream not only fails to obey our will but very often stands in flagrant opposition to our conscious intentions.*[218]

In his late work *Man and His Symbols*, Jung makes the similarity between the experience of the dream and that of God explicit when he states, "We are so captivated by and entangled in our subjective consciousness that we have forgotten the age-old fact that God speaks chiefly through dreams and visions."[219]

One way to think about this connection between the experience of God and the activity of the dream would be to understand our ideas, thoughts, images, and feelings about God as projections of the human psyche. This is certainly an acceptable framework that works and, moreover, feels comfortable for many people. But there is also another way to understand this connection. This would be to recognize that our capacity to experience God (setting aside the question of just what exactly "God" is), as well as the possibility for that experience to have a living reality for us, is directly proportional to our capacity to take seriously the manifestations of the psyche.

Look again at the first part of that last quote from Jung: "We are so captivated by and entangled in our subjective consciousness." Jung is pointing to the fact that we make ourselves responsible for, indeed we arrogate to ourselves, the creative power to produce everything that appears on the screen of our minds and imaginations. Our technical mastery in so many areas of life has fooled us into thinking that we have a similar mastery over ourselves. And yet we are visited every night by images and symbols that we do not will and do not create. Even in our waking life, there is some power in us that visits us with psychological events—thoughts, feelings, images, and fantasies—that we do not initiate.

That there is some connection between the experience of the psyche and the experience we call God is not a new idea. It is not the case that it is only now, in this time of human history, that we must seek for what was once called God in our own psychological experience. Rather, this is a return to a universal and primal human experience. The connection between dreams and the experience of the divine is an ancient one that is well established in many religious traditions. In fact, dreams play an integral role not only in the various narratives of the religions, but often in their development, as well. Throughout the stories of the Bible, for instance, in both the Old and New Testaments, God's will is revealed through dreams. Likewise, in Buddhism, tradition holds that the birth of the Buddha was announced to his mother, Queen Maya, in a dream. The prophet Muhammad's revelations that became the Qu'ran were said to have been preceded by a series of dreams full of divine inspiration. To these examples can be added the Aboriginal experience of the dreamtime, as well as the understanding of the Kalahari Bushmen, as reported by Joseph Campbell, that "there is a dream dreaming us."[220] In all parts of the world and at all times, the feeling of the relationship between dreaming and the divine has persisted.

What all these traditions attest, and what Jung sought to recover, is the experience that the dream is a kind of presence. If we are to receive the deepest benefit of the dreaming psyche, we must find a way to allow this presence to become real for us. Throughout his writings, Jung pushes back against what he calls the "nothing but" explanation, which he sees as a modern prejudice and a constant temptation of a solely rational approach to the psyche. This manifests as a merely reductive response to the dream, as the impulse to brush it away apotropaically with the magical phrase, "It's only a dream." Instead, we have to learn to experience the dream, and not just analyze it. Jung believed that dreams must be taken seriously, by which he presumably meant that they were not just objects of intellectual curiosity, but rather had their own fundamental reality in which our very being was implicated in a radical and transformative way.

## Active Imagination

This "taking seriously" of the dream finds its ultimate fulfillment in a technique that Jung called active imagination. The essence of active imagination is the direct engagement with the images and experiences of the unconscious in a kind of dialogue. Instead of merely thinking about one's dreams and reflecting on their meanings, active imagination is a more participatory activity of interacting with the deep imagination. For example, one might focus on a mood or a dream image, holding it in one's consciousness in such a way that it is allowed its own initiative. Any spontaneous changes or developments are observed and responded to by the individual, leading, in turn, to new developments and new responses, and so on. Jung called this technique a kind of dreaming "with open eyes."[221] With active imagination, we have the clearest indication of just what Jung was aiming at in the practice of his psychology—the full engagement and participation of the individual in the movements and manifestations of her own psyche.

In *Jung on Active Imagination*, Joan Chodorow identifies two main components or stages of active imagination: "First, *letting the unconscious come up;* and second, *coming to terms with the unconscious.*"[222] The first stage involves the surprisingly difficult task of getting out of the way of the operation of the normal image-producing process of the psyche. Generally, as we go about our daily lives, the concerns and tasks of everyday living, as well as our interactions with others, push this activity of the creative imagination far into the background. Perhaps we experience the occasional stray thought or unusual image, but we are quite adept at ignoring it (even when we get caught up in it!) and redirecting our energy back to the task at hand—driving the car, writing the email, cooking the meal, or checking the Facebook feed. In the practice of active imagination, it is exactly that "stray" thought or image that is given our attention, while the daily concerns are relegated to the background.

The second phase—coming to terms with the unconscious— means allowing ourselves some kind of response to what we encounter in the psyche. In other words, one engages and experiences the image with the whole of one's being—thoughts, feelings, physical reactions, beliefs, hopes, and fears. This personal investment is crucial says Jung. "The piece that is being played does not want merely to be watched impartially, it wants to compel [our] participation."[223]

It would not be too much to say that active imagination is a contemplative discipline, much like meditation or certain forms of prayer. Take an image and contemplate it, advises Jung, when he describes the process. It is essential that this practice not be understood as an intellectual exercise. To contemplate something is to enter into a state of deep reflection, to set aside one's will, allowing the initiative to arise from the image itself. It is, in fact, a discipline of listening— listening to an "Other" within. The primary intention is not to manipulate the material of the unconscious or to shape it in a particular or predetermined way. "Don't try to make it into something," advises Jung, "just *do nothing* but observe what its spontaneous changes are."[224]

Active imagination is a discipline that requires patience and receptivity. The goal of this work is not to analyze the images of the psyche, but to "give your unconscious a chance to analyse yourself."[225] This is an extraordinary reversal of our usual mode of approach. We are not trying to interpret our psychological material, but rather allowing the psyche to teach us about ourselves. It is not so much that we are working on ourselves as it is that we are learning to let ourselves *be worked on.*

Chodorow notes that the sequence of letting the unconscious come up and then coming to terms with it is not necessarily a discreet sequence of activity. "It is a natural sequence that may go on over many years."[226] This suggests that it is not a "method," but rather a relationship. More than that, it is a way of life. As in a long-term committed relationship, it is an ongoing dialogue, an ongoing process of learning, listening, growing, and adapting to one another, but in this case the other is one's own psyche and ultimately, the Self.

For Jung, the activities of religion, dreams, and active imagination are all to be understood as different means by which we engage something that is absolutely real. They are not to be approached with meager intellectual or conceptual considerations, like curiosities preserved in formaldehyde. Rather, they are to be encountered as experiential realities that make a claim on our being. Jung's move was not to reduce religion to a psychological construct, to exchange symbols for concepts. His was not the "nothing but" approach. On the contrary, his attempt was to recover for the individual the way to experience the full psychic reality of religious symbols. "No one has any obligations to a concept," Jung wrote at the end of his life, "the spirit does not dwell in concepts."[227] We are not simply meant to know *about* the spirit, but to *live* it. For Jung, we are meant to feel an obligation to that aspect of life that discloses itself to us in symbolic dress. When we can do this, we become true participants in life and not mere observers.

# Chapter 9
## What Religion Teaches

At this time in our culture in which "spiritual but not religious" sensibilities are on the rise, it is fairly commonplace to speak critically of "institutional" or "organized" religion. Such criticism, however justified it often may be, is frequently given out in such a reflexive and stereotyped manner as to be almost clichéd in its expression. For many, the rigidity or authoritarianism of "organized religion" is an established truism. It is just the unreflective and automatic nature of this assumption, however, that calls it into doubt. What *is* true is that through the lens of contemporary, secular culture, there is much about religious institutions that appears anachronistic, lifeless, or dying.

Jung himself was an early voice in the criticism of institutional religion, which, as I discussed earlier, he preferred to call a "creed," in order to differentiate it from "religion," which he understood to be a vital activity of the human psyche. A creed, in Jung's sense, is the public institution that has grown out of an original religious experience. Properly meant to keep its members in touch with this experience of the *numinosum,* the creed too often devolves into an habitual activity by which the original numinous experience becomes increasingly occluded.

A creed, then, can be understood as the performance of religion that has become self-justifying and that has lost much of its power to mediate the experience of the divine. As a result, participation in a creed, wrote Jung, is more often a social matter than a religious one—just another obligation to fulfill, but lacking the capacity of being able to provide a firm psychological or spiritual foundation for the individual. An example of this level of religious participation was vividly portrayed to me recently by a churchgoer who explained her three reasons for going to church: an edifying sermon, beautiful music, and fellowship. All of these, of course, have their inherent virtues, and one should not doubt the value they possessed for this individual.

Notably missing in this list of reasons, however, is any mention of God—that is, of the experience of the numinous or transcendent.

Although there is much of which to be critical in the institutions of religion, it is also true that without them it is highly likely that an incalculable wealth of human wisdom would have been lost to the ages, a fact that Jung readily acknowledges. I recall here Jung's reflection, quoted in Chapter 3, on the religious symbols that have been handed down through human history and, regarding which, he is moved to suggest that we owe a gratitude "to the institution which has not only conserved them, but developed them dogmatically."

At any rate, it seems undeniable that it is a human tendency—an archetypal tendency, in fact—to raise up institutions around powerful and meaningful aspects of human life and community. Given this fact, we might begin to ask what values and advantages, beyond merely being an archive of human wisdom, could be discerned in the structures and forms of organized, institutional religion.

## Institution as Symbol

In Chapter 2, I noted that one of the functions of ritual is toward what Jung called "the consolidation of consciousness." To remain in connection to our differentiated human consciousness amidst all the powerful impulses and instincts of the human psyche has always required ongoing and consistent effort. Jung showed that, in the context of more traditional cultures, the maintenance and renewal of consciousness required that the ritual actions supporting it had to be regularly repeated. This is one of the foundations for the building up of religious institutions—the need to regularly engage in life-sustaining rituals.

Religion is first and foremost a practice. It is easy to see that it would be a natural progression for a ritual practice, performed in the context of a community and repeated on a regular basis, to form a structure, a kind of institution. And, as human beings tend to reflect on their actions, it is also easy to imagine that, over time, this same community begins to formulate some ideas and understandings regarding their practices. Eventually, these ideas would find further definition in the form of doctrines, theological assertions, and shared statements of faith. In this way an organized system of beliefs would grow up around the religious practices of a community.

Although Jung was critical of the merely social reasons that many people have for their adherence to a religious community, the fact remains that human beings are social creatures by nature. It is reasonable to think that some shared structure and system of beliefs— that is, some form of institution supporting spiritual and religious matters—is a human necessity. That said, it is important to recognize that the institution is not the creator of religious experience. It is, as I have shown, the response to such experience. Original experience is prior to the building up of the institution, and even though there are undoubted challenges and problems inherent in this institutionalization, the innate capacity for individual religious experience remains despite them.

I am suggesting here that just as we can miss the symbolic nature of the images and stories of religion by reading them too concretely and literally, so we can miss that the institution, too, has symbolic value. In other words, religious institutions ultimately point beyond themselves to something essentially unknowable. The difficulty, of course, is that an institution presents itself in a much more concrete form than an image or a story can. However, if we can revisit our interpretations of and assumptions about "institutional religion," we can begin to recover the ways in which an institution supports an individual's connection with the transcendent and is not necessarily an obstacle to it.

## The Relationship of the Individual to the Institution

If we imagine that our relationship to a religious institution can come only at the cost of our autonomy, our personal experience, and the independence of our minds and hearts, then any institution will be perceived to be an agent of oppression and not of the liberation that is the intended aspiration of all religious traditions. We will then see the institution as that which aims to dictate the content and quality of our individual experience.

Raimon Panikkar offers an alternate vision for our perception of religious institutions:

> We should interpret institutions not as a refuge that would spare us or permit us experience but as a stimulus to make that experience grow, be nourished and reawakened. This requires a considerable degree of maturity.[228]

From this point of view, the institution is neither the obstacle to, nor is it the agent of, religious experience. It does not "spare us or permit us experience." In other words, our experience of our institutions *depends on the quality of relationship that we make to them*. In Panikkar's vision, the individual is not simply to be the passive receiver of that which the institution gives out. To approach the institution in this way would be to make of it either a benevolent or a withholding parent. Either attitude leaves the individual in an infantile state of relationship to the institution.

If, on the other hand, the institution is related to as an aid to the cultivation of an experience that takes place *within the individual*, the quality of relationship is very different. This is why Panikkar says that it "requires a considerable degree of maturity." From this perspective, the individual does not give up either autonomy or responsibility for her experience, but instead enters into a relationship that challenges, stimulates, inspires, and, yes, even at times, frustrates. In this way, the institution becomes a kind of mirror in which one's inner experiences, replete with conflicts and triumphs, can be, in a sense, externalized, observed, and enacted.

What Panikkar is ultimately suggesting is that the quality of a person's relationship to "institutional religion" depends, in large part, on the psychology of that individual. It reflects the level of psychological and spiritual development of the individual. This is not to deny that institutionalization has problems. There is always a tendency to cling to what has been established and to a fixing and hardening of the creed, which then, as has already been noted, becomes an obstacle to a living experience of the transcendent. This tendency notwithstanding, I would contend that phrases such as *institutional religion* and *organized religion* are so general and sweeping in their connotation that, for the most part, their use reveals a lack of reflection and differentiation. In other words, they reflect a relationship to the structures of religion that is essentially unconscious.

The hallmark of this kind of an unconscious relationship is that it is expressed in a stereotyped and reactive manner. This expression is then accepted or rejected uncritically and automatically. What I am attempting here is to move beyond the stereotype of "institutional religion" in order to recover a sense of its *archetypal* value. To put it another way, the goal is to evolve from prejudice to mature judgment, and from reactivity to responsiveness. This requires recognizing that the particular institution is not synonymous with the religion it houses. It is not an equation without remainder. Religious experience does not come to an end with its structure, though it is certainly true that the structure can facilitate religious experience.

If the institution is to be a faithful exponent of the numinous experience that informs it, both the individuals involved and the structures that have been established need to maintain an openness, each within themselves, as well as toward each other.[229] In other words, we cannot simply be dependent on the institution, but must become co-creators with it, transforming it as we allow it to transform us.

## The Elements of Institutional Religions

The essence of the symbolic life is that we need markers (symbols) to direct our consciousness to that which exceeds conceptualization and even understanding. We need structures and forms to direct us to what is ultimately beyond form or structure. Approached as symbols, we can experience the institutions of religion as guides that help us go beyond the institution itself. To institute something is to "set up" or establish a certain order or structure around it. The word *institute* comes from the Latin root *statuere*, meaning "to cause to stand" or "to make firm." If we understand this in terms of one's relationship to religious experience, then we might wonder what the elements are that religious institutions employ that allow for the firming up of the relationship between the individual and the transcendent dimension to which they point? What advantages do they offer for the facilitation and practice of the symbolic life?

The first element, and the one that underlies and supports all the rest, is an ordering and organizing of human life—its times and seasons. Each tradition, for instance, has its religious calendar—a cycle of holy days, feasts, or festivals—that guide the practitioner throughout the year. Within that larger yearly cycle may be nested a set of smaller cycles, such as a schedule of weekly worship and even a daily schedule of prayer or meditation. This structure provides a profound orientation for the individual, not only in regard to the seasons of the particular religion but more importantly to the seasons of life. The measure of time according to such calendars is not so much a mechanical or sequential one as it is a rhythmical one. The cycle of holy days provides a lens through which the individual can reflect on and relate to the rhythms of the year and their relationship to one's own individual life.

The second element that is present in all religious traditions is some system of techniques designed to aid the individual in accessing the divine or transcendent dimension. Prayer, meditation, worship, fasting, and pilgrimage are examples of the many practices that have been used to support and to foster the religious life of the individual and the community. The main intent of these practices is a relativization of the individual sense of self, bringing the narrow ego of the individual in touch with, or in service to, a center of life that is understood to be more comprehensive.

This more comprehensive dimension of life is mediated through a differentiated set of images, symbols, and stories, which comprise the third element of religion. Every religious tradition has its specific symbolic universe, its unique form of mediating and expressing its understanding of the divine realm. This is the element, of course, that most people identify with the institutions of religion. Of the several elements that I am identifying here, this is the one that is often experienced as the most restrictive, particularly when it is framed as a literal truth that must be believed in, to the exclusion of all other points of view. In this regard, we might reasonably question what value there could be today, in our increasingly pluralistic world, in privileging one set of symbols over the rest? We live at a time when the sacred texts of the world's religious traditions are available and accessible—often in multiple translations—like never before. Why limit oneself to having a primary focus on just one jewel in this storehouse of treasures, especially if we are not among those who are inclined to declare one set of symbols as true and the rest as false?

The answer is that it is not about truth; rather, it is about depth. A limited focus allows for a depth of discovery that would be impossible otherwise, whereas a lack of focus or commitment remains too diffuse to enable an effective symbolic field to be constellated. The focus on and commitment to one symbol system lends a vitalizing intensity to the religious statement. In other words, one's investment in the particular images and symbols of a particular tradition increases their power and value for that person. We can understand this by the analogy of a person's choice of and commitment to a romantic partner. Such a commitment increases the partner's value *for the individual in question*, not to mention the impact—both the joys and the challenges—that the relationship will have in one's life.

The fourth element that can be discerned among the religious traditions is some kind of sacred space associated with its practice. Church, synagogue, mosque, temple, meditation cushion, and prayer mat all mark off the division between the ordinary, everyday world and the realm of the eternal. This setting aside of a separate space for the sacred, for acts of devotion, helps to carry the worshiper and practitioner into the appropriate psychological "space" in which one can encounter and experience the transcendent.

Finally, religious institutions are religious communities. One of the challenges of being human is navigating the boundary between the private and the public, the individual and the collective, the inner world and the outer world. This is no less true in the religious domain than in any other domain of living. Even the stories of the desert monks—those early Christians who went into the desert to live as hermits away from the social world—are filled with anecdotes of seeking each other out for spiritual instruction and experience. The religious life seems to need communities where ideas and experiences can be tried and tested in the public sphere. To meet with another clarifies, affirms, or corrects the thoughts and images we encounter in our private inner world. It takes us out of a solipsistic loop and gives depth and substance to the content of our inner lives.

These five elements—structure, techniques, symbols, sacred space, and community—are the essential building blocks, then, for a vital and functioning symbolic life. They also make clear that the practice of religion, the cultivation of spiritual experience, is a discipline. It is not something that simply happens, but rather it requires the right conditions, as well as focused and consistent action on the part of the individual. This is, of course, true in any field of endeavor. One does not become an elite athlete, an accomplished musician, or a renowned physicist, for example, without fulfilling, each in their own manner, these five conditions of practice.

Whether one seeks to live one's symbolic life within a specific religious tradition or must seek it without the support of an established tradition, this aspect of discipline cannot be avoided. "Spirituality is not a vague luminous glow," writes Diana Eck, "it is a very specific practice. It requires the daily discipline and attention that playing the piano requires: it requires practice."[230] Pastor and author Lillian Daniel concurs, stating concisely, "Religion is rigorous."[231]

## A Symbolic Field

The way we imagine religious institutions affects our under-standing of the nature of religion and vice versa. Much of the contemporary public discourse around religion centers on the question of belief, what a person confesses as opposed to what a person experiences. Writing about the Christian experience, Daniel notes, for example, "When the fundamentalist movement commandeered the word 'Christian,' faith came to be associated with intellectual certainty."[232] The institutions associated with such a religion of certainty are more likely to be experienced as more or less fixed authorities to which a person is meant to submit. What I have been developing in this chapter is an understanding of the institutions of religion, not as possessors of a truth that must be acquired and assented to, but as structures and supports for practice and for the development of a personal relationship with a vital—and vitalizing—dimension of human experience.

The structures of religion, I have contended, are as much symbols as are the images and stories contained within a religion. The purpose of those structures is to evoke a particular psychological state in the individual that is receptive to an aspect of experience that is on the margins of ordinary conscious life. In other words, the institution of religion points us to the quality of consciousness in which the divine or transcendent can be recognized and received.

At the same time as they are supporting the state of consciousness needed to *enter* into the experience of the transcendent, religious institutions also point to the experience of order and coherence that *emerges* through the encounter with the transcendent. A central component of religious experience is that it is not composed of randomness and chaos, but of order and meaning. This fact might indeed lend a different connotation to the phrase "organized religion."

James Fowler suggests that the structures of religion are properly understood as "guides for the construction of contemporary ways of *seeing* and *being*."[233] Like maps, they give an indication of a path to travel, its landmarks, challenges, and maybe even alternate routes. But they are not themselves the destination, nor are they the experience, which must be had firsthand and is always, ultimately, an individual one. As such, religious institutions should not be seen as "repositories of truth," but instead as opportunities for the individual's own "experiments with truth."[234]

One way to conceptualize the institutions of religion might be in terms of what the Jungian analyst D. Stephenson Bond calls a "symbolic field."[235] A symbolic field is "an organizational pattern of psychic energy" in which the psychological work of transformation can be achieved. It is a psychological state in which psychic material is "suspended between consciousness and the unconscious" giving each domain access to the other, which, in turn, leads to a mutual transformation of each other. The symbolic field both facilitates and, at the same time, *is* a psychological state of "sufficient intensity" in which the encounter with the symbolic dimension takes place. It is in and through the experience of the symbolic field that an image becomes a true symbol—that is, something lived and living.

Taking this idea, we can understand that the elements of religious institutions—structures, techniques, symbols, sacred space, and community—are the means by which a symbolic field is created in which the individual can encounter and have experience of the transcendent. In other words, they are the means by which the transcendent becomes immanent and a relationship between the individual and the divine dimension is facilitated.

There is, finally, one more necessary condition for the realization of the symbolic field. This is the quality of consciousness brought to it by the individual. I will turn to the examination of this aspect in the next chapter.

# Chapter 10
# Experiential Consciousness

In the last chapter, I looked at the structures of religion as a kind of infrastructure for the practice of the symbolic life. There, I used the analogy of a map, suggesting that rather than seeing institutional religions as repositories of fixed truths, they could be understood as guides for the individual's *experience* of truth, an opportunity, as I noted, for what James Fowler calls "experiments with truth." The cultivation of the symbolic life does not require membership in a particular religious tradition, but to ignore the paths by which generations past have found their way to this experience, or to reject the hard-won wisdom of the past out of hand, seems foolhardy at best and an unsupportable arrogance at worst.

I suggested that religious institutions act as "symbolic fields" in which the individual is potentially brought into contact with the vitalizing energies of the transcendent. However, as I also noted, the institutions of religion in and of themselves are insufficient to produce any lasting effect in the individual. This requires the participation of a receiving consciousness. In other words, a symbolic field *becomes* a symbolic field when it is engaged by a consciousness that is open to the experience of the symbolic. The symbolic life is simultaneously a meeting ground and a work. We cannot come to it, as we have been trained to do by our contemporary culture, merely as passive consumers.

## Ways of Knowing

The quality of consciousness necessary for participating in such a symbolic field is of a different order from that of the scientific consciousness through which we are in the habit of viewing and interpreting the world. In the scientific approach the world is seen as being separate from the human being who is confronting it. The world, to put it simply, is object to our subject. Thus, for this mindset, knowledge is the product of operations performed by our consciousness on the world "out there." In applying this approach, scientific consciousness has been, without question, extremely effective and successful in increasing our knowledge of the mechanics of the world in which we live.

The symbolic life, conversely, seeks to understand the world, not from without but from within. As such, it is a very different way of knowing from the way of science. Knowledge is not gained from a position of impersonal distance, but from one of personal participation. Instead of subjecting the world to the operations of our consciousness, our consciousness becomes subject to the operation of the world with its unknown and unknowable depths. Stated another way, *we do not operate on the world; it operates on us.*

For scientific consciousness, knowledge is separate from the individual. Any knowledge gained—any fact—remains what it is regardless of whatever impact it may have on the one who gains the knowledge. The individual's investment in, rejection of, or indifference to such knowledge has no relation to its objective existence. For the religious way of knowing, the situation is exactly the reverse. The knowledge gained through the practice of the symbolic life changes the one who gains it. That change, in fact, *is* the knowledge. Karen Armstrong writes that exactly that which would be considered to be the foundation of good scientific practice—"first you establish a principle; only then can you apply it"[236]—would be, in the religious context, a case of putting the cart before the horse. For religious consciousness, knowledge is only achieved through a commitment to and a disciplined practice of the religious life. To discover the truth of the transcendent, whether that is understood as knowing God, gaining Buddha consciousness, being in Tao, or putting on the mind of Christ, one first has to engage one's particular religious path as if it were true.

Armstrong insists on the importance of the practice of religion for discovering its truth:

> Religion is a practical discipline that teaches us to discover new capacities of mind and heart. ... It is no use magisterially weighing up the teachings of religion to judge their truth or

falsehood before embarking on a religious way of life. You will discover their truth—or lack of it—only if you translate these doctrines into ritual and ethical action.[237]

This statement is in complete alignment with Jung, who felt that it was only in the *experience* of the manifestations of the unconscious—dreams, fantasies, visions—that we could approach an understanding of them. Without that experience as a foundation, any intellectual formulation of, say, the meaning of dreams would be unconvincing, or would be likely to seem arbitrary, overly complicated, and ultimately something that strains our credulity.

For Jung, it is essential to engage the unconscious with the whole of our being—not just the mind, but the body as well. An authentic encounter with the unconscious requires approaching the images it produces as if they were fully real, which also means bringing our own full reality to them. "Something works behind the veil of fantastic images …" says Jung. "It is something real, and for this reason its manifestations must be taken seriously."[238]

The quality of consciousness with which we approach the symbolic dimension, then, is an important and determining factor. This is true whether we are talking about a religious practice, such as prayer, or a psychological practice, such as dream work. The "realness" of the particular reality being approached cannot be known directly. We cannot first establish the truth of its existence before we enter into an engagement with it. We must engage with it first in order to truly experience its existence. In other words, we must act as if it were real if we are to know something of its reality. This quality of consciousness that we must bring to the symbolic life, then, could be properly called experiential consciousness.[239] Through experiential consciousness, what is transcendent of the conscious psyche is discovered to have an experiential reality that manifests in the space between our being and the "something behind the veil."

Another way of expressing this idea is that such a reality is both pre-existent ("something real behind the veil"), and at the same time, a kind of arising that proceeds from our engagement with the reality. This reality announces itself, so to speak, through the psychological image and becomes—again, so to speak—a lived reality in and through our real and lived encounter with that image.

## Experiential Consciousness

Because of the difficulty we naturally have in thinking about a reality that is both existent *and* emergent, two potential dangers exist regarding how we approach and think about the image that expresses this reality. In such a case, we are prone to either concretism or negation. On the one hand, says Jung, we must be careful of taking a psychological image literally and mistaking it for the dynamism operating in the background of which the image is an expression. This is the error of concretism. On the other hand, when we engage with such an image, it "cannot be taken literally enough" lest we fall prey to the error of negation.[240] As I read Jung here, I think that he is trying to convey the kind of dual consciousness that I have been exploring not only in this chapter, but throughout this book. The image is, in a sense, "real but not real." To put it another way, the image should not be understood as a "thing" but rather as an experience. To properly encounter it, then, requires what I am calling an experiential consciousness, which is a willed suspension of disbelief in regard to one's engagement with the manifestations of the transcendent. At the same time, we must also be ready to bring our reflective capacities to bear upon the experience and remain, at least in part, objective toward it.

This is a difficult state of consciousness to describe, hence my use of the phrases *so to speak* and *in a sense* when trying to put this experience into language. The psychoanalyst D. W. Winnicott called such a state of consciousness "play."[241] This level of experiencing takes place in "potential space," which is a paradoxical psychological state in which self and other, inner world and external world, are simultaneously joined and separated. We could understand Winnicott's notion of play by analogy to the performance of an actor on the stage. The job of the actor also involves maintaining a kind of dual consciousness. The actor must fully and authentically inhabit the reality of the character being portrayed, while at the same time remaining conscious of the technical aspects of the performance, such as knowing where his marks are on the stage.

For his part, Jung describes this experiential consciousness as one of "unprejudiced objectivity," which he states is an attitude of having "deep respect for the facts."[242] This is significantly different from our conventional sense of "being objective," that quality of detached observation and analysis in which subjective and feeling states are bracketed out of the picture. This latter attitude is one we might call *prejudiced* objectivity. In contrast, Jung's "unprejudiced objectivity" is an attitude of taking the presentations—the images—of the unconscious as they are, as they present themselves. It is a "feeling-into" and not a standing apart, a participation in the psychic movement. Ultimately, it is an attitude by which the psychic image is treated as a Thou, that is, as an Other with its own inviolable being, which yet has a connection to one's own being, and not simply as an It, a mere thing, an object that is subject to one's willful manipulations.

Thus, our "coming to terms" with the unconscious, as it was described in relation to the practice of active imagination, is not so much a process of categorization and conceptualization as it is a suffering of the experience. One takes note of how the encounter affects him. He reflects on it, feels into it, thinks about it, imagines it further, while all the time maintaining an awareness of the mystery at the heart of the experience. Experiential consciousness, in other words, involves bringing a religious attitude to one's experience.

This mode of attention, as I said, is a dual consciousness. This is a hard state of consciousness to hold and a harder one to describe, since to describe it we are forced by language and by reason to state first one thing and then another, while the actual experience is made up of both elements (the "real" and the "not real") simultaneously. It is both the presence and the absence of belief, the absence and presence of disbelief. It is an awareness of "This is It" while holding the knowledge that "It is *not* this." It is a recognition that though the symbol and what it symbolizes are, in one sense, inseparable, the meaning (the symbolized) is not trapped in the symbol, and they must also remain distinguished one from the other.

Experiential consciousness, then, is the capacity to sense more than what is contained in the image, without thereby denying the value of the image. What conveys that sense of "something more" is not just any image, but this specific image, which is related to the "more-ness" to which it points. The reality of the "something more" to which the symbolic image points can only be known by exposing or opening oneself to it—the opening of one being to another being in which the irreducible mystery of the other is encountered. Anything less than this full investment of oneself remains at the level of the recognition of a theoretical possibility but does not open out into the full experience of a lived reality.

## Active versus Passive Consciousness

Experiential consciousness consists of a state of mind and being that is similar to many "emptiness" practices as found in the contemplative streams of the world's religious traditions. The practice of emptiness is one of opening oneself to the transcendent depths of reality without preconceived ideas or pragmatic concerns.[243] This is exactly the quality of consciousness that Jung advocates, for instance, for the practice of active imagination, which I discussed in Chapter 8. As I noted there, active imagination is first of all a discipline of receptivity. Recall the advice that Jung gives regarding this practice: "Do nothing but observe."

Whether it is in the psychological practice of active imagination or in the religious discipline of prayer, the location of agency, ultimately, is not in oneself. We are not the creator and director of the experience of the symbolic dimension. It is more a question of letting oneself be open to the action of the transcendent. The psyche, we might say, is the receiver through which the "signal" of the depths sounds. Panikkar speaks of letting oneself "be fertilized"[244] and Jung writes of letting oneself by analyzed by the unconscious.[245] It is a passive, as opposed to an active, consciousness.

All of this, of course, should be understood as qualitatively different from the passivity fostered by our entertainment culture, in which the imagination is barraged by a clutter of images 24 hours a day. In this instance it is important to distinguish between what we might call a dead (or passive) passivity in contrast to a living (or active) passivity. Although it is unquestionably true that good drama, art, and music can speak to us and stir us at the depths, and that this experience can even manifest through the thinnest of entertainments, the vast majority of the entertainment that is pushed at us is meant to be consumed in what can only be called a state of agitated indifference.

To let ourselves be fertilized—or to allow ourselves to be analyzed—is to let the transcendent into our lives in a way that changes us. The purpose of entertainment is distraction. As such, it merely washes over us, never penetrating beneath the surface. We remain fundamentally unchanged by the experience. This is what distinguishes symbolic experience from more superficial engagements with the imagination: The symbolic life, whether it is experienced through religion, psychology, or art, is inherently transformative.

Transformation cannot happen if we hold ourselves back from the experience of the images and symbols we encounter. If we approach them with a merely intellectual curiosity, then we are trying to dominate the image, rather than letting ourselves be dominated *by* it. And this, in turn, can happen only if we suspend our "knowing" that what we experience is "nothing but" an image. We have to allow it to be an active presence with its own subjectivity. We have to *experience* it.

This is the fundamental work of both depth psychology and of religion—the recognition and the experience of the fact that what we are is far greater in scope than our conscious sense of ourselves. It is the awareness that there are demands and impingements on us that are not necessarily in alignment with our conscious plans and goals. "The mystery of the psyche," writes D. Stephenson Bond, "is that we are haunted not by what we want out of life, but by what life wants out of us."[246] This involves a complete revolution of our normal way of conceiving of symbolic material. The images and symbols of the psyche, which include, of course, religious symbolism, are not so much "products" of the imagination as they are *presences within the field of imagination*. They are not reflections of ourselves; rather, *we* are reflections of them.

## Postcritical Consciousness and the Ironic Imagination

The concept of experiential consciousness is not a new idea, but one that has been put forward in many different guises. I have already noted, for instance, Karen Armstrong's observation that one's commitment to religious practice must precede the experience of transcendence, Winnicott's notion of play and "potential space," and Jung's insistence on "unprejudiced objectivity."

Philosopher Michael Polanyi makes the point that the determination of the truth or untruth of any system of thought is the result of nonrational commitment. "It is," he says, "a fiduciary act which cannot be analysed in non-committal terms."[247] In other words, the participation, the assent, and the commitment of the individual is an inherent part of *any* approach to knowledge. To formulate this another way, we could say that every truth investment involves some element of faith. Polanyi further points out that all learning occurs through one's submergence into an experience of the material being learned and not through an act of distancing oneself from it. We do not confront a unit of knowledge as a separate object; instead, we feel into it through a process of "visceral identification." As Berman summarizes this process, "Rationality, as it turns out, begins to play a role only after the knowledge has been obtained viscerally."[248] This is essentially the process articulated by Jung regarding active imagination: First there is an encounter with the material, then we come to terms with it.

Another framework is provided by Paul Ricoeur, who speaks of the difference between "first naïveté" and "second naïveté" (or "willed naïveté.")[249] As Fowler describes, first naïveté is an attitude that is rooted in a precritical consciousness that experiences no distinction between the symbol and the symbolized. This precritical stage is a childlike level of faith that sees and accepts religious and psychological symbols as concrete realities. First naïveté begins to break down with the rise of critical consciousness, when the individual begins to ask questions of the symbols being encountered.

Much of the perceived conflict between science and religion takes place between the critical consciousness of scientific materialism and the precritical consciousness of a fundamentalist or literalist approach to religion. Experiential consciousness, as I have been developing it in this chapter, is not to be understood as a regression to first naïveté. Rather, it is to be regarded as a move beyond critical consciousness to a postcritical consciousness, which brings with it the possibility of a second naïveté.

Critical consciousness can lead to important and interesting insights in its examination of the symbols of transcendence, but these tend to be prescribed and limited within the confines of the conscious assumptions with which these symbols are examined. The initiative of inquiry, in other words, remains with the conscious mind. This has its place and its value, but because consciousness takes the initiative, any potential transformation of consciousness is precluded. In contrast to this, second naïveté reflects a "postcritical desire to resubmit to the initiative of the symbolic."[250] It releases, as far as is possible, all preconceived notions and allows the symbol to be what Fowler aptly calls self-authenticating—that is, an experiential fact with which the individual is confronted. Second naïveté is the ability, described earlier in this chapter, to experience the symbol and the symbolized as being both inseparable and yet, at the same time, differentiated from each other.

From the psychological point of view, a postcritical consciousness is one that takes seriously the manifestations of the unconscious, respecting their autonomy (initiative), and approaching them on their own terms instead of reducing them to the terms of consciousness. In this way, one's sense of self becomes less fixed—one thing confronting another thing, as in consciousness confronting the unconscious—and is experienced instead as more fluid, consisting of *both* conscious and unconscious. This latter understanding is a recognition of the truth that we are more than we can know about ourselves.[251]

Fowler associates this postcritical stage of consciousness with the emergence of the ironic imagination, which he understands as the ability to recognize the relativity and partiality of one's symbolic commitments, even as one is able to live within them and experience their power and truth. The ironic imagination is that form of apperception that de-absolutizes experience, holding together the contraries of "real" and "not-real," for instance, such that things are neither absolutely true (literalism) nor absolutely false (positivism).[252]

For his part, Jung does not use the terms *postcritical, second naïveté,* or *ironic imagination,* but in his own words describes the essence of the experience denoted by these terms. In his essay on "A Psychological Approach to the Dogma of the Trinity," he states:

> Spiritual transformation does not mean that one should remain a child, but that the adult should summon up enough honest self-criticism admixed with humility to see where, and in relation to what, he must behave as a child—irrationally, and with unreflecting receptivity.[253]

This is exactly the description of a second or willed naïveté—to see where one must "behave as a child ... with unreflecting receptivity." There is a dual sacrifice involved here. On the one hand, the development of self-reflection and maturity requires leaving behind the dependence that belongs to childhood. On the other hand, the possibility of a mature spiritual transformation requires an equal sacrifice of one's *independence*, insofar as it has become merely an isolated and enclosed self-reliance. In other words, in order to experience the fullness of our humanity, we must learn to recognize both our independence from, and simultaneous dependence on, the unconscious, the transcendent. This is the essence and the goal of experiential consciousness.

# Chapter 11
## Psychology as *Religio*

Throughout Jung's *Collected Works*, one repeatedly finds him reminding his readers that the way to an understanding of the human soul, both collectively and personally, is not to be reached through a merely rational attitude. Symbols and images are not concepts and therefore cannot simply be addressed with the critical intellect, which is, in the end, inadequate for dealing with the very thing it would be trying to grasp in this case. Symbols are not rational facts but rather psychic phenomena. Furthermore, symbols are enveloped by a penumbra of ambiguity and uncertainty that reason is unequipped to handle on its own.

Jung's approach to the symbolic is a postcritical one. It does not so much abandon the rational, nor eliminate critical judgment, as it supplements these with a kind of empathic engagement. Such an engagement approaches the phenomena of the psyche on its own terms. To proceed empathically is to suspend one's own categories of knowing and even one's particular worldview in an attempt to get an "inside view" of the self-presentation of that which is transcendent of consciousness.

One of the remarkable aspects of Jung's thought is his awareness of and respect for the ultimate mystery of the psyche and the limits of human knowledge. "The psyche," he wrote, "is part of the inmost mystery of life."[254] Our thoughts, Jung insisted, are not made by the conscious mind; rather, they are "objective occurrences"[255]—events that happen to us. This means that there is no final resting place of knowledge, no destination that we arrive at intellectually, no quantity of knowledge or information that we finally possess. There is only the ongoing encounter with life in the worlds within, without, and beyond.

When we approach our psychological experience with empathy and respect, we begin to recognize that we cannot take possession of our inner life. I would even go so far as saying that we begin to recognize that the inner life is not *our* inner life as much as it is our inner experience *of life*. It is for this reason that Jung often makes use of religious language to describe the activity of the psyche. As I have noted previously, religious and mythic language give the most adequate expression to the autonomy and the power of the psychological experiences that daily confront us. At the same time, it is important to remember that religious language does not capture the full reality of the inner life; it merely gives us a point of meeting it. We cannot force the inner life to reside within a particular set of images and symbols. Its ultimate existence is independent of the symbol, even though it is intimately tied to it. The task for each one of us is to seek those images and those symbols in which the pulse of one's own inner life resides.

## *Religio*: Careful Observation of the Numinous

The stated goal of Jung's psychological approach is the meeting of the conscious personality and the unconscious. Through this meeting, one experiences wholeness, or, what Jung calls elsewhere, a participation in a "wider personality."[256] The union of conscious and unconscious is both the path to the goal and, at the same time, the goal itself. The word that Jung often turns to throughout his writings to express this encounter is the Latin word *religio*.

The term *religio* is the basis from which our word *religion* is derived. According to Jung, there are competing etymologies of *religio*, each of which lead, in turn, to different ways of understanding religion and its function in human life. Because this is the word from which Jung derives his own specific definition and understanding of religion, it is worth taking a closer look at this etymological background.

The distinction between these understandings of religion that Jung notes rests on a very subtle difference—the difference between the words *religare* and *religere*, each of which has been suggested, in different contexts, as the root of the word we are looking at here, *religio*. In his own research, Jung came upon the divergence of meaning and intention that flow from these two separate streams. He refers to it repeatedly in scattered footnotes throughout his *Collected Works* in order to try to clearly differentiate his usage of the word *religion* from more common understandings of the word.

As Jung points out, the word *religare* is used in the writings of the early Church Fathers and carries the sense of "reconnecting" or "linking back."[257] The root of *religare* is *lig-*, the same root as that found in the word *ligament*. The connotation of *religare* is of "binding together," "connecting," or "linking." Occasionally in his writings, Jung uses the word *religio* with this understanding in mind, as he does, for instance, in his essay on *The Psychology of the Child Archetype*. In that essay, he points out that all psychological explanations of religious or mythological symbols are "only more or less successful translations into another metaphorical language,"[258] because both the religious symbol and the psychological explanation are, in fact, pointing to the unknowable archetype and its vital energy. It is the ultimately irrepresentable archetypes that are the "real and invisible roots of consciousness."[259] Connection (linking) with these archetypal roots is what is of primary importance. Psychologically, the quality of this linking or connecting with these roots is affected for good or for ill by the quality of our explanations of the religious and mythological symbols that express them. "A bad explanation means a correspondingly bad attitude to this organ, which may thus be injured."[260] In other words, religious symbols "link" or "reconnect" us to the archetypal depths of our own nature, and this link is only as strong as our interpretations and understanding will allow.

More frequently, however, Jung relies on an understanding of *religio* that is derived from the root *religere* (with an *e*, not an *a*). His sources for this etymological stream are the classical writers, particularly Cicero. The word *religere* means "to go through again, to think over, to recollect."[261] Jung renders the definition of *religio* as derived from this root as the "careful consideration and observation of certain dynamic factors,"[262] or, alternately, "a careful observation and taking account of … the numinous."[263] This is Jung's preferred definition throughout the *Collected Works*, and it essentially becomes his exclusive definition from around 1950 on.

Though perhaps similar to the former definition of "linking back," *religio* as "careful consideration," "carefully observing," and "taking account" adds an important emphasis. The first definition—*religio* as "reconnecting"—places the attention on *that which connects*, the thing that does the linking; that is, the symbol that mediates the archetype. The second definition, however—*religio* as careful consideration— places more emphasis on the *observer of the symbol*. Careful consideration is human reflection on the archetypal image and the dynamic that it represents. The careful observation and taking account of the invisible factors of the psyche reflects what Jung called, in German, the *Auseinandersetzung*—the confrontation or dialogue— between the conscious and the unconscious, which was such a crucial aspect of his psychological approach.[264] In other words, what Jung is emphasizing with his use of the word *religio* is not just the symbol but *the symbolic life*, the engagement of the individual with the symbolic dimension, through the use of one's experiential consciousness.

## Religious Attitude versus Religious Belief

There is still a further differentiation to be noted on this point. The description of the difference between the meanings of *religio* as derived from either the words *religare* or *religere* is taken from statements in Jung's writings that are primarily confined, as I have said, to a few footnotes in his *Collected Works*. Fortunately, we also have the writings found in a great number of Jung's letters. In one such letter from 1959, he writes more extensively about the differences of these two derivations. This letter provides us with more context that can help to give a better sense of what Jung is aiming for in his particular understanding of *religio*.

The first sense of *religio*, that of "linking" or "binding," Jung suggests in his letter, is reflected in the Judeo-Christian notion of the covenant, or marriage, with God. *Religio*, in this sense, then, is best understood as that which *binds* us in fidelity to God. This, he points out, comes with the possibility, and even the likelihood, of unfaithfulness on the part of humanity. The occurrence of such human infidelity would, in turn, call forth God's vengeance, resulting in a disconnection between God and humankind. Hence, there would arise the need for a "re-connecting."[265]

In contrast with this understanding, *religio* approached as "to consider," "to take account," or "to observe" reflects the attitude of earlier "pagan" religions. "Here," Jung writes, "religion means a watchful, wary, thoughtful, careful, prudent, expedient, and calculating attitude towards the powers-that-be, with not a trace of that legal and emotional contract which can be broken like a marriage."[266]

There is certainly room for disagreement with Jung regarding his view of marriage as a merely contractual agreement and his interpretation of the Judeo-Christian covenant. However, if we look past the specifics of this interpretation to its underlying implication, it is clear that what Jung is trying to emphasize, with his preference for *religio* as "careful consideration," is the religious attitude that attends to the "powers-that-be" in whatever form they may arise. This he prefers in contrast to a more fixed system of beliefs—that is, to a binding obligation that one might make in relation to only one particular form of these powers. We could say that, for Jung, one understanding of *religio*—that of "linking"—leads to a more fixed experience of religion, whereas the other leads to a more open and fluid engagement with religion. In other words, with his emphasis on the "careful consideration of the numinous," Jung is advocating for the development of a religious *attitude* and not that of a religious *belief*. To have *religio*, then, is to be religious but not religious. One is religious in the sense of having a reverent or respectful attitude toward one's deepest experiences, but not religious in the sense of holding, in a rigid way, to a fixed and particular belief system.[267]

## The God-Experience

Jung's concept of *religio* stands in stark contrast to the focus on goals and outcomes—the productivity mindset—that dominates so much of our current cultural worldview. The "careful observation and consideration" of the many powers that beset us is not done for the sake of problem solving, not for the sake of knowing, not even for the sake of healing. For Jung, the aim of analytic treatment is not in finding a cure for one's symptoms; it is in the development of an attitude toward the psyche, and toward life, that enables the individual to better face the challenges and struggles of living that are an inevitable part of any human life.

*Religio*, then, is not a method that one applies in order to achieve a finite goal. It is a way of living in the world. We do not engage in dream interpretation or active imagination, for instance, in order to extract information from the psyche that we can then apply in a technical way to the problems of living, thereby increasing our productivity, becoming a better lover, or achieving whatever other goal we may have for ourselves. We engage in these activities in order to overcome our alienation from the psyche, from the foundations of our own being, from the life seeking to live itself in us. The goal, in other words, is nothing short of the transformation of the individual. We do not apply a method. Through the practice of *religio*, we *become our own method*.

One could say that Jung's notion of *religio* acknowledges God as a psychological experience, all the while recognizing that it is ultimately beyond one's human capacity to know anything definitive beyond that experience. Throughout his writings, Jung makes a distinction between God and what he calls the God-image. This distinction is meant to differentiate between a metaphysical understanding of God on the one hand and the psychological approach to God on the other. The problem with the phrase *God-image*, however, is that it tends to give the impression that what we are dealing with is but a picture, a way of describing God that is somewhat arbitrary and, ultimately, in-substantial.

This does not do justice to what Jung is pointing to, and therefore it is important to recall what he means by the word *image*, which is best understood as a psychological *experience*. An image is not just a picture in the mind, but an experience that touches the whole person—one's thoughts, feelings, sensations, and intuitions. The distinction, then, that we are discussing here is probably better rendered as the difference between God and the *God-experience:* "From time immemorial," writes Jung, "man has called anything he feels or experiences as stronger than he is 'divine' or 'daemonic.' God is the Stronger in him."[268] This "Stronger in us" is that which we cannot master by an act of will or reason—indeed, that we cannot master at all. All we can do is find a way to submit to the reality of the "Stronger" and work toward a reconciliation with the powerful energies with which it confronts us. This work is the work of *religio*.

Through this work, the "divine or daemonic" other-experience of the "Stronger in us" is held together with, and brought into relationship with, the self-experience. And this self-experience is none other than the field on which the encounter with the divine or daemonic other occurs. "We are the point of contact," says Panikkar.[269] "God becomes manifest in the human act of reflection," echoes Jung.[270]

## A Consecration of Oneself

*Religio*, then, proceeds by reflection, which itself has a particular meaning and quality for Jung. It does not just refer to the act of thinking about something but rather is an attitude that one holds. Reflection leads us out of the realm of the natural and into the spiritual. It is that which moves us from *bios* to *zoê*. In other words, it is the unique human capacity by which one steps back from one's automatic impulses and instinctive reactions and, in doing so, effectively dissolves one's identity with those reactions. Through the act of reflection, we can hold our experiences in mind, relate to them, and come to accept them. This is what it means to become conscious. In essence, it is what gives us a psychological foothold outside of the mere reactivity of our organism. I would describe this as the difference between the fullness of the experience of life and the condition of being alive. It is in our capacity for reflection that experience truly becomes experience. Prior to that, it is merely "what happens to us."

This shaping of experience out of that which happens to us describes another dimension of the function and quality of *religio*—it brings cohesion and ordering to our encounter with life. All religions give some symbolic expression to the fullness, the wholeness, the unity of the divine, as well as to the foundation, the ground, and the refuge that it provides. This experience of wholeness stands in opposition to the more fragmented and diffuse pattern of living that tends to be constellated and amplified by life in the modern world, marked as it is by chronic distraction and the paralysis that attends the dubious gift of a world of limitless choice.

The experience of *religio*, in contrast, is that which comes by way of focus and commitment. Through it we clarify those things that have value and meaning for us and to which we want our lives to be directed. The word that Jung uses for this quality of commitment is the Greek New Testament word for faith, πίστις *(pistis)*. *Pistis* is both a trust in and a loyalty to our deepest experiences. Faith, so understood, is not to be confused with belief, but recognized, rather, as a commitment to particular meanings and values, as well as a loyalty to that commitment. The πίστις of *religio*, then, is a consecration of oneself, a self-dedication to a center, or centers, of value. As such, it contrasts with the compulsion toward novelty and the prodigal collecting of increasingly stimulating "experiences" that is sanctioned by contemporary mores.

## What We Serve

In a few places in his writings, Jung will state that one of his patients "had *religio*." He notes that the possession of this attitude toward their experiences was an essential factor in their treatment. To "have *religio*" means, in part, that I do not take responsibility for the presence of powerful feelings and energies that beset me. That is, I don't identify with them, on the one hand, and I don't try to reassert control by overpowering them, on the other. Instead, I "carefully take account" of these energies, making a "careful consideration and observation" of my experience. Another way of saying this is that rather than pushing powerful, and often difficult, psychological experiences away, I make every effort to welcome them in. This does not, however, mean acquiescing to or indulging in the energy, fantasy, or feeling that is being experienced, but rather getting curious about it, watching it, and perhaps even engaging it in a kind of dialogue. It means recognizing that these experiences are part of the "Stronger in me," that they have some relation to me, and then asking why they are presenting themselves to me in this way and at this time.

*Religio*, ultimately, is an attitude of respect and awe for the powers and agencies that act upon our psyches. It is a response to the experience that there are things outside of our will that impinge on us, such as patterns of reaction that we can't shake, insoluble problems that we can't seem to resolve and that return in various disguises, and powerful images and fantasies that can be either terrible or beautiful, and sometimes both at the same time.

The welcoming act of *religio* corresponds to what Fowler calls "dialogical knowing," which is a way of encountering a phenomenon—particularly in regard to numinous or religious experience—as an "Other" in its own right. This "Other" is given an opportunity to reveal itself according to its own structure, to which, in turn, one "accommodates her or his knowing"[271] before bringing to bear one's own framework of understanding to the encounter. To "accommodate one's knowing" to the structure of that being known is a good way of describing the recentering from the personal to the transpersonal that occurs in the practice of *religio*. Our perspective shifts, in a sense, from looking for what serves us to discovering what we serve, as the following example illustrates.

A man with whom I worked had struggled for much of the first year of his becoming a father. Prior to the birth of his first child, a good percentage of our work together had been given to wrestling with his relationship with his own father, and his frustrations and disappointments with the way he had been fathered. What had been particularly wounding for him was his father's emotional distance. When he was a younger man, he would often try to challenge his father to meet him on a feeling and emotional level, but that would only be met by a further withdrawal of his father's emotional presence. His father's attitude toward life and work, he told me, was one of passivity—a resigned acceptance of his lot in life. As a consequence, my patient struggled with his own place in the world and with his confidence in being able to take up the adventure of life.

When his child was born, his ambivalent relationship to the archetypal energy of fathering was constellated in a powerful way. It was clear that he deeply loved his child and strove to be, and in fact was, a good, loving, and available father. Nevertheless, he felt unready to dedicate himself to fatherhood because he felt he hadn't yet sorted out his own place in the world. Furthermore, he found himself feeling displaced. The care, concern, and support that he received from his wife, and still longed for, was now being directed primarily to their child. He felt resentful and, at the same time, deep guilt at feeling such resentment. This conflict gnawed at him in the form of relentless ruminations.

Together we sat with his struggles and the conflict that was eating away at him and that, at times, felt insoluble. This sticking with the conflict is an essential part of *religio*—it is a commitment, a *pistis*, to the problem that the conflict stirs up without the attempt to shut it down with quick fixes or with simple but unsatisfying solutions. This kind of commitment is hard to give and hard to bear, and it can often feel like running on a hamster wheel—going over the same issues, the same struggles, again and again. Sometimes, because of this, he would get apologetic and say to me, "I feel like I keep saying the same thing!" Still, he was the kind of person who could not ignore the struggle of his soul nor the existential puzzles of life. And so, he pushed on, carefully observing his reactions to his experience, and reflecting deeply on them and the way they expressed themselves in his dreams and fantasies. In other words, he had *religio*.

The stalemate was broken with the experience of a dream that he was eager to share with me:

> *He had been walking in the street and seen a dead bird that was being gnawed at by rats. At first, he walked by, like all the other people around him. Later, however, he came back and chased the rats away, even though it seemed futile to do so. The rats tried to return, but he stood his ground. Then he was in his home and a beautiful, multicolored bird entered his house. His first thought was to release it, but it clung to him and would not fly off. At this point he realized that the bird was dehydrated and that he needed to care for it.*

This is a beautiful dream of the recovery of a spiritual potential—symbolized by the multicolored bird—which had been almost completely devoured. Because he refused to abandon this deep need within himself, he was eventually able to stand his ground against those factors that had been gnawing away at his soul. He discovered that not only did he need to be connected to this manifestation of the spirit but *it needed him,* it needed his nurturing. The image of the multicolored bird here is reminiscent of the alchemical idea of the *cauda pavonis,* the "peacock's tail." Jung associates this image with the emergence of the Philosopher's Stone—the goal of the alchemical opus—and by extension, his own concept of the Self.[272] The dream, then, heralds the possibility for my patient of living in connection with the Self.

Around the time of his telling this dream to me, he also noted that he had had a kind of epiphany about the role that he needed and wanted to play in his family. His job, he saw, was to be a support to his wife in ways that made it easier for her to make the necessary sacrifices that come with motherhood, and that, in this way, they could nurture and build their family together. About this idea he said, "I feel like this is my place of service." Through the *religio* of his inner work, his giving careful attention to his inner conflict, he was led to discover that family and fatherhood were crucial aspects of his place of service, and an important aspect of his spiritual work.

Of course, this was not the end of the story for this man. He was not immediately freed from his doubts and conflicts. This new awareness, however, became a kind of anchor point for him. It gave a focus and meaning to his ongoing struggles, as well as a "place" to return to and to remember when he would inevitably forget, as we all do, and get submerged in his ruminations once again. Interestingly, shortly after this dream and its accompanying epiphany, he began to develop an interest in renewing his engagement with the religious tradition of his youth. At first, he started by reading the stories of the Old Testament patriarchs. He could not articulate why he was drawn to these stories but sensed there was something invaluable in them, something he might be able to take from them about living a human life. It seemed to me as if this interest in the biblical patriarchs was an expression of his need to be connected to the archetypal roots of fathering that these stories, in part, represented and imaged.

Over time, this interest began to include a felt need to participate in the seasonal rituals of the church: Christmas, Lent, Easter. As he described it to me, this feeling was not about becoming a "believing Christian" but in participating in something that expressed the rhythms and seasons, not only of the year but also of the full sweep of human life. The rituals connected him to a source of wisdom and gave some foundation to the day-to-day life of work and family. They allowed him to be religious but not religious.

The question arises: Did his dream create his new attitude, or did his new attitude result in this impressive dream? This question, however, approaches the situation with the wrong intention—one that seeks to understand the mechanism, and not the quality, of the experience. What is most important here is the capacity to hold a symbolic attitude. In his struggle, my analysand sensed a "something" that he could not identify, but that he knew was important for his life. It manifested in his dissatisfaction at work, his struggles as a father, and later in his interest in religious stories and rituals. This holding to the unknown, and the attempt to come into relationship with it, constellates the very relationship it seeks. Bond puts it this way:

> The imagination is … a vehicle of relationship to what lies on the other side of imagination—autonomous psyche. It is as if as we lay hold of [our] images … all of a sudden one day something lays hold of us.[273]

The dream and the new attitude, we might say, are part of a mutual arising, which we can understand as the shifting of the center from the ego to the Self. Because it is a relational dynamic between the personal and the impersonal, or the conscious and the unconscious, it does not proceed only from one direction or the other, but both together act as co-creators of the new experience of meaning. Jung describes just this dynamic of the co-creation of transformation, using the symbolism of the Philosopher's Stone as illustration. He states:

> It is a phenomenon of consciousness, a product of human effort, and at the same time a *donum gratiae*, a gift of God's grace. It is always stressed that it is impossible to do it on one's own, it can only be given *per gratiam dei*, but man still has to make the effort to make this structure.[274]

And so we move, we might say, from the *religio* of effort, involving *pistis* and commitment, to the experience of *Religio*, "the gift of God's grace," which is the felt experience of the arising of vocation, the place of one's service in the world.

# Conclusion
## Opening a Space for Wonder

The question of the value of the religious life poses something of a dilemma in our modern world. On the one hand, as I have shown, the lack of an organizing and meaningful center by which one's life can be oriented, and which religion provides, can lead to the experience of emotional suffering, and in some cases even become life-threatening. Furthermore, by remaining unconscious of the religious dimension of life, we risk the inflation of our sense of ourselves as human beings to a kind of god-like status. On the other hand, the scientific rationalism in which our world and our minds are steeped has made it nearly impossible for increasing numbers of people to experience a naive relationship with religion, its forms, and its symbols.

We seem to have forgotten how to wonder about the meaningfulness of life. The discourse about God and religion has devolved into a shouting match of one rigid and fixed idea against another equally rigid and fixed idea. As Diana Eck observes, "Today there is perhaps too much certainty, too little pondering, among both the religious and the irreligious."[275]

## The Activity of Religious Consciousness

Carl Jung asserted that an essential aspect of his work was to "teach people the art of seeing."[276] That is, he sought to articulate a means by which people could experience the truth inherent in the symbols of religion through an understanding of their psychological roots. He saw his psychology as providing a way out of both an arid rationalism and a metaphysical concretism. There is much in modern theology that has come a long way toward Jung's psychological approach. Religion, too, has felt the need to dissolve its own rigid formulations and put forward understandings that have the capacity to connect people to the essential truths—the experiential truths—which lie at its heart.

With his notion of *religio*, Jung lays emphasis on the activity of a religious consciousness, in contradistinction to the object of religion. The symbol is not an object, but rather an experience, and it is in the experiencing—the careful consideration, the taking into account—of the symbol that the transformation of consciousness is made possible. In taking the emphasis off the object and putting it onto the experience, the temptation to see religion as an end—that is, as a destination or a goal— is dissolved. Through this attitude, religion as a set of symbols, practices, and orienting beliefs becomes instead a doorway that leads beyond itself to religion as an experience, an encounter with the depths of life.

The perspective of Raimon Panikkar is instructive here. He suggests that Being (that is, God) should be understood as a verb and not as a noun. In the light of this idea, religion, properly understood, is not something that one possesses but something that *propels one toward* religious experience, toward a deeper encounter with life. If we hold to the "thingness" of religion too tightly, a process of petrification sets in and we are in danger of losing the religious life that it expresses.[277]

## The Empty Center

Jung was impressed with the parallels that he discovered between the images that appeared in the dreams of his patients and those that made up the symbolic language of the world's religious traditions. As I discussed in Chapter 8, one symbol that had particular impact on Jung's work and thought was that of the mandala. The production of mandalas by his patients provided evidence for him of an archetypal religious process in the human psyche. At the same time, the particular forms that his patients' mandalas took seemed to him to be an indication of a development or evolution of the god-image itself.

In particular, Jung found that instead of depicting a god in the center of the mandala, as had historically been the case in religious mandala images, the center of these modern mandalas produced by his patients were empty. For Jung, the emptiness of the center did not mean the denial or absence of God; rather, it pointed to the growing experience of "something unknowable which is endorsed with the highest intensity."[278] It was the appearance in the psyche of this "unknowable something" that Jung gave the name of the Self.

## Emptiness and Kenosis

This psychological experience of an empty center finds resonance in virtually every religious tradition, if not always within a religion's mainstream expression, then certainly through the contemplative or mystical aspect of that tradition. In this regard, we find the concept of *sunyata* in Buddhism, the Void in Taoism, *nirguna Brahman* in Hinduism, *Ayin* in mystical Judaism, and the aspect of Allah as *al-Batin* ("the Hidden One") in Islam. Each of these symbols is an expression of "Nothingness" or "Emptiness," which is not to be understood here as a negation; rather, it should be regarded as the source and fullness of all things that yet cannot be known or named within the field of consciousness.

The Christian tradition, too, has its expression of emptiness in the form of the theological idea of *kenosis*, which is derived from the phrase in Paul's letter to the Philippians, where he states that Christ "emptied himself" of his divinity in order to become a human being (Phil. 2:7). Kenosis is worth looking at here in more detail, as it provides an archetypally grounded image of a living essence that becomes more fully realized in that act of giving itself up or of going beyond itself. A quick survey of the qualities used to describe kenosis will show some of the contours of this important symbolic idea. Kenosis is described as a self-emptying, a humbling, and a pouring out. It is said to proceed through self-limitation rather than self-interest, letting go rather than clinging, and giving away rather than possessing. At the same time, this self-surrender is also a self-realization, a letting go of a false self so that a true self can emerge.

The paradoxical nature of kenosis is nicely articulated by Alan Watts, who offers an essential insight into the kenotic dimensions of Christianity when he says, "The basic theme of the Christ-story is that this 'express image' of God becomes the source of life in the very act of being destroyed."[279] This is the paradox spoken by Jesus himself to his disciples when he taught them that "those who try to make their life secure will lose it, but those who lose their life will keep it" (Luke 17:33).

In the symbol of kenosis, then, we have an image of the self-presentation of the Divine that simultaneously points away from itself. In other words, kenosis, in particular, and Emptiness, more generally, as expressed in *all* religious traditions, can be understood as the archetypal background of what is conveyed in the phrase *religious but not religious*.

The religious attitude is properly empty—kenotic. It maintains an awareness of the ultimate mystery of life and does not cling to the forms through which that mystery is sensed. It understands that although we need structures with which we can meet the contingencies of life, and through which we can gain some understanding of its depths, ultimately what we call *Truth*, or *Knowledge*, or *Reality*, or *God* exceeds what those names and structures are able to contain. We cannot do without our structures—language, image, theory, symbol, story—all these are points of orientation without which we would be lost in the chaos of the infinite stimuli of living, a chaos we only reinforce through our current preoccupation with the proliferation of data and information. Nevertheless, we must be willing to let our structures go, or else they can become barriers to the individual adventure of being alive.

Jung was acutely aware that all our structures, be they religious symbols or psychological concepts, were, in the end, but "human veils and curtains concealing the abysmal darkness of the Unknowable."[280] The best that human beings could do in the face of the transcendent mystery of life, Jung felt, was "to paint the world with divine colours."[281] We find ourselves in a position, in other words, in which we must learn what I would call the art of knowing but not knowing. We must find ways to know (be in relationship with) what cannot be known (a possession of the mind).

Ultimately, it is not what we know that matters but what we live. Our concepts and ideas—whether psychological or spiritual, scientific or religious—are like mirrors in which the reflection of truth can be glimpsed, though not fully known as in a face-to-face encounter. At best, they are partial and incomplete expressions of the experiences they are attempting to describe. This means it is not so important that we are in possession of an ultimate and final truth, as that will always remain beyond our grasp. What is important is that we are able to *experience* a truth that brings us more alive, one that awakens the heart to love, the soul to beauty, and the mind to the wonder of life.

# Notes

# Introduction: The Decisive Question

[1] From "About Us," The Guild of Pastoral Psychology, http://www.guildofpastoralpsychology.org.uk/index.php/about-us (Accessed 4 Mar. 2018).

[2] From "The Symbolic Life," by C.G. Jung, 1939/1976a, *The Collected Works of C.G. Jung*, Vol. 18, par. 627, NJ: Princeton University Press.

[3] *Neurosis*, for Jung, refers to a class of psychological suffering characterized by symptoms that develop when aspects of one's personality become dissociated, or split off, from conscious awareness. This is often due to the individual's inability to tolerate or integrate these aspects in one's conscious living. Neuroses disrupt and disturb, as with depression or anxiety, but they do not threaten the personality as a whole, as does psychosis. The term *neurosis* is no longer used widely in contemporary psychology, having been removed from the *Diagnostic and Statistical Manual of Mental Disorders* in 1980.

[4] See, for example, Edinger, 1972; von Franz, 1996; Stein, 2009.

[5] See, for example, *Chapter 1 Symbols and the Symbolic* for an in-depth explanation of the nature of the symbol.

[6] The Jungian understanding of the word *psyche* is much broader than simply "mind." It refers to the totality of psychic processes, both conscious and unconscious. These include cognition, feeling, imagination, dreams, emotions, sensations, and more. In this way, the psyche for Jung was much closer to the original Greek meaning of the word—soul or animating principle—than the more restricted contemporary understanding of mental activity. Because it is through the psyche that we come to know the psyche, its ultimate essence remains a mystery.

[7] The *unconscious* is the name given to the existence of psychological contents and experiences that are not conscious and yet produce effects in the conscious experience of the individual. The contents of the unconscious consist not only of those elements that were at one time conscious and have become suppressed or repressed but also those aspects of the psyche that have *never* been conscious. For Jung, the unconscious is the matrix out of which the conscious mind emerges and not simply the repository of those things discarded by consciousness.

[8] From "Five Lectures on Psycho-Analysis," by Sigmund Freud, 1909/2001a, *The Standard Edition of the Complete Psychological Works of Sigmund Freud*, Vol. 11, p. 33, London: Vintage.

[9] The word *ego* is a translation of what Freud, in his writing, called "the I." It is therefore meant to refer to that part of the psyche that we identify with ourselves—the conscious willing self and core of our identity. For Jung, the ego is the center of consciousness—we are conscious of something when it has a relationship to the ego.

[10] From "A Difficulty in the Path of Psycho-Analysis," by Sigmund Freud, 1917/2001b, *The Standard Edition of the Complete Psychological Works of Sigmund Freud*, Vol. 17, p. 143, London: Vintage.

[11] The *archetype* is a deep pattern of thought and behavior. It expresses the timeless history of the human psyche through collective images, such as those found in religious and mythological motifs. Archetypes express universal patterns of human functioning—those aspects of living common to all, such as the experiences of the Mother, the Mentor, the Child, Birth, Death, and Transcendence, to name just a few.

[12] From "Freud and Jung: Contrasts," by C.G. Jung, 1929/1961, *The Collected Works of C.G. Jung*, Vol. 4, par. 781, NJ: Princeton University Press.

[13] Edinger, E. F. (1972). *Ego and Archetype: Individuation and the Religious Function of the Psyche*. Boston: Shambhala.

[14] Procrustes was a figure from Greek mythology who offered a bed for travelers to sleep on. He required them to fit the bed exactly. Those who were too short were stretched and

those who were too long for the bed had their legs cut off. Thus, the dictionary definition of Procrustean bed is "a plan or scheme to produce uniformity or conformity by arbitrary or violent methods."

[15] This treatment emphasis is vividly described in a 2011 article from the *New York Times*. It describes the experience of a Dr. Donald Levin, a psychiatrist who once offered psychotherapy to his patients, but now, like many in his profession, felt forced for financial reasons to limit his practice to the prescribing of psychiatric medications: "Then, he knew his patients' inner lives better than he knew his wife's; now, he often cannot remember their names. Then, his goal was to help his patients become happy and fulfilled; now, it is just to keep them functional." From *Talk Doesn't Pay, So Psychiatry Turns Instead to Drug Therapy*, http://www.nytimes.com/2011/03/06/health/policy/06doctors.html (Accessed 18 Nov. 2019).

[16] Emphasis mine. From "The Psychology of the Child Archetype," by C.G. Jung, 1951/1968a, *The Collected Works of C.G. Jung*, Vol. 9i, par. 271, NJ: Princeton University Press.

[17] From *The Ritual Process: Structure and Anti-Structure* (p. 2), by Victor Turner, 1969, New York: Aldine de Gruyter.

[18] Ibid., p. 4.

[19] Polanyi, M. (1966). *The Tacit Dimension*. Chicago: University of Chicago Press.

[20] Gottschall, J. (2012). *The Storytelling Animal: How Stories Make Us Human*. New York: Houghton Mifflin Harcourt.

[21] From *Encountering God: A Spiritual Journey from Bozeman to Banaras* (p. 47), by Diana L. Eck, 1993, Boston: Beacon Press.

[22] Fowler, J. (1981). *Stages of Faith*. New York: HarperCollins.

[23] Jung, C.G. (1997). *Visions: Notes of Seminar Given in 1930–1934* (C. Douglas, Ed.). NJ: Princeton University Press.

[24] From *Encountering God* (p. 15), by Diana L. Eck.

[25] From *Memories, Dreams, Reflections* (p. 325), by C.G. Jung, 1961/1989a, New York: Vintage.

## Chapter 1  Symbols

[26] Jung, C.G. (1950/1966c). "Psychology and Literature," *The Collected Works of C.G. Jung*, Vol. 15, NJ: Princeton University Press.

[27] Jung, C.G. (1921/1976). "Psychological Types," *The Collected Works of C.G. Jung*, Vol. 6, NJ: Princeton University Press.

[28] From "Answer to Job," by C.G. Jung, 1952/1969c, *The Collected Works of C.G. Jung*, Vol. 11, par. 555, NJ: Princeton University Press.

[29] Ibid.

[30] Quoted in *The Shallows: What the Internet Is Doing to Our Brains* (p. 46), by Nicholas G. Carr, 2011, New York: Norton.

[31] Watts, A. (2003). *Become What You Are* (M. Watts, Ed.). Boston: Shambhala.

[32] All quotes from the *Tao Te Ching* are taken from a translation by J. H. McDonald, published online at: http://www.wright-house.com/religions/taoism/tao-te-ching.html (Accessed 18 Nov. 2019).

[33] From "The Stages of Life" by C.G. Jung, 1931/1969, *The Collected Works of C.G. Jung*, Vol. 8, par. 794, NJ: Princeton University Press.

[34] Jung, C.G. (1968c). "Approaching the Unconscious." In C.G. Jung & M.-L. von Franz (Eds.), *Man and His Symbols* (pp. 1–94). New York: Dell.

[35] From *the Experience of God: Icons of the Mystery* (p. 28), by Raimon Panikkar, 2006, Minneapolis, MN: Augsburg Fortress.

[36] "This reality is more than what is disclosed by my senses and my rational life, it is Being...If we, our mind, feelings, sense of ego, or whatever, ask for ways to discern reality, we are already 'outside' reality on what we take to be a firmer ground than reality itself." (From *The Rhythm of Being: The Unbroken Trinity*, pp. 78–79, by Raimon Panikkar, 2010, Maryknoll, New York: Orbis.

[37] From *Way to Wisdom: An Introduction to Philosophy* (p. 34), by Karl Jaspers, 1954, New Haven, CT: Yale University Press.

[38] Jung, C.G. (1951/1970). "Foreword to Werblowsky's 'Lucifer and Pometheus,'" *The Collected Works of C.G. Jung*, Vol. 11, NJ: Princeton University Press.

[39] Edinger, E. F. (1972). *Ego and Archetype: Individuation and the Religious Function of the Psyche*. Boston: Shambhala.

[40] The Self is the archetype of wholeness that includes both the conscious and unconscious aspects of the psyche. As such, it transcends the ego, which is understood to be the center of the conscious mind. The Self is the totality of the personality, much of which remains unknown because it is unconscious. Jung often describes the Self as the center and the circumference of the personality. Because of its transcendent nature, symbols of the Self often take the form of God-images.

[41] From "Psychological Types," by C.G. Jung, par. 816.

[42] Jung, C.G. (1917/1966a). "On the Psychology of the Unconscious," *The Collected Works of C.G. Jung*, Vol. 7, NJ: Princeton University Press.

[43] Psychic reality is an intermediate realm between and including both the physical and the mental or spiritual realms: "It is characteristic of Western man that he has split apart the physical and the spiritual for epistemological purposes. But these opposites exist together in the psyche and psychology must recognize this fact. 'Psychic' means physical *and* spiritual." (From "Commentary on 'The Secret of the Golden Flower,'" by C.G. Jung, 1957/1967a, *The Collected Works of C.G. Jung*. Vol. 13, par 76n, NJ: Princeton University Press.)

[44] Jung. C.G. (1968c). "Approaching the Unconscious," in *Man and His Symbols*.

[45] From *Jungian Psychotherapy and Contemporary Infant Research: Basic Patterns of Emotional Exchange* (p. 98), by Mario Jacoby, 1999, London and New York: Routledge. (It would take us too far afield to go into an in-depth description of the archetype of the father. I would refer the reader to Jacoby's excellent exposition of this realm of experience.)

[46] Jung, C.G. (1968c). "Approaching the Unconscious," in *Man and His Symbols*.

[47] From "Freedom Not to Choose Is a Faith Worth Believing In" by David Mitchell, The Guardian, https://www.theguardian.com/commentisfree/2017/oct/15/living-without-shared-religion-neil-macgregor-living-with-gods-radio-4 (Accessed 16 Oct. 2017).

[48] Edinger, E. F. (1972). *Ego and Archetype*.

[49] Jung, C.G. (1968c). "Approaching the Unconscious." In *Man and His Symbols*.

[50] Jung extended the notion of psychic energy, or libido, beyond Freud's limited focus on sexuality. For Jung, libido was better understood as a more generalized "psychic energy" that could become manifest in multiple impulses and instincts. With the concept of psychic energy, the movements of the psyche are seen as purposive—that is, aimed toward the fulfillment of certain ends, and not merely reactive. Psychic energy determines the direction of one's attention, interest, motivation, or desire.

[51] Edinger, E. F. (1972). *Ego and Archetype*.

[52] From *The Psychology of Kundalini Yoga: Notes of the Seminar Given in 1952* (p. 61), by C.G. Jung, 1996, NJ: Princeton University Press.

[53] From *The Idea of the Holy: An Inquiry into the Non-Rational Factor in the Idea of The Divine and Its Relation to the Rational* (p. 146), by Rudolf Otto, 1958, New York: Oxford University Press (A Galaxy Book).

[54] See, for example, Eck, 1993; Fowler, 1981; Panikkar, 2006.

## Chapter 2  Ritual: The Embodied Symbolic

[55] From "The Symbolic Life," by C.G. Jung, 1939/1976a, *The Collected Works of C.G. Jung*, Vol. 18, par. 625, NJ: Princeton University Press.

[56] Turner, V. (1969). *The Ritual Process: Structure and Anti-Structure.* New York: Aldine de Gruyter.

[57] From *Emotionally Engaged: A Bride's Guide to Surviving the "Happiest" Time of Her Life* (p. 33), by Allison Moir-Smith, 2006, New York: Hudson Street Press.

[58] From *The Joseph Campbell Companion: Reflections on the Art of Living* (p. 90), by Joseph Campbell, 1991, New York: HarperCollins.

[59] From *Psychology and Religion* (p. 58), by C.G. Jung, 1938, New Haven, CT: Yale University Press.

[60] In Jung's model, psychic energy, like physical energy, follows a similar law of conservation—psychic energy never disappears, but takes on another form. Psychic energy that should be available for consciousness, but is unable to find adequate expression or outlet, accumulates in the unconscious and produces various symptoms.

[61] From "The Sacrament of Penance and Reconciliation," Catechism of the Catholic Church, http://www.vatican.va/archive/ccc_css/archive/catechism/p2s2c2a4.htm (Accessed 20 Oct. 2017).

[62] From Gino, F. & Norton, M. I. (2013, May 13). "Why Rituals Work," Scientific American, https://www.scientificamerican.com/article/why-rituals-work/ (Accessed 20 Oct. 2017).

[63] Emphasis mine. From "Archetypes of the Collective Unconscious," by C.G. Jung, 1934/1968, *The Collected Works of C.G. Jung*, Vol. 9i, par. 47, NJ: Princeton University Press.

[64] From *The Sabbath* (p. 60), by Abraham Joshua Heschel, 1951a/1975, New York: Noonday Press.

[65] From "Sin," Catechism of the Catholic Church, http://www.vatican.va/archive/ccc_css/archive/catechism/p3s1c1a8.htm (Accessed 22 Oct. 2017).

[66] Sedgwick, M. J. (2000). *Sufism: The Essentials.* New York: The American University in Cairo Press.

[67] "Building Block No. 6: Nefesh HaBahamis (Animal Soul), Nefesh HoElokis (G-dly Soul)," Chabed.org, https://www.chabad.org/library/article_cdo/aid/80970/jewish/Nefesh-HaBahamis-Animal-Soul-Nefesh-HoElokis-G-dly-Soul.htm (Accessed 25 March 2019).

[68] From *The Ritual Process* (pp. 25-26), by Victor Turner.

[69] Otto, R. (1959). *The Idea of the Holy: An Inquiry into the Non-Rational Factor in the Idea of The Divine and Its Relation to the Rational.* New York: Oxford University Press (A Galaxy Book).

[70] Panikkar uses the term *homeomorphic equivalents* to describe analogous forms of "comparable importance and function in the context of another religious or cultural system." [From *A Dwelling Place for Wisdom* (p. 173), by Raimon Panikkar, 1993, Louisville, KY: Westminster/John Knox Press.] The Ndembu relationship to ritual and our own are homeomorphic equivalents that can be compared and contrasted with each other, though not identified.

[71] From "The Stages of Life" by C.G. Jung, 1931/1969, *The Collected Works of C.G. Jung*, Vol. 8, par. 794, NJ: Princeton University Press.

[72] From "The Symbolic Life," by C.G. Jung, par. 628.

[73] Eck, D. L. (1998). *Darśan: Seeing the Divine Image in India.* New York: Columbia University Press.

[74] Jung, C.G. (1961/1989). *Memories, Dreams, Reflections.* New York: Vintage.

[75] Jung, C.G. (1921/1976). "Psychological Types," *The Collected Works of C.G. Jung*, Vol. 6, NJ: Princeton University Press.

[76] Watts, A. (n.d.). *Alan Watts—On Prickles and Goo.* YouTube: https://www.youtube.com/watch?v=D4vHnM8WPvU (Accessed 15 Feb. 2018).

[77] From *The Ritual Process* (p. 113), by Victor Turner.

[78] Ibid., p. 129.

[79] From *The Power of Myth* (p. 115), by Joseph Campbell & Bill Moyers, 1991, New York: Anchor Books.

[80] "Native American Church," The Pluralistic Project, http://pluralism.org/religions/native-american-traditions/native-peoples-experience/native-american-church/ (Accessed 17 Feb. 2019).

# Chapter 3 Religion: The Lived Symbolic

[81] From *The Reenchantment of the World* (p. 40), by Morris Berman, 1981, Ithaca, NY: Cornell University Press.

[82] From *Random House Compact Unabridged Dictionary, Special Second Edition* (p. 1628), New York: Random House.

[83] From "The Undiscovered Self (Present and Future)," by C.G. Jung, 1957/1970b, *The Collected Works of C.G. Jung*, Vol. 10, par. 505, NJ: Princeton University Press.

[84] From *Man Is Not Alone: A Philosophy of Religion* (p. 128), by Abraham Joshua Heschel, 1951, New York: Farrar, Straus and Giroux.

[85] Ibid, pp. 128–129.

[86] From *Way to Wisdom* (p. 51), by Karl Jaspers, 1954, New Haven, CT: Yale University Press.

[87] From *Self-Emptying of Christ and the Christian: Three Essays on Kenosis* (p. 109), by John B. Lounibos, 2011, Eugene, OR: Wipf & Stock.

[88] From *The Idea of the Holy: An Inquiry into the Non-Rational Factor in the Idea of The Divine and Its Relation to the Rational* (p. 11), by Rudolf Otto, 1958, New York: Oxford University Press (A Galaxy Book).

[89] From *Psychology and Religion* (p. 4), by C.G. Jung, 1938, New Haven, CT: Yale University Press.

[90] From *The Idea of the Holy* (p. 6), by Rudolf Otto.

[91] I do not intend in any way to diminish the experience of the anxiety sufferer. It is a debilitating experience that can cause great suffering. I simply want to suggest that our current reductive understanding of such experiences reflects a failure of imagination that tends to increase suffering. It is no accident, I believe, that many current approaches to anxiety, such as mindfulness practices, for instance, have their origins in the religious traditions.

[92] See, for example: Gnaulati, E. (2018). *Saving Talk Therapy: How Health Insurers, Big Pharma, and Slanted Science are Ruining Good Mental Health Care.* Boston: Beacon Press.

[93] See, for example: Mark, K. P., Janssen, E., & Milhausen, R. R. (2011, October). Infidelity in heterosexual couples: Demographic, interpersonal, and personality-related predictors of extradyadic sex. *Archives of Sexual Behavior, 40*(5), 971–982. https://doi.org/10.1007/s10508-011-9771-z

[94] Waldenfels, H. (1976). *Absolute Nothingness: Foundations for a Buddhist-Christian Dialogue.* New York: Paulist Press.

[95] From *Psychology and Religion* (p. 6), by C.G. Jung.

[96] From "A Psychological Approach to the Dogma of the Trinity," by C.G. Jung, 1948/1969b, *The Collected Works of C.G. Jung*, Vol. 11, par. 293, NJ: Princeton University Press.

[97] Panikkar, R. (2006). *The Experience of God: Icons of the Mystery*. Minneapolis, MN: Augsburg Fortress.

[98] Emphasis mine. From *Psychology and Religion* (p. 6), by C.G. Jung.

[99] Quoted in *Stages of Faith* (p. 11), by James Fowler, 1981, New York: HarperCollins.

## Chapter 4  The State of Religion

[100] Armstrong, K. (1993). *A History of God: The 4000-Year Quest of Judaism, Christianity, and Islam*. New York: Knopf.

[101] MacCulloch, D. (2010). *Christianity: The First Three Thousand Years*. New York: Viking Penguin.

[102] From *The Case for God* (p. 292), by Karen Armstrong, 2009, New York: Knopf.

[103] From *Heraclitus* (p. 68), by Philip Wheelwright, 1959, NJ: Princeton University Press.

[104] Dourley, J. (2006). "Rerooting in the Mother: The Numinosity of the Night." In A. Casement and D. Tacey (Eds.), *The Idea of the Numinous: Contemporary Jungian and Psychoanalytic Perspectives* (pp. 171–185). London and New York: Routledge.

[105] From "Psychology and Alchemy," by C.G. Jung, 1968d, *The Collected Works of C.G. Jung*, Vol. 12, par. 14, NJ: Princeton University Press.

[106] "U.S. Public Becoming Less Religious," Pew Research Center, 3 Nov. 2015, http://www.pewforum.org/2015/11/03/u-s-public-becoming-less-religious/ (Accessed 14 Nov. 2017).

[107] Daniel, L. (2016). *Tired of Apologizing for a Church I Don't Belong To*. New York: FaithWords.

[108] From "U.S. Public Becoming Less Religious," http://www.pewforum.org/2015/11/03/u-s-public-becoming-less-religious/

[109] "Why People with No Religion Are Projected to Decline as a Share of the World's Population," Pew Research Center, 7 Apr. 2017, http://www.pewresearch.org/fact-tank/2017/04/07/why-people-with-no-religion-are-projected-to-decline-as-a-share-of-the-worlds-population/ (Accessed 14 Nov. 2017).

[110] See, for example, Campbell, J. (1964/1976); Campbell, J. (2004); Campbell, J. & Moyers, B. (1991).

[111] From *The Hero with a Thousand Faces* (p. 3), by Joseph Campbell, 1949/1972, NJ: Princeton University Press.

[112] Campbell's differentiation of mythology and religion is essentially equal to Jung's distinction between religion and creed. What Jung means by the word *creed*, Campbell calls *religion*, whereas Jung's use of the word *religion* correlates to what Campbell chooses to designate with the word *mythology*. For reasons laid out in this book, I follow Jung's usage of *religion* to refer to the relationship with, and experience of, the transcendent.

[113] From *The Masks of God: Occidental Mythology* (p. 519), by Joseph Campbell, 1964/1976, New York: Penguin.

[114] Ibid., p. 519.

[115] Ibid., p. 520.

[116] Ibid., p. 521.

[117] Fowler, J. (1981). *Stages of Faith*. New York: HarperCollins.

[118] From "The Development of Personality," by C.G. Jung, 1934/1954, *The Collected Works of C.G. Jung*, Vol. 17, par. 284, NJ: Princeton University Press.

[119] Emphasis mine. From *Stages of Faith* (p. 18), by James Fowler.

[120] Ibid, p. 249.

[121] From "The Development of Personality," by C.G. Jung, par. 284.

[122] Cox, D. (2016, Aug. 23). "Religious Diversity May Be Making America Less Religious," FiveThirtyEight, https://fivethirtyeight.com/features/religious-diversity-may-be-making-america-less-religious/ (Accessed 17 Nov. 2017).

[123] Ibid.

[124] Ibid.

[125] Ibid.

[126] C.G. Jung (1957/1970b). "The Undiscovered Self (Present and Future)." *The Collected Works of C.G. Jung*, Vol. 10, NJ: Princeton University Press.

[127] "Americans Significantly Inflate Religious Participation, New Study Finds," Public Religion Research Institute, 19 May 2014, https://www.prri.org/press-release/news-release-aapor-2014/ (Accessed 17 Nov. 2017).

[128] Ibid.

[129] For example: Armstrong, K. (2010). *Twelve Steps to a Compassionate Life*. New York: Knopf.

[130] From *Tired of Apologizing for a Church I Don't Belong To* (p. 165), by Lillian Daniel.

[131] Eck, D. L. (n.d.). "What Is Pluralism?" The Pluralism Project, http://www.pluralism.org/pluralism/what_is_pluralism/ (Accessed 3 Mar. 2015).

[132] From *The Masks of God: Occidental Mythology* (p. 519), by Joseph Campbell.

[133] The Hindu cosmology is one exception to this statement. It possesses a vastness that is equal to and mirrors that which is being offered to us from Astronomy and Physics.

[134] Jaggard, V. (2014, Sept. 15). "What Is the Universe? Real Physics Has Some Mind-Bending Answers," Smithsonian.com, http://www.smithsonianmag.com/science/what-universe-real-physics-has-some-mind-bending-answers-180952699/ (Accessed 18 Nov. 2017).

[135] For example: Polkinghorne, J. (2005). *Quarks, Chaos, & Christianity: Questions to Science and Religion*. New York: Crossroads.

[136] Brian Swimme, quoted in *The Rhythm of Being: The Unbroken Trinity* (p. 375), by Raimon Panikkar, 2010, Maryknoll, NY: Orbis.

[137] From *I Asked for Wonder: A Spiritual Anthology* (p. 63), by Abraham Joshua Heschel, 1983, New York: Crossroads.

[138] From *The Experience of God: Icons of the Mystery* (p. 131), by Raimon Panikkar, 2006, Minneapolis, MN: Augsburg Fortress.

[139] From *The Idea of the Holy: An Inquiry into the Non-Rational Factor in the Idea of The Divine and Its Relation to the Rational* (p. 42), by Rudolf Otto, 1958, New York: Oxford University Press (A Galaxy Book).

[140] From *Stages of Faith* (pp. 163–164), by James Fowler.

[141] Routledge, C. (2017, July 21). "Don't Believe in God? Maybe You'll Try U.F.O.s," *The New York Times*, https://www.nytimes.com/2017/07/21/opinion/sunday/dont-believe-in-god-maybe-youll-try-ufos.html (Accessed 19 Nov. 2017).

[142] Ibid.

[143] From "Flying Saucers: A Modern Myth of Things Seen in the Skies," by C.G. Jung, 1959/1970c, *The Collected Works of C.G. Jung*, Vol. 10, par. 624, NJ: Princeton University Press.

[144] From "On the Psychology of the Unconscious," by C.G. Jung, 1917/1966a, *The Collected Works of C.G. Jung*, Vol. 7, par. 199, NJ: Princeton University Press.

[145] Schore, A. (2012). *The Science and the Art of Psychotherapy*. New York: Norton.

[146] Panikkar, R. (2006).

# Chapter 5  Loss of Symbols

[147] That this is the case is shown by Jung's account of the moment when his calling dramatically presented itself to him as he began to read through a textbook on psychiatry. He suddenly realized in a kind of epiphany that psychiatry was a field of study that was concerned with both the biological and the spiritual dimension of human nature. It was

in that moment, and for that reason, that he knew that psychiatry was the profession he would pursue. (See: Jung, C. G., 1961/1989).

[148] From "Good and Evil in Analytical Psychology," by C.G. Jung, 1960/1970d, *The Collected Works of C.G. Jung*, Vol. 10, par. 864, NJ: Princeton University Press.

[149] Ibid., par. 864.

[150] From *Memories, Dreams, Reflections* (p. 177), by C.G. Jung, 1961/1989a, New York: Vintage.

[151] See, for example, "Latest APA Survey Reveals Deepening Concerns about Connection Between Chronic Disease and Stress," American Psychological Association, https://www.apa.org/news/press/releases/2012/01/chronic-disease (Accessed 10 Dec. 2018).

[152] From *Jung's Seminar on Nietzsche's Zarathustra, Abridged Edition* (p. 311), by C.G. Jung, 1998, NJ: Princeton University Press.

[153] Ibid., p. 311.

[154] From *Ego and Archetype* (p. 64), by Edward F. Edinger, 1972, Boston: Shambhala.

[155] Ibid., p. 64.

[156] Emphasis mine. Ibid., p. 64.

[157] From *Traveling Mercies: Some Thoughts on Faith* (p. 49), by Anne Lamott, 1999, New York: Pantheon.

[158] From "The Psychology of the Transference," by C.G. Jung, 1946/1966b, *The Collected Works of C.G. Jung*, Vol. 16, par. 460, NJ: Princeton University Press.

[159] From *Loose Ends: Primary Papers in Archetypal Psychology* (p. 1), by James Hillman, 1975, Dallas, TX: Spring Publications.

[160] There is growing evidence that the cognitive behavioral approach has some serious limitations. Psychodynamic approaches that focus on unconscious and relational processes are proving to have greater effectiveness and longer-lasting effects. See, for example, "The Efficacy of Psychodynamic Psychotherapy," by Jonathan Shedler, 2010, https://www.apa.org/pubs/journals/releases/amp-65-2-98.pdf and *The Science and the Art of Psychotherapy*, by Allan N. Schore, 2012.

## Chapter 6  Religion and Psyche

[161] Adler, G., & Jaffé, A. (Eds.). (1973). *C.G. Jung Letters* (Vol. 2). (R. F. C. Hull, Trans.), NJ: Princeton University Press.

[162] Jung, C.G. (1933). *Modern Man in Search of a Soul*. New York: Harcourt Brace.

[163] Malone, K. M., Oquendo, M. A., Haas, G. L., Ellis, S. P., Li, S., & Mann, J. J. (2000). "Protective Factors Against Suicidal Acts in Major Depression: Reasons for Living." *American Journal of Psychiatry*, 157 (no.7), 1084–88. doi:10.1176/appi.ajp, Retrieved from ResearchGate: https://www.researchgate.net/publication/12444871_Protective_Factors_Against_Suicidal_Acts_in_Major_Depression_Reasons_for_Living (Accessed 2 Dec. 2017).

[164] Ibid.

[165] Emphasis mine. Ibid.

[166] Bakhiyi, C. L., Calati, R., Guillaume, S., & Courtet, P. (2016, June). "Do Reasons for Living Protect Against Suicidal Thoughts and Behaviors? A Systematic Review of the Literature." *Journal of Psychiatric Research*, 77, 92–108.

[167] From *Man's Search for Meaning* (p. 135), by Victor Frankl, 1985, New York: Washington Square Press.

[168] From *Memories, Dreams, Reflections* (p. 340), by C.G. Jung, 1961/1989a, New York: Vintage.

[169] Dervic, K. et al. (2004, Dec. 1). "Religious Affiliation and Suicide Attempt," *American Journal of Psychiatry*. http://ajp.psychiatryonline.org/doi/full/10.1176/appi.ajp.161.12.2303 (Accessed 2 Dec. 2017).

[170] Ibid.

[171] Ibid.

[172] Ibid.

[173] From *Modern Man in Search of a Soul* (p. 229), by C.G. Jung.

[174] From *The Will to Believe and Other Essays in Popular Philosophy* (p. 32), by William James, 1956, New York: Dover Publications.

[175] Tillich, P. (1952). *The Courage to Be*. New Haven, CT: Yale University Press.

[176] From "Commentary on 'The Secret of the Golden Flower,'" by C.G. Jung, 1957/1967a, *The Collected Works of C.G. Jung*, Vol. 13, par. 71, NJ: Princeton University Press.

[177] Moore, T. (1994). *Care of the Soul: A Guide for Cultivating Depth and Sacredness in Everyday Life*. New York: HarperPerennial.

[178] Jung, C.G. (1933).

[179] From *Ego and Archetype* (p. 108), by Edward F. Edinger, 1972, Boston: Shambhala.

[180] Ibid., p. 108.

[181] From *The Rhythm of Being* (p. 247), by Raimon Panikkar, 2010, Maryknoll, NY: Orbis.

[182] Ibid., p. 247.

[183] From "Foreword to White's 'God and the Unconscious,'" by C.G. Jung, 1952/1969d, *The Collected Works of C.G. Jung*, Vol. 11, par. 452, NJ: Princeton University Press.

[184] Eck, D. L. (1993). *Encountering God: A Spiritual Journey from Bozeman to Banaras*. Boston: Beacon Press.

[185] See Chapter 11 *Psychology as* Religio.

[186] From "Freud and Jung: Contrasts," by C.G. Jung, 1929/1961. *The Collected Works of C.G. Jung*, Vol. 4, par. 780, NJ: Princeton University Press.

## Chapter 7  The Role of Religion

[187] From "Approaching the Unconscious," by C.G. Jung, 1968c, *Man and His Symbols* (p. 75), New York: Dell.

[188] Corbin, H. (1969). *Alone with the Alone: Creative Imagination in the Sūfism of Ibn 'Arabī*. NJ: Princeton University Press.

[189] Jung, C.G. (1933). *Modern Man in Search of a Soul*. New York: Harcourt Brace.

[190] "Growing Up in the Universe: Ultraviolet Garden," by Richard Dawkins, 1991, The Royal Institution: https://www.rigb.org/christmas-lectures/watch/1991/growing-up-in-the-universe/ultraviolet-garden (Accessed 15 Dec. 2017).

[191] Panikkar, R. (2006). *The Experience of God: Icons of the Mystery*. Minneapolis, MN: Augsburg Fortress.

[192] Ibid., p. 52.

[193] Fowler, J. (1981). *Stages of Faith*. New York: HarperCollins.

[194] From *Man Is Not Alone: A Philosophy of Religion* (p. 257), by Abraham Joshua Heschel, 1951, New York: Farrar, Straus and Giroux.

Quoted in "Arnold Eisen: The Opposite of Good Is Indifference," On Being: https://onbeing.org/programs/arnold-eisen-the-opposite-of-good-is-indifference-sep2017/ (Accessed 4 Jan. 2018).

From *Stages of Faith* (p. 18), by James Fowler.

From *Small Is Beautiful: Economics as if People Mattered* (p. 34), by E. F. Schumacher, 1973, New York: Harper & Row.

Csikszentmihalyi, M. (1991). *Flow: The Psychology of Optimal Experience*. New York: HarperPerennial.

From *Dictionary of Latin and Greek Theological Terms* (p. 335), by Richard A. Muller, 1985, Grand Rapids, MI: Baker Book House.

Jung, C.G. (1939/1976a). "The Symbolic Life," *The Collected Works of C.G. Jung*, Vol. 18, NJ: Princeton University Press.

From *Small Is Beautiful* (pp. 33–34), by E. F. Schumacher.

[202] From *Psychology and Religion* (p. 113), by C.G. Jung, 1938, New Haven, CT: Yale University Press.

[203] From *The Reenchantment of the World* (p. 51), by Morris Berman, 1981, Ithaca, NY: Cornell University Press.

[204] From *Memories, Dreams, Reflections* (p. 252), by C.G. Jung, 1961/1989a, New York: Vintage.

[205] Ibid., p. 252.

[206] Ibid., p. 255.

[207] Ibid., p. 256.

## Chapter 8  What Jung Teaches

[208] Armstrong, K. (2009). *The Case for God*. New York: Knopf.

[209] From *Modern Man in Search of a Soul* (p. 226), by C.G. Jung, 1933, New York: Harcourt Brace.

[210] Ibid., p. 226.

[211] From *Visions: Notes of Seminar Given in 1930–1934* (p. 41), by C.G. Jung, 1997, NJ: Princeton University Press.

[212] From *C.G. Jung Speaking: Interviews and Encounters* (p. 448), W. McGuire & R. F. C. Hull (Eds.), 1977, NJ: Princeton University Press.

[213] From "The Symbolic Life," by C.G. Jung, 1939/1976a, *The Collected Works of C.G. Jung*, Vol. 18, par. 635, NJ: Princeton University Press.

[214] Ibid., par. 636.

[215] From *Psychology and Religion* (p. 72), by C.G. Jung, 1938, New Haven, CT: Yale University Press.

[216] From *C.G. Jung Speaking* (p. 71), by C.G. Jung.

[217] Quoted in *Ego and Archetype* (p. 101), by Edward F. Edinger, 1972, Boston: Shambhala.

[218] Emphasis mine. From "On the Nature of Dreams," by C.G. Jung, 1945/1969a, *The Collected Works of C.G. Jung*, Vol. 8, par. 545, NJ: Princeton University Press.

[219] From "Approaching the Unconscious," by C.G. Jung, 1968c, *Man and His Symbols* (p. 92), New York: Dell.

[220] Campbell, J. (1974). *The Mythic Image*. NJ: Princeton University Press.

[221] From "Mysterium Coniunctionis," by C.G. Jung, 1955/1970a, *The Collected Works of C.G. Jung*, Vol. 14, par. 706, NJ: Princeton University Press.

[222] From *Jung on Active Imagination* (p. 10), by Joan Chodorow (Ed.), 1997, NJ: Princeton University Press.

[223] From "Mysterium Coniunctionis," by C.G. Jung, par. 706.

[224] Emphasis mine. From *Jung on Active Imagination* (p. 164).

[225] Ibid., p. 164.

[226] Ibid., p. 10.

[227] From *Memories, Dreams, Reflections* (p. 144), by C.G. Jung, 1961/1989a, New York: Vintage.

## Chapter 9  What Religion Teaches

[228] From *The Experience of God* (p. 32), by Raimon Panikkar, 2006, Minneapolis, MN: Augsburg Fortress.

[229] This, of course, is true of all institutions, including marriage, education, government, and, yes, schools and theories of psychology.

[230] From *Encountering God: A Spiritual Journey from Bozeman to Banaras* (p. 157), by Diana L. Eck, 1993, Boston: Beacon Press.

[231] From *Tired of Apologizing for a Church I Don't Belong To* (p. 123), by Lillian Daniel, 2016, New York: FaithWords.

[232] Ibid., p. 101.

[233] From *Stages of Faith* (p. 295), by James Fowler, 1981, New York: HarperCollins.

[234] Ibid., p. 295. All that has been said in this chapter about institutional religion can, of course, also be said about the institution of Jungian Psychology. The theories and concepts developed by Jung and elaborated by his early followers represent the encounters with the psyche that were had by this particular group of people. These theories and the experiences that inspired them have, since the time of their original development, become invitations to scores of others in subsequent generations to engage in their own "experiments with truth." Furthermore, one can see the five elements identified in organized religion as also being present in the practice of Jungian analysis. There is, for instance, a structure, which includes the frequency and length of sessions. There are techniques for accessing non-ordinary states of consciousness, such as dream analysis and active imagination. For the attention to stories and symbols, there are the stories of the person's history, the developing narrative of the person's sense of self, and the dream symbols that may herald her growth and development. The consulting office provides the "sacred" space in which the analysis takes place, and finally, the encounter between analyst and analysand fulfills the aspect of community.

[235] From *Living Myth: Personal Meaning as a Way of Life* (p. 105), by D. Stephenson Bond, 1993, Boston: Shambhala.

## Chapter 10  Experiential Consciousness

[236] From *The Great Transformation: The Beginning of Our Religious Traditions* (p. xiv), by Karen Armstrong, 2006, New York: Knopf.

[237] From *The Case for God* (p. xiii), by Karen Armstrong, 2009, New York: Knopf.

[238] From "The Relations Between the Ego and the Unconscious," by C.G. Jung, 1916/1966, *The Collected Works of C.G. Jung*, Vol. 7, par. 353, NJ: Princeton University Press.

[239] The term *experiential consciousness* is indebted to similar concepts suggested by D. Stephenson Bond and Morris Berman. Bond (1993) speaks of *symbolic consciousness* and Berman (1981) of *participating consciousness.*

[240] From "The Relations Between the Ego and the Unconscious," by C.G. Jung, par. 353.

[241] Winnicott, D. W. (1971/1989). *Playing and Reality.* London and New York: Routledge.

[242] From *Modern Man in Search of a Soul* (p. 234), by C.G. Jung, 1933, New York: Harcourt Brace.

[243] "Nine Ways Not to Talk about God," by Raimon Panikkar, 1997, http://www.crosscurrents.org/panikkar.htm (Accessed 4 Jan. 2018).

[244] From *The Experience of God: Icons of the Mystery* (p. 57), by Raimon Panikkar, 2006, Minneapolis, MN: Augsburg Fortress.

[245] Chodorow, J. (Ed.) (1997). *Jung on Active Imagination.* NJ: Princeton University Press.

[246] From *Living Myth: Personal Meaning as a Way of Life* (p. 117), by D. Stephenson Bond, 1993, Boston: Shambhala.

[247] Quoted in *The Reenchantment of the World* (p. 136), by Morris Berman, 1981, Ithaca, NY: Cornell University Press.

[248] Ibid., p. 139.

[249] Quoted in *Stages of Faith* (p. 187), by James Fowler, 1981, New York: HarperCollins.

[250] Ibid., pp. 187–189.

[251] Compare Karl Jaspers: "Man is fundamentally more than he can know about himself." From *Way to Wisdom* (p. 63), by Karl Jaspers, 1954, New Haven, CT: Yale University Press.

[252] Bednar, G. J. (1996). *Faith as Imagination: The Contribution of William F. Lynch, S. J.,* Kansas City, MO: Sheed & Ward.

[253] From "A Psychological Approach to the Dogma of the Trinity," by C.G. Jung, 1948/1969b, *The Collected Works of C.G. Jung*, Vol. 11, par. 273, NJ: Princeton University Press.

## Chapter 11 Psychology as *Religio*

[254] From "Psychological Aspects of the Mother Archetype," by C.G. Jung, 1954/1968b, *The Collected Works of C.G. Jung*, Vol. 9i, par. 187, NJ: Princeton University Press.

[255] From "The Relations Between the Ego and the Unconscious," by C.G. Jung, 1916/1966, *The Collected Works of C.G. Jung*, Vol. 7, par. 323, NJ: Princeton University Press.

[256] From "On the Nature of Dreams," by C.G. Jung, 1945/1969a, *The Collected Works of C.G. Jung*, Vol. 8, par. 557, NJ: Princeton University Press.

[257] From "Symbols of Transformation," by C.G. Jung, 1967b, *The Collected Works of C.G. Jung*, Vol. 5, par. 669, NJ: Princeton University Press.

[258] From "The Psychology of the Child Archetype," by C.G. Jung, 1951/1968a, *The Collected Works of C.G. Jung*, Vol. 9i, par. 271, NJ: Princeton University Press.

[259] Ibid., par. 271.

[260] Ibid., par 271.

[261] From "Symbols of Transformation," by C.G. Jung, par. 669, n.71.

[262] From *Psychology and Religion* (p. 5), by C.G. Jung, 1938, New Haven, CT: Yale University Press.

[263] From "Foreword," by C.G. Jung, 1950/1967, *The I Ching or Book of Changes* by Richard Wilhelm, p. xxviii, NJ: Princeton University Press.

[264] See, for example, Jacoby, 1999; Stein, 1998.

[265] Adler, G., & Jaffé, A. (Eds.). (1973). *C.G. Jung Letters* (Vol. 2). (R. F. C. Hull, Trans.), NJ: Princeton University Press.

[266] Ibid., p. 483.

[267] Compare the words of a contemporary Christian theologian: "The fact that we *merely believe* in a statement does not make us christians. If I believe that Jesus has risen yet do not take part in this resurrection process, my faith will only be theoretical…. Faith is not a thought process, not a mere assumption of facts. Instead, faith denotes the existential participation in the fate of Jesus Christ, in his experience and reality." From *A Dwelling Place for Wisdom* (p. 70), by Raimon Panikkar, 1993, Louisville, KY: Westminster/John Knox Press.

[268] From *C.G. Jung Letters* (Vol. 2, p. 272).

[269] From *The Experience of God: Icons of the Mystery* (p. 136) by Raimon Panikkar, 2006, Minneapolis, MN: Augsburg Fortress.

[270] From "A Psychological Approach to the Dogma of the Trinity," by C.G. Jung, 1948/1969b, *The Collected Works of C.G. Jung*, Vol. 11, par. 238, NJ: Princeton University Press.

[271] From *Stages of Faith* (p. 185), by James Fowler, 1981, New York: HarperCollins.

[272] Jung, C.G. (1955/1970a). "Mysterium Coniunctionis," in H. Read, et al. (Ed.), *The Collected Works of C.G. Jung* (R. F. C. Hull, Trans.), Vol. 14, NJ: Princeton University Press.
[273] From *Living Myth: Personal Meaning as a Way of Life* (p. 120), by D. Stephenson Bond, 1993, Boston: Shambhala.
[274] From *Children's Dreams: Notes from the Seminar Given in 1936–1940* (p. 222), by C.G. Jung, 2008, NJ: Princeton University Press.

## Conclusion: Opening a Space for Wonder

[275] From *Encountering God: A Spiritual Journey from Bozeman to Banaras* (p. 103), by Diana L. Eck, 1993, Boston: Beacon Press.
[276] From "Psychology and Alchemy," by C.G. Jung, 1968d, *The Collected Works of C.G. Jung*, Vol. 12, par. 14, NJ: Princeton University Press.
[277] Panikkar, R. (2006). *The Experience of God: Icons of the Mystery*. Minneapolis, MN: Augsburg Fortress.
[278] Quoted in "Dying to be Born," by Gordon Wallace, 2009, in *Self and No-Self: Continuing the Dialogue Between Buddhism and Psychotherapy* (p. 150), London and New York: Routledge.
[279] From *The Wisdom of Insecurity: A Message for the Age of Anxiety* (pp. 26–27), by Alan Watts, 1951, New York: Vintage.
[280] From *C.G. Jung Letters* (Vol. 1, p. 57), edited by Gerhard Adler & Aniela Jaffé, 1976, NJ: Princeton University Press.
[281] Ibid., p. 57.

# References

*About Us*. (n.d.). Retrieved from The Guild of Pastoral Psychology: http://www.guildofpastoralpsychology.org.uk/index.php/about-us

Adler, G., & Jaffé, A. (Eds.). (1973). *C.G. Jung letters*. (R. F. C. Hull, Trans.) NJ: Princeton University Press.

*Americans significantly inflate religious participation*. (2014, May 19). Retrieved from Public Religion Research Institute (PRRI): https://www.prri.org/press-release/news-release-aapor-2014/

Armstrong, K. (1994). *A history of God: The 4000-year quest of Judaism, Christianity, and Islam*. New York: Knopf.

Armstrong, K. (2006). *The great transformation: The beginning of our religious traditions*. New York: Knopf.

Armstrong, K. (2009). *The case for God*. New York: Knopf.

Armstrong, K. (2010). *Twelve steps to a compassionate life*. New York: Knopf.

*Arnold Eisen: The opposite of good is indifference*. (2008, June 5). Retrieved from On Being: https://onbeing.org/programs/arnold-eisen-the-opposite-of-good-is-indifference-sep2017/

Bakhiyi, C. L., Calati, R., Guillaume, S., & Courtet, P. (2016, June). Do reasons for living protect against suicidal thoughts and behaviors? A systematic review of the literature. *Journal of Psychiatric Research, 77*, 92–108.

Bednar, G. J. (1996). *Faith as imagination: The contribution of William F. Lynch, S.J.* Kansas City, MO: Sheed & Ward.

Berman, M. (1981). *The reenchantment of the world*. Ithaca, NY: Cornell University Press.

Bond, D. S. (1993). *Living myth: Personal meaning as a way of life*. Boston: Shambhala.

Campbell, J. (1949/1972). *The hero with a thousand faces*. NJ: Princeton University Press.

Campbell, J. (1964/1976). *The masks of God: Occidental mythology.* New York: Penguin Books.

Campbell, J. (1974). *The mythic image.* NJ: Princeton University Press.

Campbell, J. (1991). *The Joseph Campbell companion: Reflections on the art of living.* (D. K. Osbon, Ed.) New York: HarperCollins.

Campbell, J. (2004). *Pathways to bliss: Mythology and personal transformation.* (D. Kudler, Ed.) Novato, CA: New World Library.

Campbell, J., & Moyers, B. (1991). *The power of myth.* (B. S. Flowers, Ed.) New York: Anchor Books.

Carr, N. G. (2011). *The shallows: What the internet is doing to our brains.* New York: Norton.

Chodorow, J. (Ed.). (1997). *Jung on active imagination.* NJ: Princeton University Press.

Corbin, H. (1969). *Alone with the alone: Creative imagination in the Sūfism of Ibn 'Arabī.* (R. Manheim, Trans.) NJ: Princeton University Press.

Cox, D. (2016, August 23). *Religious diversity may be making America less religious.* Retrieved from FiveThirtyEight: https://fivethirtyeight.com/features/religious-diversity-may-be-making-america-less-religious/

Csikszentmihalyi, M. (1991). *Flow: The psychology of optimal experience.* New York: HarperPerennial.

Daniel, L. (2016). *Tired of apologizing for a church I don't belong to.* New York: FaithWords.

Dawkins, R. (1991). *Growing up in the universe: Ultraviolet garden.* Retrieved from The Royal Institution: https://www.rigb.org/christmas-lectures/watch/1991/growing-up-in-the-universe/ultraviolet-garden

Dervic, K., Oquendo, M. A., Grunebaum, M. F., Steve, E., Burke, A. K., & Mann, J. J. (2004). Religious affiliation and suicide attempt. *American Journal of Psychiatry, 161*(12), 2303–08. doi:10.1176/appi.ajp.161.12.2303

Dourley, J. (2006). Rerooting in the mother: The numinosity of the night. In A. Casement & D. Tacey (Eds.), *The idea of the numinous: Contemporary Jungian and psychoanalytic perspectives* (pp. 171–185). London and New York: Routledge.

Eck, D. L. (1993). *Encountering God: A spiritual journey from Bozeman to Banaras.* Boston: Beacon Press.

Eck, D. L. (1998). *Darśan: Seeing the divine image in India.* New York: Columbia University Press.

Eck, D. L. (n.d.). *What is pluralism?* Retrieved March 3, 2015, from The Pluralism Project at Harvard University: http://www.pluralism.org/pluralism/what_is_pluralism

Edinger, E. F. (1972). *Ego and archetype: Individuation and the religious function of the psyche.* Boston: Shambhala.

Fowler, J. (1981). *Stages of faith: The psychology of human development and the quest for meaning.* New York: HarperCollins.

Frankl, V. E. (1985). *Man's search for meaning.* New York: Washington Square Press.

Freud, S. (1909/2001). Five lectures on psycho-analysis. In J. Strachey & A. Freud (Eds.), *The standard edition of the complete psychological works of Sigmund Freud* (J. Strachey, Trans., Vol. 11, pp. 7–55). London: Vintage.

Freud, S. (1917/2001a). A difficulty in the path of psycho-analysis. In J. Strachey & A. Freud (Eds.), *The standard edition of the complete psychological works of Sigmund Freud* (J. Strachey, Trans., Vol. 17, pp. 135–144). London: Vintage.

Gino, F., & Norton, M. I. (2013, May 14). *Why rituals work.* Retrieved October 20, 2017, from Scientific American: https://www.scientificamerican.com/article/why-rituals-work/

Gnaulati, E. (2018). *Saving talk therapy: How health insurers, big pharma, and slanted science are ruining good mental health care.* Boston: Beacon Press.

Gottschall, J. (2012). *The storytelling animal: How stories make us human.* New York: Houghton Mifflin Harcourt.

Harris, G. (2011, March 5). *Talk doesn't pay, so psychiatry turns instead to drug therapy.* Retrieved from New York Times: http://www.nytimes.com/2011/03/06/health/policy/06doctors.html

Heschel, A. J. (1951). *Man is not alone: A philosophy of religion*. New York: Farrar, Straus and Giroux.

Heschel, A. J. (1951a/1975). *The sabbath*. New York: Noonday Press.

Heschel, A. J. (1983). *I asked for wonder: A spiritual anthology*. (S. H. Dresner, Ed.) New York: Crossroad.

Hillman, J. (1975). *Loose ends: Primary papers in archetypal psychology*. Dallas, TX: Spring Publications.

Jacobi, J. (1971). *Complex/archetype/symbol in the psychology of C.G. Jung*. (R. Manheim, Trans.) NJ: Princeton University Press.

Jacoby, M. (1999). *Jungian psychotherapy and contemporary infant research: Basic patterns of emotional exchange*. (R. Weathers, Trans.) London and New York: Routledge.

Jaggard, V. (2014, September 15). *What is the universe? Real physics has some mind-bending answers*. Retrieved from Smithsonian.com: https://www.smithsonianmag.com/science/what-universe-real-physics-has-some-mind-bending-answers-180952699/

James, W. (1956). *The will to believe: And other essays in popular philosophy*. New York: Dover Publications.

Jaspers, K. (1954). *Way to wisdom: An introduction to philosophy*. (R. Manheim, Trans.) New Haven, CT: Yale University Press.

Jung, C.G. (1916/1966). The relations between the ego and the unconscious. In H. Read, et al. (Eds.), *The collected works of C.G. Jung* (R. F. C. Hull, Trans., vol. 7, pp. 121–241). NJ: Princeton University Press.

Jung, C.G. (1917/1966a). On the psychology of the unconscious. In H. Read, et al. (Eds.), *The collected works of C.G. Jung* (R. F. C. Hull, Trans., vol. 7, pp. 1–119). NJ: Princeton University Press.

Jung, C.G. (1921/1976). Psychological types. In H. Read, et al. (Eds.), *The collected works of C.G. Jung* (R. F. C. Hull, Trans., vol. 6). NJ: Princeton University Press.

Jung, C.G. (1929/1961). Freud and Jung: Contrasts. In H. Read, et al. (Eds.), *The collected works of C.G. Jung* (R. F. C. Hull, Trans., vol. 4, pp. 333–342). NJ: Princeton University Press.

Jung, C.G. (1931/1969). The stages of life. In H. Read, et al. (Eds.), *The collected works of C.G. Jung* (R. F. C. Hull, Trans., vol. 8, pp. 387–415). NJ: Princeton University Press.

Jung, C.G. (1933). *Modern man in search of a soul.* New York: Harcourt Brace & Company.

Jung, C.G. (1934/1954). The development of personality. In H. Read, et al. (Eds.), *The collected works of C.G. Jung* (R. F. C. Hull, Trans., vol. 17, pp. 167–186). NJ: Princeton University Press.

Jung, C.G. (1934/1968). Archetypes of the collective unconscious. In H. Read, et al. (Eds.), *The collected works of C.G. Jung* (R. F. C. Hull, Trans., vol. 9i, pp. 3-41). NJ: Princeton University Press.

Jung, C.G. (1938). *Psychology and religion.* New Haven, CT: Yale University Press.

Jung, C.G. (1939/1976a). The symbolic life. In H. Read, et al. (Eds.), *The collected works of C.G. Jung* (R. F. C. Hull, Trans., vol. 18, pp. 265–290). NJ: Princeton University Press.

Jung, C.G. (1945/1969a). On the nature of dreams. In H. Read, et al. (Eds.), *The collected works of C.G. Jung* (R. F. C. Hull, Trans., Vol. 8, pp. 281-297). NJ: Princeton University Press.

Jung, C.G. (1946/1966b). The psychology of the transference. In H. Read, et al. (Eds.), *The collected works of C.G. Jung* (R. F. C. Hull, Trans., Vol. 16, pp. 163-323). NJ: Princeton University Press.

Jung, C.G. (1948/1969b). A psychological approach to the dogma of the trinity. In H. Read, et al. (Eds.), *The collected works of C.G. Jung* (R. F. C. Hull, Trans., vol. 11, pp. 107–200). NJ: Princeton University Press.

Jung, C.G. (1950/1966c). Psychology and literature. In H. Read, et al. (Eds.), *The collected works of C.G. Jung* (R. F. C. Hull, Trans., vol. 15, pp. 84–105). NJ: Princeton University Press.

Jung, C.G. (1950/1967). Foreword. In R. Wilhelm, *The I Ching or Book of Changes* (C. F. Baynes, Trans., pp. xxi-xxxix). NJ: Princeton University Press.

Jung, C.G. (1951/1968a). The psychology of the child archetype. In H. Read, et al. (Eds.), *The collected works of C.G. Jung* (R. F. C. Hull, Trans., vol. 9i, pp. 151–181). NJ: Princeton University Press.

Jung, C.G. (1951/1970). Foreword to Werblowsky's "Lucifer and Prometheus." In H. Read, et al. (Eds.), *The collected works of C.G. Jung* (R. F. C. Hull, Trans., vol. 11, pp. 311–315). NJ: Princeton University Press.

Jung, C.G. (1952/1969c). Answer to Job. In H. Read, et al. (Eds.), *The collected works of C.G. Jung* (R. F. C. Hull, Trans., vol. 11, pp. 355–470). NJ: Princeton University Press.

Jung, C.G. (1952/1969d). Foreword to White's "God and the unconscious." In H. Read, et al. (Eds.), *The collected works of C.G. Jung* (R. F. C. Hull, Trans., vol. 11, pp. 299–310). NJ: Princeton University Press.

Jung, C.G. (1954/1968b). Psychological aspects of the mother archetype. In H. Read, et al. (Eds.), *The collected works of C.G. Jung* (R. F. C. Hull, Trans., vol. 9i, pp. 73–110). NJ: Princeton University Press.

Jung, C.G. (1955/1970a). Mysterium coniunctionis. In H. Read, et al. (Eds.), *The collected works of C.G. Jung* (R. F. C. Hull, Trans., vol. 14). NJ: Princeton University Press.

Jung, C.G. (1957/1967a). Commentary on the secret of the golden flower. In H. Read, et al. (Eds.), *The collected works of C.G. Jung* (R. F. C. Hull, Trans., vol. 13, pp. 1–56). NJ: Princeton University Press.

Jung, C.G. (1957/1970b). The undiscovered self (present and future). In H. Read, et al. (Eds.), *The collected works of C.G. Jung* (R. F. C. Hull, Trans., vol. 10, pp. 245–305). NJ: Princeton University Press.

Jung, C.G. (1959/1970c). Flying saucers: A modern myth of things seen in the skies. In H. Read, et al. (Eds.), *The collected works of C.G. Jung* (R. F. C. Hull, Trans., vol. 10, pp. 307–433). NJ: Princeton University Press.

Jung, C.G. (1960/1970d). Good and evil in analytical psychology. In H. Read, et al. (Eds.), *The collected works of C.G. Jung* (R. F. C. Hull, Trans., vol. 10, pp. 456–468). NJ: Princeton University Press.

Jung, C.G. (1961/1989). *Memories, dreams, reflections.* (A. Jaffé, Ed., R. Winston & C. Winston, Trans.) New York: Vintage.

Jung, C.G. (1967b). Symbols of Transformation. In H. Read, et al. (Eds.), *The collected works of C.G. Jung* (R. F. C. Hull, Trans., 2nd ed., vol. 5). NJ: Princeton University Press.

Jung, C.G. (1968c). Approaching the unconscious. In C.G. Jung, & M.-L. von Franz (Eds.), *Man and his symbols* (pp. 1–94). New York: Dell.

Jung, C.G. (1968d). Psychology and alchemy. In H. Read, et al. (Eds.), *The collected works of C.G. Jung* (R. F. C. Hull, Trans., vol. 12). NJ: Princeton University Press.

Jung, C.G. (1996). *The psychology of kundalini yoga: Notes of the seminar given in 1952 by C.G. Jung* (S. Shamdasani, Ed.) NJ: Princeton University Press.

Jung, C.G. (1997). *Visions: Notes of the seminar given in 1930–1934.* (C. Douglas, Eds.) NJ: Princeton University Press.

Jung, C.G. (1998). *Jung's seminar on Nietzsche's Zarathustra, abridged edition.* (J. L. Jarrett, Ed.) NJ: Princeton University Press.

Jung, C.G. (2008). *Children's dreams: Notes from the seminar given in 1936–1940.* (L. Jung & M. Meyer-Grass, Eds.; E. Falzeder & T. Woolfson, Trans.) NJ: Princeton University Press.

Kremnizer, R. (n.d.). *Building Block No. 6: Nefesh HaBahamis (Animal Soul), Nefesh HoElokis (G-dly Soul).* Retrieved from Chabad.org: https://www.chabad.org/library/article_cdo/aid/80970/jewish/Nefesh-HaBahamis-Animal-Soul-Nefesh-Ho-Elokis-G-dly-Soul.htm

Lamott, A. (1999). *Traveling mercies: Some thoughts about faith.* New York: Pantheon.

Lao-Tzu. (1996). *Tao te ching.* (J. H. McDonald, Trans.): http://www.wright-house.com./religions/taoism/tao-te-ching.html (Accessed 18 Nov. 2019).

*Latest APA survey reveals deepening concerns about connection between chronic disease and stress.* (2012, January 11). Retrieved from American Psychological Association: https://www.apa.org/news/press/releases/2012/01/chronic-disease

Lipka, M., & McClendon, D. (2017, April 7). *Why people with no religion are projected to decline as a share of the world's*

*population.* Retrieved from Pew Research Center: https://www.
pewresearch.org/fact-tank/2017/04/07/why-people-with-no-
religion-are-projected-to-decline-as-a-share-of-the-worlds-po
pulation/

Lounibos, J. B. (2011). *Self-emptying of Christ and the Christian: Three essays on kenosis.* Eugene, OR: Wipf & Stock.

MacCulloch, D. (2010). *Christianity: The first three thousand years.* New York: Viking Penguin.

Malone, K. M., Oquendo, M. A., Haas, G. L., Ellis, S. P., Li, S., & Mann, J. J. (2000). Protective factors against suicidal acts in major depression: reasons for living. *American Journal of Psychiatry, 157*(7), 1084-88. doi:10.1176/appi.ajp

Mark, K. P., Janssen, E., & Milhausen, R. R. (2011, October), Infidelity in heterosexual couples: Demographic, interpersonal, and personality-related predictors of extradyadic sex. *Archives of Sexual Behavior, 40*(5), 971–982.

McGuire, W., & Hull, R. F. C. (Eds.). (1977). *C.G. Jung speaking: Interviews and encounters.* NJ: Princeton University Press.

Mitchell, D. (2017, October 15). *Freedom not to choose is a faith worth believing in.* Retrieved October 16, 2017, from The Guardian: https://www.theguardian.com/commentisfree/2017/oct/15/livi
ng-without-shared-religion-neil-macgregor-living-with-gods-
radio-4

Moir-Smith, A. (2006). *Emotionally engaged: A bride's guide to surviving the "happiest" time of her life.* New York: Hudson Street Press.

Moore, T. (1994). *Care of the soul: A guide for cultivating depth and sacredness in everyday life.* New York: HarperPerennial.

Muller, R. A. (1985). *Dictionary of Latin and Greek theological terms.* Grand Rapids, MI: Baker Book House.

*Native American Church.* (n.d.). Retrieved from The Pluralism Project: http://pluralism.org/religions/native-american-
traditions/native-peoples-experience/native-american-church/

Otto, R. (1958). *The idea of the holy: An inquiry into the non-rational factor in the idea of the divine and its relation to the rational.* (J.

H. Harvey, Trans.) New York: Oxford University Press (A Galaxy Book).

Panikkar, R. (1993). *A dwelling place for wisdom.* (A. S. Kidder, Trans.) Louisville, KY: Westminster/John Knox Press.

Panikkar, R. (1997). *Nine ways not to talk about God.* Retrieved from Cross Currents: http://www.crosscurrents.org/panikkar.htm

Panikkar, R. (2006). *The experience of God: Icons of the mystery.* (J. Cunneen, Trans.) Minneapolis, MN: Augsburg Fortress.

Panikkar, R. (2010). *The rhythm of being: The unbroken trinity.* Maryknoll, NY: Orbis.

Polanyi, M. (1966). *The tacit dimension.* IL: University of Chicago Press.

Polkinghorne, J. (2005). *Quarks, chaos, & christianity: Questions to science and religion.* New York: Crossroad Publishing.

*Random House compact unabridged dictionary, special second edition.* (1987). New York: Random House.

Routledge, C. (2017, July 21). *Don't believe in God? Maybe you'll try U.F.O.s.* Retrieved from *The New York Times:* https://www.nytimes.com/2017/07/21/opinion/sunday/dont-believe-in-god-maybe-youll-try-ufos.html?auth=login-email&login=email

*Sacrament of penance and reconciliation, The.* (n.d.). Retrieved October 20, 2017, from Catechism of the Catholic Church, part two: The celebration of the Christian mystery: http://www.vatican.va/archive/ccc_css/archive/catechism/p2s2c2a4.htm

Schore, A. N. (2012). *The science and the art of psychotherapy.* New York: Norton.

Schumacher, E. F. (1973). *Small is beautiful: Economics as if people mattered.* New York: Harper & Row.

Sedgwick, M. J. (2000). *Sufism: The essentials.* New York: The American University in Cairo Press.

Shedler, J. (2010, February 1). *The efficacy of psychodynamic psychotherapy.* Retrieved from American Psychological Association: https://www.apa.org/pubs/journals/releases/amp-65-2-98.pdf

*Sin.* (n.d.). Retrieved October 22, 2017, from Catechism of the Catholic Church, part three: Life in Christ: http://www.vatican.va/archive/ccc_css/archive/catechism/p3s1c1a8.htm

Stein, M. (1998). *Jung's map of the soul: An introduction.* Chicago: Open Court.

Stein, M. (Ed.). (2009). *Spring: A journal of archetype and culture (Book 82: Symbolic life 2009).* New Orleans, LA: Spring Journal, Inc.

Tillich, P. (1952). *The courage to be.* New Haven, CT: Yale University Press.

Turner, V. (1969). *The ritual process: Structure and anti-structure.* New York: Aldine de Gruyter.

*U.S. public becoming less religious.* (2015, November 3). Retrieved from Pew Research Center: https://www.pewforum.org/2015/11/03/u-s-public-becoming-less-religious/

von Franz, M.-L. (1996). *The interpretation of fairy tales.* Boston: Shambhala.

Waldenfels, H. (1976). *Absolute nothingness: Foundations for a Buddhist-Christian dialogue.* (J. W. Heisig, Trans.) New York: Paulist Press.

Wallace, G. (2009). Dying to be born. In D. Mathers, M. E. Miller, & O. Ando (Eds.), *Self and no-self: Continuing the dialogue between Buddhism and psychotherapy* (pp. 143–152). London and New York: Routledge.

Watts, A. (2003). *Become what you are.* (M. Watts, Ed.) Boston: Shambhala.

Watts, A. (n.d.). *Alan Watts—On prickles and goo.* Retrieved February 15, 2018, from YouTube: https://www.youtube.com/watch?v=D4vHnM8WPvU

Watts, A. W. (1951). *The wisdom of insecurity: A message for the age of anxiety.* New York: Vintage.

Wheelwright, P. (1959). *Heraclitus.* NJ: Princeton University Press.

Winnicott, D. W. (1971/1989). *Playing and reality.* London and New York: Routledge.

# Acknowledgments

There are several people I would like to thank whose help was essential to the realization of this book.

This material was initially presented in a lecture format. I am grateful to both the C.G. Jung Institute-Boston and to the Jung Association of Western Massachusetts for providing me with a forum in which to explore these ideas. I am equally grateful to the people who attended those talks and engaged with me and with this material in ways that helped me focus my thinking, deepen my understanding, and clarify my communication of these ideas.

Francine Lorimer and Christiane Alsop read through an early draft of this book. I am indebted to both of these remarkable women for their generosity of time, the care with which they read the manuscript, and their thoughtful reflections and suggestions. They both encouraged me and challenged me, and the final result is significantly more than it might have been without their invaluable insights. Lynda Griffiths added the finishing touches with her keen editor's eye.

Every day I have the honor of working with my clients as we navigate the difficult, intimate, and enriching process of Jungian analysis. Every day I learn something new from them about what it means to be a human being. I am privileged to be able to do this work, and this book is infused by the spirit of all of these encounters. Several of my clients gave me permission to use material from our work together. A special note of gratitude is due to them.

Finally, I would like to say thank you to my family—Allison, Annabel, and Atticus. Their patience, support, interest, and love through this long writing process have been a priceless gift to me. Writing can be lonely, but knowing that they were always there, ready and eager to receive me, helped keep me grounded through this time. I am beyond blessed. Special thanks are owed to my wife, Allison Moir-Smith, who has been a reader, an editor, a coach, and a confidante. I do not have the words to express the gratitude I feel for her unwavering support, nor the great good fortune that has been mine ever since she agreed to share her life with mine. This is, without question, the best possible life.

Each and every one of these people has contributed to making this book so much better than it could have been without them. The responsibility for its deficiencies lies solely with me.

# About the Author

Jason E. Smith is a Jungian analyst. He is a past president of the C.G. Jung Institute-Boston and currently serves as a training analyst and core faculty member in its analytic training program. Jason has a private practice in Manchester-by-the-Sea, Massachusetts, where he lives with his family.

CPSIA information can be obtained
at www.ICGtesting.com
Printed in the USA
LVHW040721100522
718380LV00002B/172